OTHER MINDS

JOHN WISDOM

OTHER MINDS

University of California Press
Berkeley and Los Angeles
1968

UNIVERSITY OF CALIFORNIA PRESS

BERKELEY AND LOS ANGELES

CALIFORNIA

ORIGINALLY PUBLISHED IN GREAT BRITAIN

IN 1952 BY BASIL BLACKWELL, OXFORD

FIRST CALIFORNIA PAPER-BOUND PRINTING, 1968,

BASED ON A SECOND EDITION PUBLISHED

BY BLACKWELL IN 1965

MANUFACTURED IN THE UNITED STATES OF AMERICA

Preface

The central aim of *Other Minds* is to indicate what it is about one person's knowledge of the mind of another which has led some philosophers to say that such knowledge is impossible, others to say that it is inevitably indirect and others to say that it is no more than knowledge of the reactions of an organism to its environment. The book is also concerned with what has led philosophers to say similar things about other sorts of knowledge: knowledge of the future, knowledge of the past, knowledge of the material world as opposed to knowledge of what at the moment appears to be so.

Philosophy and Psychoanalysis treats of ethical and aesthetic judgement, probability, degrees of logical connection and other matters. But it has three main aims. The first is a better understanding of what is wanted by the philosopher who raises questions as to the nature of this or that sort of knowledge. The second is a better recognition of the power of thought to give us the knowledge we want, not only when we are asking questions as to what is or is not possible but also when we are concerned with what in fact is so. The third aim is a better recognition of our power to form new concepts, new habits of thought, when those we have already are inadequate.

Contents

Acknowledgments

The thanks of the author and the publisher are due to the Editor of *Mind* for permission to reprint *Other Minds* I–VIII and to the Editor of *The Aristotelian Society* for permission to reprint *Symposium: Other Minds, Synopsis of Paper: Other Minds, The Concept of Mind*, and *Metaphysics*.

The author is very grateful to Mr Renford Bambrough for seeing the Second Edition through the press.

Note on the Second Edition

Although the contents of this edition have not been changed, the opportunity has been taken to correct printing errors and wrong references.

Other Minds I

1. *Natural doubts and philosophical doubts.* At a recent meeting of the Moral Sciences Club at Cambridge, Mr Isaiah Berlin read a paper in which he raised, in a very interesting way, what I venture to call the Inner-Outer metaphysical doubts. At this meeting we contrasted two cases of doubt as to whether a certain man, Smith say, believes that flowers feel, namely (1) a case of *natural* doubt arising because the doubter knows only that Smith has once at a party said, 'I believe flowers feel', and thinks that Smith might have been saying this for the sake of something to say; and (2) a case of *philosophical* doubt arising because the doubter knows only *outward* signs of Smith's *inward* state, and feels that from these he can never be sure what that state is.

2. *Two sources of philosophical doubt.* This philosophical doubt as to Smith's inward state must be distinguished from another philosophical doubt as to his inner state,[1] one which arises from

[1] Or, if you like, the doubt is the same and we have to distinguish between two sources of the philosophical doubt. It was Wittgenstein who first drew my attention to the need to distinguish between these two sources of doubt about other people's states of mind.

How much in this paper is due to Wittgenstein will be appreciated only by people who have listened to him. My debt to him is enormous and is by no means to be measured by the few places where I happen to mention that such and such a point comes from him or put a W. against an example of his. At the same time I do not think that my way of doing things would quite meet with his approval—it's not sufficiently hard working—a bit cheap and flash.

I make no apology for mentioning this sort of point. For this is the sort of criticism of philosophical work which I find appropriate. Those who deplore so 'personal' an attitude and say, 'Who cares whether so and so likes what is said, what we want to know is whether it is true', emphasize the objectivity of philosophy to the point of turning it into a science. I, remember with what relish I once heard McTaggart say in a discussion, 'What we want to know is not why he said it but what reason he had for saying it'. But I didn't then realize how near to reasons are some causes which aren't reasons and how beside the point are many reasons.

To continue, I want to say: There are three sources of chronic doubt as to whether S is P.

1. The doubt may arise from the infinity of the criteria as to whether S is P. Because of the infinity of the criteria it can never be said that all are present. At the same time there are no groups, short of all, of which we unhesitatingly say, 'With these enough are present'. This is the philosophical doubt most directly connected with an anxiety doubt, 'Are the taps turned off?', 'Have I turned out the

I

lights?', and thus with obsessional duties, 'I must go and make sure I have turned out the lights, turned off the taps, locked the doors, got a visa for heaven, made sure of security'. Is this water or a mirage? Is this love or infatuation? I don't know yet. I can't ever know. I don't know with Annabel, I can never know with anyone, How I'll feel tomorrow, How she'll feel tomorrow, Whether it's really love.

2. The doubt may arise from conflict among the criteria for S's being P. 'Can you play chess without the queen?' (W.). 'Is a tomato a fruit or a vegetable?' (W.). 'Can you unintentionally keep a promise?'

3. The doubt may arise from hesitation at the jump from the criteria, even the infinite all, to S is P, e.g. from the outer (bodily) to the inner (spiritual), from the present to the past, from the actual to the potential, from possibilities of sensation to physical things. These are the doubts which may take form in the idea of an arch-deceiver whose performance always goes without a hitch.

There is a connection between (1) and (2) which is indicated by the phrase, 'There is no definite line where we say that enough criteria are present for us to say that S is P'. There is a connection between (2) and (3) in that hesitation as to whether to doubt in the way the third class of sceptic doubts is hesitation as to whether, in view of conflicting criteria, one should say with these sceptics that s_1, $s_2 \ldots s\infty$ entail or mean that S is P or not—conflicting criteria, I mean, for the presence of entailment or identity of meaning.

A doubt such as 'I can never really know what another person is feeling' may arise from more than one of these sources. This over-determination of sceptical symptoms complicates their cure. The treatment is like psychoanalytic treatment (to enlarge on Wittgenstein's analogy) in that the treatment is the diagnosis and the diagnosis is the description, the very full description, of the symptoms.

What I mean is this: When in psychoanalysis it is said of a patient 'He is like this because when he was a child he wished for sexual contact with his mother', this means, 'If we analyse him, i.e. let him talk on, he will talk in such and such a way and then feel better'.

It may be said that the analyst cures by recommending a certain view of the patient's case. But the explaining to the patient what is wrong with him consists in allowing the patient to describe his own case, but not in 'septic' general terms, such as 'I have always suffered from a weak heart', 'I have always been treated unfairly', but in an 'aseptic' story language, e.g. 'I remember once when I was carrying all the things for a picnic and my sister wasn't carrying anything, suddenly at the top of the hill I felt a stabbing pain over my heart. . . .'

In like way a philosophical difficulty such as 'What then, do you say that philosophical questions are meaningless?', 'Do we know that dogs hear whistles too high for us to hear?' may be removed by getting the patient to describe himself. He must then describe fully the sort of question or statement he is considering. By the time he has described this, e.g. has described a philosophical question, he has set it in its place on the language map with regard to all other questions. And thus he has answered his own question. He is like the man who first saw a zebra and came back and said, 'I saw an animal with hoofs like a donkey but in shape rather more like a pony than a donkey. What sort of animal was it? Would you say it was a kind of donkey?' His friend said, 'Tell me, what sort of coat had it? Like a pony or like a donkey? Like a pony you say. Well I should say it was a sort of pony. But what sort of ears had it? Long ears? Oh! well then . . . But neighs like a horse?' And so on. It appears that the man who asked the question was best placed for answering it.

In the same way every philosophical question, when it isn't half asked, answers itself; when it is fully asked, answers itself.

Of course it is not necessary always to adopt this *entirely* 'aseptic' technique, to borrow a metaphor from Dr. George Pegge, an analyst. (I have hinted at the meaning of 'aseptic' above.) One may gently, surreptitiously, introduce a septic but beneficent notation which shall help towards the grasp and arrangement which so slowly comes from repeating again and again in this order and that the stories which give the setting of the patient's difficulties.

the infinite corrigibility of 'Smith believes that flowers feel', an infinite corrigibility which it shares with any statement about people and things, indeed any statement having infinite corrigibility! The difference between these two philosophical doubts is sometimes brought out thus: The inner-outer doubter is saying that even though he knows not only what Smith's behaviour has actually been but also what it will be and what it would be if this or that were to happen and what it would have been if this or that had happened, that even though he has all this knowledge, and it is all in favour of Smith's believing that flowers feel, still he doesn't know that Smith believes that flowers feel. With such extensive knowledge he is provided against surprise but not against the fact that his evidence is about outward and visible things while his conclusion is about an inward and invisible state.

3. *Another chronic doubt.* Both the philosophical doubts just described must be distinguished from and likened to another sort of doubt which I venture to call 'philosophical,'[1] though I cannot here present all the excuses for stretching the word to cover

1 The excuse for doing so is that all philosophical questions register conflict, that all philosophical doubts are requests for decision. In note 1, page 1, on the sorts of chronic doubt, I have represented philosophical doubts as some of them conflict doubts and some not. Here I want to say that all are, but some in one way and some in another. I must explain myself. The doubts I call *conflict doubts* in the note to page 1 are of the form, 'Given $s_1, s_2 \ldots s_{n-m}$ and given that not s_{n-m} to s_n shall we say that Σ?' I call this a request for a decision as to the use of 'Σ'. Here $s_1 \ldots s_n$ may be a typical group of criteria for Σ (a text-book case of schizophrenia) or may be a group of all consistent criteria for Σ. Examples in addition to those I have given are: 'Is Jack's promise keeping promise keeping?' 'Is philosophical doubt doubt?'.

The doubts I call on page 1 *doubts from infinite corrigibility* are of the form, 'We know that $s_1 \ldots s_n$ but do not know that $s_n \ldots s\infty$, do we know that Σ? where $s_1 \ldots s_n$ make a text-book case of Σ although $s_n \ldots s\infty$ are other tests for Σ which have not been carried out. These are requests for decision as to the use of 'know' *although ordinarily it would be unhesitatingly applied.*

The doubts I call on page 2 *doubts arising from the jump from criteria to that of which they are criteria* I now call requests for decision as to the use of 'means the same'.

But now a warning is necessary. From the fact that a man describes a non-typical and borderline case of Σ and asks, 'Is this Σ?' one may well and wisely guess that he is requesting a decision on the use of 'Σ'. But this *may* not be so. On inquiry you may find that he regards himself as having described a typical case of Σ, so that what he is really concerned with is the relation between an infinite or utterly first class group of criteria for Σ and Σ. Thus, if a man describes a non-typical case of belief or love in behaviouristic terms and asks, 'Is it belief?', 'Is it love?', then you can't be sure whether what bothers him is (1) its non-typicalness, or (2) the jump from the outer criteria to the inner state, or (3) the everlasting possibility of something turning up which would make us waver as to whether there was real conviction, real love.

all doubts of this sort. Examples of doubts of this sort are, 'Can a man keep a promise by mistake?', 'Is a zebra without stripes a zebra?'

A doubt of this sort may arise, of course, as to the presence of doubt or belief. Just as one may hesitate as to whether Annabel loves or hates Bertram because in some ways she does and in some ways she doesn't, so one may hesitate when asked whether Colonel Fawcett's wife really believes he's still alive somewhere in Brazil. True, she always swears she does when you ask, and no doubt she then honestly feels she does; but it's so many years ago now that he disappeared, as she well knows; and wouldn't she be as astonished as anyone to see him come up the garden path? One may say, 'She does and she doesn't believe it'. If someone asks of Annabel and Bertram 'Does she love him or hate him?' someone, *even someone who knows them well*, may answer 'I can't make out which it is'. This difficulty, this ignorance, can be removed, not by saying 'You *do* know', but by saying 'Yes, you don't know. But what sort of not knowing is this?[1] It's like not knowing whether a leopard without spots is a leopard, whether an axe of sugar which breaks when you use it is an axe'.

4. *The inner-outer doubts.* What concerned Mr. Berlin were some of the inner-outer doubts. 'Surely from information, however complete, about a man's bodily condition and behaviour I can never know how he's feeling or even that he's feeling?' It is worth noticing how these doubts as to the quality, and finally as to the existence, of 'experiences' behind the faces of others may grow from a milder scepticism which amounts to no more than a relativity in psychology. One may say: 'We can never tell the absolute quantities of desire and feeling which others have. We can't, for example, be sure that Napoleon got a very great thrill from success. True, we know that he was prepared to sacrifice thousands of lives in order to gain it. But then all this proves is that the ratio of his desire for success to his desire for the safety of his fellows was abnormal, and this may have been because he didn't care as much about his fellows as most people do, and not because he had a very strong desire for success. True, he showed

---

[1] The line between a man who asks, 'Does she love him?' as an empirical question and one who asks it as an *a priori* question is not sharp. For a man may be induced to decide partly by giving him new information and partly by reminding him of information he has already.

signs of concern for his fellows when riding over the battlefield, but then perhaps he was a man who *showed* such feelings more readily than most men in those days. True, he divorced Josephine. But then this only proves that the ratio of his desire for success to his love for one he loved best wasn't normal. And this may have been because he didn't love anyone *very* much, and not because he loved success more than you or I. Maybe you and I want success just as much, only from love, or nobly, we resist our inclinations to set this before the welfare of those near to us. No, we can't tell, not for certain at any rate, whether it is that Smith feels things more intensely than Jones, or that he gives vent to them more readily. We can't say: "He loves music very much"; only that "the ratio of his desire for music to his other desires and aversions is abnormally high".'

Having said all this, then very readily the embarrassing idea occurs to one that for all we know the very feeling which we call aversion and which makes us act in one way is what makes Smith act as if he desired a thing. Specialists once were puzzled by a girl in Vienna who cried when she was glad and laughed when she was sad. How did they know she was sad? They watched her eyes and so on. But might not her eyes and all her other reactions have been misleading like her laughter? Unlikely, of course, and of course it would then never be found out. But just as there is nothing impossible in *some* of the reactions usually associated with happiness being associated with unhappiness, so there is nothing impossible in *all* of the reactions associated with happiness being associated with unhappiness. And if this happened in the case of a man called Smith, say, why then we should never know. We should clap him on the back and congratulate him just when, though he was grinning and kept trying for more of what he'd had, he was feeling wretched. Something like this does sometimes nearly happen, and then hardly anyone knows. And surely a man might just be able to tell *no* one that really it made him wretched. And if he didn't *no* one would know. So we don't know but what many of our friends are like this all unknown to us. It may be unlikely but we can't be certain[1] it isn't so. How can we tell, for example,

---

[1] And if it isn't ever certain how can it sometimes be probable that behind A is *a*?

whether the colour which makes Smith call a thing red is the
colour which makes us call a thing red? If he saw green just
where we saw red and vice versa we should never know. He
would match things just as we do, and if asked to paint something would paint it so it looked green to him, that is so it would
look red to us. So we shouldn't know there was anything wrong.
When Smith says he sees a red flag all we know is that he sees a
flag of a colour which stops him and which he calls red. But we
don't know what colour he sees. And when Smith says he believes that flowers feel, then, however consistently he acts, how
can we be sure that he isn't pulling our leg and never slipping up
on it? We can't be sure. There must always be some doubt,
practically negligible if you like, but still some doubt as to what
is going on in the mind of another. What lies behind the smiling
face, pleasure or pain, or nothing?

5. *But now what sort of ignorance is this? What sort of doubt?* If we
try to use the doubt it turns to dust. If we say, 'So perhaps Smith
won't sigh when he hears the young plants are dying', then the
Sceptic says, 'No, I am sure he'll sigh'. The usual case in which
we speak of doubting is one in which the doubt does not turn to
dust when it is used. But the sceptic doesn't even half expect to
find Smith treating flowers callously nor to find in his diary after
he is dead the words, 'Made them all think I thought flowers
feel'. He has explained that he expects nothing of the sort. But
now isn't faith without works dead? And isn't doubt without
works dead? 'He swears that he loves her but he does nothing
for her though she's so ill—it's a queer sort of love.'[1]

6. *The contemplating of a possibility?* The Sceptic may say, 'Well,

---

[1] Another way of treating this would be to say: I doubt whether you doubt
whether Smith believes flowers feel. Consider my doubt as to your doubt. Of what
am I ignorant about you? I doubt (don't you?) whether my doubt is doubt. Now
our doubt about my doubt is also not a matter of ignorance. Your doubt about
Smith may be like ours because just as we are in doubt because we are inclined to
say both that I doubt and that I don't, so you may be inclined to say both that
Smith believes flowers feel and that he doesn't. This will be the case if your doubt
arises because Smith's doubt is philosophical and peculiar and queer. If it doesn't
arise like this but arises like the doubt as to whether he is in pain because he groans,
etc., then it is less like our doubt, which arises because of the queerness of my doubt,
and less like my doubt about you, which arises in the same way. But still your doubt
will be like ours in that it is peculiar in that it is not a matter of ignorance, not a
matter of not knowing what to expect of Smith.

It may be replied, 'But my doubt as to Smith *is* a matter of ignorance'. But this
point in these discussions will be reached later in the text.

perhaps my doubt is a queer doubt. It is not so much a doubt as the contemplating of a possibility'.

7. *I must protest that this is a very inadequate description of this dead doubt.* It at once goes too far and not far enough. It represents the doubt as less like a live doubt than it is and also as more like. It represents the doubts, 'Is there within this body a soul which controls it?' and 'Is there within this machine a man who manipulates it?' as less like each other than they are and also as more like. It represents them as less like than they are because when someone says, 'But can you be sure that there are any feelings behind the behaviour of others?' I feel a qualm just like I feel when someone says, 'You thought that was an attendant who nodded in answer to your question but it was an ingenious waxwork figure'.

On the other hand, to say that the philosophical doubt is the contemplating of a possibility makes it too like a live doubt. The doubt as to whether the figure was an attendant or a waxwork can be settled by watching, by further experiments, though maybe we shan't have time or opportunity to do them. But the doubt whether within Smith's body is a soul cannot be settled by further watching and listening. For, of course, watching and listening would reveal only further outward signs. Yet unfortunately no other means are available. It isn't that there is another means, a psychometer or telepathizer say, which with other people tells us what their inner states are but isn't available for Smith because of the expense. On the contrary, there is no test which *if we did carry it out* would tell us Smith's inner state. Our ignorance is not removable by watching his face under a microscope nor by questioning him for hours nor by waiting in a dark room for a telepathic revelation.[1] This is why I say that to speak of our doubt as *the contemplating of a possibility, the imagining of a possibility*, makes it look more like than it is to the doubt whether this figure is an attendant or a waxwork. For this latter doubt *is* connected with the possibility that further experiments on the figure will give results against saying that he is an attendant, it *is* connected with the possibility that though he

[1] Or it is removable in this way. And then it is. And that is the solution. Then to say, 'We don't know what is in the minds of others' is to say, 'We haven't the power of telepathy'. The answer to this empirical lament is, 'Some of us have sometimes', or 'Yes, isn't it a pity', or 'Yes, isn't it a good thing'.

answers 'This way to the chamber of horrors?' with a nod, he fails to answer any other question. And just as I call the doubt whether Smith believes flowers feel, when he is known to have given infinite and perfect evidence of belief that flowers feel, a queer doubt, so I call the contemplating of the possibility that Smith does not believe flowers feel, a queer contemplating of a possibility—What possibility?

The answer sometimes given is, 'The possibility that Smith does not believe that flowers feel, that his inward state does not fit his outward behaviour'. And this same answer may be given to 'What is in doubt?'

But there is something very dissatisfying about this answer. The Sceptic says, 'I doubt whether he really believes that flowers feel'. We say, 'You mean that possibly if we look in his diary after he's dead . . . ?' The Sceptic says, 'No'. We say, 'Then what is it you have in mind?'. The Sceptic says, 'I have in mind the possibility that after all he doesn't believe that flowers feel'. Suppose a Sceptic says, 'I doubt whether these nations are at war'. We say, 'You mean that possibly although guns are being placed in position and aeroplanes are flying overhead the gunners will all refuse to fire when ordered to do so?' The Sceptic says, 'No'. We say, 'What then?' The Sceptic says, 'All we know is that these men are moving these guns about. But after all the nations are not these men. I am just doubting whether the nations themselves are at war'. What does he mean? What is he doubting? He expects all we expect. Is he really doubting?

Suppose someone says of Smith who, after a long illness, breathes his last, 'I wonder if he's dead'. We say, 'You mean, is it a sort of coma, a sort of suspended animation?' He says, 'No, I don't mean he will come to life again, as we say. I mean is the essential Smith perhaps alive all the time? I know in the ordinary way we should say he's dead. But after all, all we know is that his body no longer moves up and down in breathing and that it won't do so. But Smith is not just his body, and I am wondering whether Smith still exists'. What does this Sceptic mean? What does he expect which we don't expect? Is he doubting?

And here remember that this issue which I, who am not a

sceptic, am raising with regard to the inner-outer sceptic, is not the issue which, as a sceptic, he is raising with regard to Smith. It happens from our selecting as an example of a statement about Smith's mind, 'Smith believes, etc.', that the same or nearly the same form of words expresses our doubts. But they are very different doubts. The Sceptic says, 'Smith gives all the normal signs of doubting the usually accepted view that flowers don't feel and I am sure that he always will give all the usual signs of doubting this, but does he doubt it?'. I say, 'Does the Sceptic, the philosophical sceptic, really doubt about the minds of others?' But I *don't* say the philosophical sceptic gives all the normal signs of doubting.[1] On the contrary, what I say is, 'He looks and feels *at the moment* as if he is doubting but the feeling will not in the usual way be accompanied by any hesistancy in preparations for the future or surprise or relief as it unrolls'. Jones while at the revival meeting sweats with conviction of eternal life but his belief isn't real, because in the morning he is afraid to die. Or shall we say that his conviction was real but very evanescent? Shall we say, 'It wasn't really love'?, or shall we say, 'It was love but love is so evanescent'? (W.). Shall we say that McTaggart[2] doubted the existence of matter but the doubt was very evanescent, or shall we say that he didn't really doubt the existence of matter? When I said 'They didn't have to amputate, I've still got both my hands' did he disbelieve this statement?

8. *Let us put the issue with an example which is less confusing.* Suppose the Sceptic says: 'Smith shows all signs of pain but is he really in pain? I can't be sure. I can't get rid of this doubt. True, Smith gives such signs of pain as I am sure will never be followed by his saying "I was pulling your leg"—there's an arrow in his chest, there is sweat on his brow. But even these are only outward signs. And surely I can *wonder whether* he feels the opposite

[1] Wittgenstein was inclined to put my question in the form: 'He gives none of the normal signs of doubt. Is he in doubt?' But this confuses doubts (2) and (3) (see note 1 to page 1), although Wittgenstein himself drew my attention to the distinction. What Wittgenstein had in mind I think was that the Sceptic gives none of the *contextual* signs of doubt. He is still just as considerate of Smith's feelings although he says with an air of doubt that he doubts their existence.

[2] McTaggart, *Some Dogmas of Religion*; Moore, 'Proof of an External World', *Proceedings of the British Academy*, Vol. XXV. To understand this we need to understand the James-Lange theory of emotion and to extend it to believing, doubting, imagining.

of what I do under these circumstances or whether he doesn't
feel at all. Surely I can *imagine* that when I see red, white and
blue he sees black, green and yellow?'

9. *Imagining the opposite inner state.* Who am I to say what the
Sceptic can imagine? No doubt he says he can imagine Smith
sees the Union Jack as black, green and yellow and telephone
boxes as black and grass as white, because he *does* imagine this.
So do I, so can I. I imagine now that Professor G. E. Moore sees
things like this. How queer it would look to me. Yet, of course,
it must seem quite ordinary to him and so it would to me if I had
always seen things that way.

10. *Rival pictures and rival hypotheses.* But there is something
queer about this imagining. Imagining that though Smith is
moaning he is quite comfortable and pleased doesn't consist in
having an image of Smith comfortable and pleased—for what I
ordinarily call having an image of Smith comfortable and
pleased includes an image of his smiling face. Nor does this
imagining that Smith, in spite of *all* appearances, is comfortable,
consist in having an image of Smith moaning and frowning and
then when no one is looking grinning all over his face. No. It is
the image (or faint sensation) of comfort which is the essential
image in imagining Smith comfortable. Now this image is not
related to what one is imagining in the way in which mostly one's
image when one is imagining is related to what one is imagining.
The image of comfort is related to one's imagining Smith being
in comfort in very much the way that one's image of a leprechaun is related to what one is imagining when one imagines
that in one's watch is an *invisible* leprechaun.

Smith, of course, when asked the colours of the Union Jack
replies, 'Red, white and blue' because he has been taught to call
the colours he then sees 'red', 'white' and 'blue'. But does he see
the same colours, red, white and blue, as we see or does he see,
say, black, green and yellow?

Here are rival pictures, one of the Union Jack in red, white
and blue and one of it in black, green and yellow, underneath
each is written 'Smith'. But these pictures are not related to my
wondering whether Smith sees the Union Jack in red, white and
blue or in black, green and yellow, in the way that my images of
a rat and a fox are related to my wondering whether it's a rat

or a fox that is causing the commotion in the hen-house. No, my pictures of the green, black and yellow Union Jack and the red, white and blue Union Jack, corresponding to the two hypotheses, (1) that it's Smith's seeing the Union Jack in red white and blue, (2) that it is his seeing it in black, green and yellow which is responsible for his behaviour, help to work these hypotheses, more in the way that my pictures of a germ in his blood and of a poison in his veins work the hypotheses (1) that it is an *invisible* germ which is making him so ill, (2) that it is an *invisible* poison which is making him so ill. The pictures of the Union Jacks lead to no expectations of seeing Union Jacks inside Smith. Nor do the pictures of the germ and the poison.

11. *The leprechaun and brownie hypotheses with 'idle' pictures.* Suppose one person says, 'This watch behaves so oddly because there's a leprechaun inside', and another says, 'No, it's a brownie'. Of course these hypotheses are related to the leprechaun and brownie pictures in a way like the hypotheses about Smith's inner state are to the pictures of a green, black and yellow flag and a red, white and blue flag, only if they lead to no expectations of seeing a leprechaun. That is, the leprechaun and brownie must be invisible like Smith's inner states. And further, if these hypotheses are to be like those about Smith then the question which of them is correct must not be settlable by indirect means either. That is, it mustn't be the case that the one hypothesis would lead us to expect one thing and the other something different. For example, though we may say, 'If it's a brownie he wears a peaked cap', and thus deduce different consequences from the brownie hypothesis from those we deduce from the leprechaun hypothesis, we must not deduce, 'If it's a brownie, he won't care for milk so it will be no good putting a saucer of milk in front of the watch in order to get it to go better; but if it's a leprechaun it will be some good.' For that would be a practical, a visible consequence. No practical consequence like that must be deducible from the one hypothesis which is not deducible from the other. Otherwise the leprechaun-brownie dispute will not be *idle*. It will be practical, like the hypothesis that Smith is colour blind *before* it reaches its philosophical condition. If in the ordinary way I say 'Smith says he sees the Union Jack in red, white and blue but I suspect he's colour blind and

sees everything in greys' this is a serious suspicion. For if I am right we cannot take him on as an engine driver. But if when you say 'Then we can't take him as an engine driver' I reply 'Oh, he's all right in that way, in fact, do what you will, you'll find no sign of his weakness', then my hypothesis has reached a philosophical condition. Likewise the dispute as to whether it is a leprechaun or a brownie who makes my watch sing may be either practical and settlable, or academic and idle. It becomes the latter when not only every tested but every testable consequence of the two hypotheses is the same.

12. *Don't say the dispute then becomes meaningless.* Don't say the question 'The watch sings fairy songs, but now *is* there a leprechaun within?' becomes meaningless. For then you will have to say that the question 'The watch sings fairy songs, but now *is* there a brownie within?' is meaningless. And yet here are two hypotheses, not one hypothesis.[1] And how could they be two if they were meaningless? To imagine the one is one thing, to imagine the other another. And they have different consequences, only these different consequences are not observable, because the fairies are by nature invisible to human eyes.

To call the question which of these hypotheses is correct meaningless is too abusive. On the other hand, to call it idle is not abusive enough. It is an idle question how many grains of sand are in my hour glass and the question 'Are there one thousand three hundred and seventy-six or one thousand three hundred and seventy-eight' means less to me than the question 'Is it a brownie with a red cap and a white owl's feather or a leprechaun in green who runs my watch?' or the question 'Is Smith in pain or is he pleased when he grins and says "Delicious!"?' Nevertheless these last two questions are idle in a way in which the idle question about the grains of sand is not. If I ask you the question about the grains of sand I request of you an effort in a certain technique which will result in your being

[1] Compare the three hypotheses with regard to the man under hypnosis who, told that he will see no *t*'s, calls out 'Blank' every time he comes to a *t* when he reads out the letters on a page of print. 'Does the hypnosis alter his sensory apparatus so that he gets a sensation as of a blank? Does hypnosis produce an eccentricity in the way he uses words so that though he says 'Blank' he sees a *t*? Does hypnosis turn him into a liar so that though he sees a *t* and knows it is called a '*t*' he consistently calls it a blank?'

able to tell me the answer, or I ask you to tell me the result of
past effort. But when I ask the question 'Is it an invisible leprechaun or an invisible brownie which produces these phenomena? Each would do so as readily as the other and there is no
experiment which would tell us which it is', then I don't ask you
to set about anything. I am not asking a question. I make an
interrogative noise which would usually act as a request to look
for certain things. But by (1) the use of 'invisible' I exclude
some of these, and by (2) saying that the outward signs would
be the same I exclude the rest.

13. *Degrees of departure from a difference in odds offered, to a picture
preference*. Between disputes which reflect no issue suitable for
betting, no difference of expectation, and disputes which reflect
only difference of expectation, i.e. disputes which will be settled
at once when a certain experiment is done, there are many
different shades of dispute. In some the betting issue predomin-
ates, in others devotion to a notation with its picture. Only when
there remains no experiment which will influence the disputants
at all has the dispute become entirely of the latter sort, so that
their assertions register not at all difference in expectations but
only devotions to different working pictures.

14. *Equality of prediction with diversity of picture produces conflict as
to equality of meaning*. Usually if two expressions differ in the
pictures with which they are worked they differ in expectation
value. And when two expressions differ in both these ways we
have no hesitation in saying that they mean something different,
and when they agree in both these ways that they mean the
same. It is when expressions differ in one of these ways, picture
say, and agree in the other, prediction say, that we get into
difficulties. Shall we say that the brownie and leprechaun
hypotheses are the same because to say that a watch is 'brownie-
driven' works on a hearer like saying that it is 'leprechaun-
driven' in the ways we have described? Or shall we say that they
are not the same because of the differences which we have described in the way they work on hearers?

Does 'The Sun is rising' mean the same as 'This part of the
earth is coming into the sun again'? Does 'The sea is angry'
mean the same as 'The waves are high'? Does 'At last a turn of
the road hid them. He turned away. His eyes filled with tears',

mean the same as 'At last a turn of the road hid them. He turned sadly away'?

15. *The issue 'Are there two hypotheses?' put again.* To put the issue again: Suppose that amongst grandfather clocks some have been quite normal, and some have been abnormal and sung fairy songs on request and disappeared on Midsummer Night. On opening these, leprechauns have been found. Next, to everyone's surprise, some watches are discovered which sing fairy songs and disappear on Midsummer Night. But of course the watches are too small for ordinary leprechauns and when they are opened no leprechauns are discovered. Someone suggests that nevertheless there are tiny, invisible leprechauns within (Puck in the churn, germs in the blood, agitated invisible particles in the table, a current in the wire) and that's why the watches behave curiously. This idea is generally accepted, but you, being philosophical, ask, 'But *are* there leprechauns in the watches?' What is it you are wondering? You are not wondering what would happen if you dipped the watch in milk or left it under the moon. You've tried all that, you know all that. But then what are you wondering? You are not wondering anything. 'But', you will say, surely I *am* wondering something. I am wondering whether there is an invisible leprechaun in this watch—or a brownie, or nothing at all. The rival images are before me. Surely I am contemplating two alternatives, two possibilities?'

To this I should reply, imitating, I hope correctly, Wittgenstein: 'All right. If that's good enough for you it's good enough for me. Let's call what you do "contemplating two possibilities". Like you, when a leprechaun and a brownie are mentioned, I have two images; and even if I don't, still, even from the first, when I hear someone say "There's an invisible leprechaun in my watch" I have some idea what he means. I expect there to be something queer about the watch and I am not surprised that it signs fairy songs, not hymns.'

15.1 *Learning the meaning of 'absolutely invisible leprechaun'.* Perhaps I am a bit puzzled at first about the 'invisible'. Why does he say 'There's a leprechaun in my watch' if there is no such thing to be seen or felt when it's opened? However, as soon as he explains that his watch sings fairy songs, etc., then I quite understand when he calls to me, 'And tomorrow I'll bring you a watch with an invisible leprechaun inside'. In just the same way I can come to quite understand if he says, 'I'll bring you a watch with an invisible brownie inside'.

Although from the first I have *some* idea what a man means when he says, 'There's an invisible leprechaun in my watch', or 'There's an invisible brownie in my watch', I don't at first know how much he means, what his statement comes to. So at first my understanding is only partial compared with my understanding of his saying crossly, 'There's a demon in my watch'. This last is different. I am used to this. I just smile. We all know what this comes to, we're very scientific nowadays and don't believe in demons. What he means is that his watch has again let him down, although he's just had it put in perfect order, and so he's pretty cross. That's what his statement comes to.[1] But what his sober statements 'There's an invisible leprechaun, there's an invisible brownie, in my watch' come to, that I don't quite know *until he has explained how his watch sings fairy songs and thus explained how much is left of the usual significance of 'There's a leprechaun in my watch', even when to it is added the destructive word 'invisible'.*

15.2 *The effect of regaining significance in this way.* But now if after explaining in this way what he means by 'There's an invisible leprechaun in this watch', 'There's an invisible brownie in this watch', he then calls out as he leaves, 'Shall I bring you a leprechaun-driven watch or a brownie-driven watch?' then I should be at a loss. I should say, 'Well, but what's the difference?' He would reply, 'One is driven by a leprechaun, the other by a brownie'. I should say, 'Yes, but as they are both invisible—what do you mean, which would I rather have?' 'There's no difference in what the watches do', he would say, 'but would you rather have a watch worked by a leprechaun or one worked by a brownie?' 'Oh', I should say, 'you choose', only now this would be a joke. Choose! How can he choose? Does he choose or doesn't he? Between the two alternatives, leprechaun, brownie, does he choose? What he does is to choose a watch which sings the fairy songs and then choose *whether to say* this is

---

[1] But is that what it means? A consideration of this case would be illuminating if only people would consider it seriously. But they say, 'Ah, *that*—that's different. There's no puzzle about that, no one could find any difficulty there.' Certainly it's different. Certainly *hardly* anyone would *for long* be *much* puzzled about it

because it's run by a leprechaun or *to say* it's because it's run by
a brownie. Maybe someone else, like those who prefer mnemic
causation to invisible twists in the brain or unconscious images
in the mind, will prefer to say, 'The watch sings fairy songs,
especially by moonlight, disappears on Midsummer Night, sings
better if offered milk or honey. We don't know why, and it's no
good pretending we do'. Someone else again, instead of telling
the long story about what the watch sings and when it sings
best, will say, 'It is *as if* this watch were possessed by a leprechaun or a brownie'. Of this we readily say that it is just another
way of describing how the watch behaves. If now someone says,
'I believe there *is* a leprechaun within or a brownie', we say,
'What do you mean? You know there isn't'. He says, 'An
invisible one I mean'. Mightn't we then say, 'A hypothetical one
you mean. You don't believe anything different from the rest of
us. With you this is only another way of describing the watch'.
'No', he says, 'I mean that there is something like a leprechaun,
the presence of which *explains* the peculiar behaviour of the
watch. I don't just mean that the watch behaves as it does. I
believe that there is a reason why it behaves so queerly and I
suggest that that reason is the presence of a leprechaun. You
know what a leprechaun is like from the ones you've seen. Well
this one is like those, only it's invisible. It is, of course, absurd to
talk of *knowing* that it is there or *knowing directly* that it is there,
because knowing directly means seeing or touching and it is
self-contradictory for an invisible leprechaun to be seen and an
intangible one touched. But what I say is there may *be* one there
though we can't see it.' 'Ah', we should say, 'we know now what
this wondering comes to with you. You expect there's a stone in
the hoof of a horse that suddenly goes lame. You don't in the
same way expect there's a leprechaun in the watch that suddenly sings. You don't expect anything different from the rest of
us, so don't try to excite us about yourself by describing yourself
in a way which might lead us to suppose you mad. And you can
call your hypotheses of a brownie and a leprechaun two different hypotheses, if you like. It doesn't matter you saying this
because now we know what this amounts to, because now we've
brought out what there is to make one say "There are two
different hypotheses". There *are*, we have seen, differences be-

tween a person who speaks of the eccentricities of the watch as caused by a leprechaun and one who speaks of them as caused by a brownie. But we have also seen that these differences are such as to make very peculiar the question, Which of these people is right, which of these hypotheses is correct?" It is a peculiarity which came out in the way "Shall I bring you a watch worked by a brownie or one worked by a leprechaun?' leaves us at a loss. The question leaves us at a loss in a way which is apt to make us say, "The question is not a question. There aren't two possibilities. There's no difference. It's only a matter of which picture you paste on the back to remind you of the same peculiarities in the watch".'

It's the same peculiarity of question which tempts one to say, 'The philosophical scientist who suddenly doubts whether a current runs in wires which give off sparks, drive trains, etc., *isn't doubting anything*'. Whether it is correct to say this is of as much and as little interest as whether unintentional promise keeping is promise keeping.

The question whether Jack yesterday kept his promise loses all interest once the relevant features of the case have been described in 'aseptic'[1] language. 'One day Jack said to Dick, "I will leave you all my money". Next day Jack was dying and he said, "I won't leave my money to Dick but to my next of kin, who is my wife". So he wrote, "All my property is to go to my next of kin". But unknown to Jack his wife had died. And this left Dick his next of kin. Did Jack keep his promise or didn't he?' The question is no longer of interest. Every philosophical question answers itself if asked aseptically and *fully* enough. And the question 'Does the philosophical scientist doubt, does he not know which of two alternatives is correct?' loses its anxiety-drive when, as we have done, we set out the conflicting forces, describe in aseptic language all the influencing features of the case.

16. *I want to explain again when and how 'Is there a leprechaun within?' isn't a question*. In the ordinary way, 'There's a leprechaun in this watch' would lead us to expect to see something extraordinary. If a man explains that when he says such a thing we needn't expect to see anything of the sort, then when he says

[1] See note 1 to page 1.

'There's a leprechaun in this watch' his remark works on us very like the first sentence of a story, 'In the clock on the stairs lives a little old gnome. . . .' And we no more ask him 'Are you *sure*? I see nothing' than we ask this of the storyteller. One might be inclined to say, 'The sentence now means little to us.' On the other hand, one might say, 'It *means* just as much as before, only now we don't take it seriously'. If we speak the latter way we are apt to assume that it still makes just as much sense to ask whether the statement is true or false, it is just false. But is it? Considering the speaker wasn't wishing to lead us to expect anything in particular was he speaking falsely?

Suppose now that we are told that 'There's a leprechaun within' isn't to be taken as mere fun, as a fairy story, that there really is something peculiar about leprechaun-driven watches, that they sing songs, disappear, etc., then the sentence begins again to work in a way which makes it not inappropriate to ask when someone utters it, 'Are you sure?', 'Is he right?' But the appropriateness returns to these questions *only in so far as* what was taken from the significance of 'There's a leprechaun within' by the story-teller is returned to it by the scientist—so far and no further. Consequently, 'Is it true?' is appropriate now only while it is still a question, 'What is its eccentric behaviour like? Is it leprechaun-like or isn't it?'

17. *There are two cases where 'Is this watch's behaviour leprechaun-like?' no longer puts a question and in which consequently 'Is there a leprechaun in this watch?' no longer puts a question.* The first case is where it would ordinarily be said to put a question but the question is a conflict question and has no answer. I want to explain why I say that this question is not a question, in order to help explain why I say in the second case that 'Is there a leprechaun within?' no longer puts a question. The second case is one in which a man who is asking 'Is this watch's behaviour leprechaun-like?' is no longer putting a question because it has been fully answered. In this case 'Is there a leprechaun within?' puts a question only in so far as there is a jump between criteria and that of which they are criteria.

As to the conflict case. It may be that the behaviour of a watch is in many ways leprechaun-like but in as many ways not. Then, if asked 'Is there a leprechaun within?' it would be quite usual to reply, 'I hardly know'. But this ignorance isn't ignorance, this doubt isn't doubt. One begins to notice the peculiarity of this ignorance when one notices its irremediableness, its logical irremediableness, how it is combined with the most perfect knowledge of, and confidence in, the watch. And then one notices how instead of replying 'I hardly know' one might have replied 'I hardly know what to say', and how again instead of this, one might have replied 'You ask "Is the behaviour of this watch leprechaun-like?" Well, it is and it isn't'. And then, if one feels a bit of a qualm at saying that, one may notice the connection between 'Is its behaviour leprechaun-like?' and 'Are its behaviours, its reactions, leprechaun-like?'. Directly we have the question in the plural like this we no longer need to reply 'I don't know', 'It is and it isn't', because we can answer, 'Some are and some aren't'.[1] And we may add, 'And whether there are enough of its reactions which are leprechaun-like to call its behaviour leprechaun-like is a matter for decision'. The anxious doubt has become a cheerful indecision; the request for information that no expert in heaven or earth can provide has become a request for a decision, a judicious decision though.

Instead of saying 'Is its behaviour leprechaun-like' isn't a question and doesn't express a doubt because it turns into indecision and choice, we might say 'Is its behaviour leprechaun-like?' expresses a doubt of a sort very *peculiar* in that it is capable of turning into indecision and choice. And this has an advantage, because the transformation from a state which at first is like doubt to a state which is like indecision[2] as to whom to award the prize to, is a very important transformation.

And just as the doubt from conflict of criteria about whether the watch's behaviour is leprechaun-like is not a doubt because it turns into indecision, so the doubt from conflict of criteria as

---

[1] This is an extremely simple case of the effectiveness of the Verification Principle. The verification for 'Is its behaviour leprechaun-like?' is 'Are its reactions leprechaun-like?' The illuminating effect of this translation is seen in the text. Dr. Dorothy Wrinch once pointed out how the question 'Does he represent the feeling of his constituency?' which is all right when the people of the constituency 'feel as one' but becomes embarrassing when some feel one way and some another, can be translated into a form which is not embarrassing in either case, namely, 'Do the persons in his constituency feel as he does?' In this way she provided an excellent example of the importance of logical constructions, levels of language and the verification principle.

[2] Or doubt! as we might also say.

to whether the watch is leprechaun-driven is not a doubt because it turns into indecision. Or, if you like, it is a doubt with the peculiar property of turning into an indecision. We may say that conflict-doubts *dissolve* into indecision—to use Wittgenstein's word.

18. *It is for the same sort of reason, namely the way they dissolve, that I call doubts when the criteria do not conflict but are all for 'Yes' or all for 'No', not real doubts. For they dissolve. Not into indecision. But into decision.* One who says 'This wire gives off sparks, drives trains, rings bells, etc., but I doubt whether there is a current running through it' is declaring against saying that 'gives off sparks, drives trains, rings bells, etc.' entails 'has an electric current running through it'. This is why it would be absurd for anyone to say, 'This wire if attached to a battery at one end and a bell at the other will ring the bell, etc., but I doubt whether it behaves *as if* a current runs through it'. For 'will ring a bell when suitably attached etc.' obviously entails 'behaves *as if* a current runs through it'. But one who says, 'All the same I doubt whether there *is* a current', *is he absurd or isn't he?* Do the features mentioned entail 'There is an electric current within'? When he says 'Accepting $s_1 \ldots s_n$ I can yet doubt whether S is P' what he does is to say that $s_1 \ldots s_n$ do not entail S is P. When a man says '$s_1 \ldots s_n$ are true but is SP?' then implicitly he denies that $s_1 \ldots s_n$ entail S is P.[1] True, there are cases where this isn't all he is doing, e.g. A man in the dark says, 'This has hands, face, and feet but is it a man or a mummy?' But, on the other hand, there are cases where this *is* all he is doing. My point is that in philosophical cases this is all he's doing, that he isn't besides asking whether S is P. To grasp how philosophy though not logic is *a priori* and though *a priori* is not logic takes one far towards dissolving its difficulties.

Let us return to 'Is there an invisible leprechaun in this watch?' where the scientist has given it back some of the meaning the story-teller took from it. We said that after the scientist had explained the meaning he gave to 'There is an invisible leprechaun in this watch' it could yield a question only while 'Is this watch's behaviour leprechaun-like?' was a question. And we said that there are two cases where this becomes no longer a

[1] See note 1 to page 1.

question. They are of course two cases where all is already known about the behaviour of the watch. The first case, which we have now noticed, is that in which some of this complete information favours an affirmaive answer and some a negative. The second case, which we have now come to, is that in which either all of this complete information favours a negative answer or all of it favours an affirmative answer. In this case, if a scientist who has told us that we needn't expect to see a leprechaun when he speaks of a leprechaun-haunted watch but need expect only what we have found, then asks 'But is this watch inhabited by a leprechaun?' we are at a loss.

Someone may say: 'Of course if the scientist has explained that all that he *means* by "Is there a leprechaun within this watch?" is "Does this watch behave as if there were a leprechaun within?" then if, knowing that it does behave so, he asks "But is there a leprechaun within?" his question is absurd. But if that is not all that the scientist means then his question is not absurd. When the housewife says "Puck's in the churn" she doesn't mean merely "The churn behaves *as if* a small ill-disposed person were in it". And the scientist who says that through wires giving electrical phenomena there runs a current, isn't merely saying that wires giving electrical phenomena give electrical phenomena. Much less is it the case—if this is what you should be driving at—that Smith sees the Union Jack in red, white, and blue means "Smith acts as if he does".'

I must protest that this is the point at issue. Those who say, 'I can still doubt whether Smith sees the Union Jack in red, white and blue however normally he behaves', sometimes put their position thus: ' "Smith sees the Union Jack in red, white and blue" doesn't *mean merely* that he says that it's red, white and blue and points to roses, snow and the sky, etc.' Since the point is sometimes put this way, I must insist that to say 'Sometimes the scientist doesn't mean merely "behaves as if, etc" ' is to claim the point at issue.

However, by all means let us consider people who speak of currents and leprechauns without explaining in so many words that all they mean by 'A current runs here' is 'It is as if a current runs here', and that all they mean by 'A leprechaun lives here' is 'It is as if a leprechaun lives here'.

There is something about these people which makes us say 'They mean an *invisible* current, an *invisible* leprechaun' just as there is something about the man who says 'Poor Smith, he always has in his head the picture of the motor smash in which his brother was killed' makes us say, 'He doesn't mean a visible picture to be found by cutting Smith's head open'.

What makes us say the scientist means an invisible current? It is the fact that, like the scientist who did say in so many words that all he meant was 'behaves as if', this scientist whom we are now considering does not expect to see a flowing stream in the wire, not even with the strongest microscope, and doesn't wish you to expect this when he tells you that that wire carries a current. He is in fact just like the scientist who said in so many words, 'All I mean by "an invisible current" is "behaves as if there is a current" ', except that (1) he didn't *say* that, and (2) he is much more likely to confuse himself or be confused by others with the question 'But *is* there an invisible current within?' But if he didn't expect to see anything why should his seeing nothing suddenly arouse his suspicions? His suspicions of what? What that he formerly had confidence in has he confidence in no longer? Not the seeing of sparks, for he is still confident of that. Not seeing a stream, for he never was confident of that. So if he now says 'A doubt has struck me', then it's a queer doubt since it involves no loss of confidence in what formerly he had confidence in. As to whether he *means the same as* the former scientist who actually *said* 'I mean by "There's an invisible current within" "It's as if there were a current within" ', I must leave you to *decide*.

The very fact that this latter scientist asks: 'The sparks fly, etc., but is there a current within?' might be taken to prove that the answer to his question is 'No'. For since he asks 'Is there a current' where he doesn't ask 'Do sparks fly, etc.?' it follows that he uses these expressions differently, i.e. that they mean something different. And if they mean something different, then the flying sparks don't *prove* the pressure of the current. Speaking this way, one will say that all philosophical questions of the form 'Does S mean S'?', 'Do I know S from S'?' answer themselves in the negative. But I don't myself wish to decide as to whether the scientist means by 'There is a current in this wire' the same as he means by 'This wire gives off sparks, etc.'

19. *In other words: what I want to insist upon is how* peculiar *it is when he suddenly says* 'I wonder if there is an invisible current in this wire'. He is like someone who suddenly says, 'Is there such a thing as a wind? I see nothing except its effects [*sic*], the hurrying clouds, the flying leaves'. And one who suddenly doubts, saying, 'I wonder whether in gold, perhaps, a negative current produces all the phenomena we associate with a positive current?' is like one who suddenly doubts, saying, 'I wonder. Perhaps on Sundays when sailing boats fly eastwards, the wind is not, as we commonly suppose, from west to east, but east to west; because perhaps on Sundays winds have opposite effects on things in the wind from what they have on other days of the week'. And now consider one who says, 'Who knows? maybe with mad people signs of melancholy are all produced by happiness. Maybe with Smith signs of seeing red are produced by seeing black'.

One might say, 'These fancies aren't absurd. It's only absurd to be serious about them, but not at all because they contemplate *very* remote possibilities. They don't'.

Someone may say, 'Though we can't say what one who believes in fairies or gods which can't be seen and never act except in accordance with the laws of nature, loses confidence in when he says "Maybe you are right and there are no spirits in the trees", still he does seem to lose confidence in something. An empty picture rises and his heart falls, very like it happens with one who really believes in visible fairies and hoped to show them to you beside the lake but now suddenly doubts whether they have gone and won't return'.

I said with regard to the question 'Does Smith, who gives all signs of believing that flowers feel, really believe this?' that the qualm it brings is like the qualm that goes with a real doubt. It is the same with the qualm and picture that goes with 'But are there invisible fairies?' It too is like the qualm that goes with a real doubt, such as 'I wonder, *are* there any orchids in this wood'. The questions '*Is* there an invisible leprechaun in this watch?', '*Is* there an invisible current in electric wires?' both come with an empty picture and an empty feeling, like 'Maybe there are no orchids now'. But what we have seen is how different nevertheless are these mock doubts from betting doubts.

A father who pretends he doesn't know what is in the parcel his child has given him, feels as if he doesn't know, feels as if he is guessing, feels as if he thought it might be alive and bite him. But he doesn't really think it might be alive, he really knows that it's chocolate, he's only pretending to wonder what it is. But since he *pretends to himself* that he doesn't know *is* he only pretending? Shall we say that for the moment he forgets he knows, that for the moment he wonders? When he turns quickly to fire on the wolves who are gaining in spite of the efforts of two exhausted rocking chairs, he is really excited. He is pretending that wolves are behind but he isn't pretending he thinks that wolves are behind. He feels they are, he sort of believes they are, he half believes it. No, it isn't that he half believes it, he doesn't. It is more that just for the moment he believes it. The illusion is fragile. It breaks if you touch it. At least it does if you touch it with an unsympathetic hand. If you ask 'How much further to the inn?' that won't break it. But if you say 'There are no wolves nowadays', then the father will say 'We meant pretence wolves'. He is like the scientist who says he meant an invisible current, so invisible that not even stronger microscopes need be expected to reveal it.

20. *Everyone can see that it's silly to ask, 'But are there any pretence wolves?'* If anyone asks this he is making an academic joke like one who says, 'Since you passed nobody on the road, nobody walks slower than you'.[1] *But people don't always laugh if you talk as follows: 'But* IS *there an invisible currrent in wires giving electrical phenomena?* We say that an electric current runs with less resistance through steel than through rubber, but all we *know* is that the phenomena at the other end are more marked. Perhaps the current is as strong, only in rubber it shows itself less.' And serious economists write articles round the text that we don't know what amounts of pleasure different people get from things. They write, 'We say that Smith got more pleasure from his last and second glass of beer than Jones got from his last and tenth glass, but all we know is that Smith would have been prepared to work longer to avoid losing it than would Jones, or that Smith would have a given a greater proportion of his possessions to avoid losing it. But maybe his other possessions gave less pleas-

[1] Adapted from *Alice Through the Looking Glass.*

ure to Jones. We know nothing about the absolute amounts of pleasure things give to other people, we only know the ratios in which they prefer them. When an economist, as such, talks of a thing giving more pleasure to one man than to another, this is only *a way of talking about* what each would give for the thing. The economist should, strictly speaking, define consumer's surplus in terms not of pleasure but of the ratio of what a man would give for a thing to what he has to give for a thing. The question whether a poor man gets more pleasure from his last pound is, strictly speaking, a psychological or metaphysical question rather than a question of economics, though it is often convenient to talk in absolute terms of amounts of pleasure and desire, just as it is often convenient to talk in terms of amounts of energy almost as if it were a subtle fluid, when really all we know is that coal will keep the room warm longer or drive an engine further than the same bulk of wood'.

21. *Well now, why is it that though few people will take seriously*[1] *the question 'But are there pretence wolves?' many will take seriously 'But are there invisible currents?' and many would take seriously 'But are there invisible leprechauns?'* One way of answering this is to say: It is much more obvious that pretence wolves are not a species of wolf than it is that invisible leprechauns or invisible wolves are not species of leprechaun or wolf, i.e. it is so much more obvious that the grammar of 'pretence wolf' differs from that of 'curly wolf' than it is that the grammar of 'invisible wolf' differs from that of 'curly wolf', i.e. it is so much more obvious that questions which make sense with 'curly wolf' and 'wolf' may make no sense with 'pretence wolf' than it is that questions which make sense with 'curly wolf' and 'wolf' may make no sense with 'invisible wolf'. And this is partly because there *is* more difference between the grammar of 'curly wolf' and 'pretence wolf' than there is between the grammar of 'curly wolf' and 'invisible wolf'. But it is also partly because there are uses of 'invisible wolf' which are not so very different in grammar from the grammar of 'curly wolf' and *these uses are not sharply separated from the use in which the grammar is very different.*

In other words: People are more inclined to take seriously the

[1] The *busy* scientist is impatient of this question because he knows that 'what he wants to mean' when he talks of invisible currents is certainly true.

question 'But are there invisible electric currents?'[1] because
very often when someone says 'There's an invisible so and so
here' it's not silly to ask 'Are you sure?' For example 'Is there
invisible ink on this paper?' It is not silly to ask 'Is there an
invisible X here?' (1) when though X's can't be seen with the
naked eye they can be seen with microscopes or after prayer and
fasting; it's not silly (2) when though there is *no* way of seeing an
X there remain tests for an X which have not yet been carried
out. The question becomes silly only when neither (1) nor (2) is
the case.

It may be said: 'There are no cases where there is no further
test to be carried out.' There is no need to dispute this. My point
is that (1) there are cases where the source of dispute is not at all
these uncarried out tests, and that (2) these cases are not sharply
separated from cases where the dispute does arise from different
expectations, but are joined to them by cases where the dispute
is partly empirical and partly *a priori*. Thus when one doctor disputes with another as to whether a child who coughs and vomits
but doesn't whoop has whooping cough, the source of the dispute is largely a matter of whether one should, in view of the
absence of the whoop, speak of whooping cough. This is an *a
priori* issue. But that there is this *a priori* difference between the
doctors is obscured by the fact that the dispute probably also *in
part* arises from different expectations as to the course the illness
will take and how it will respond to this treatment or that. It is
obscured, too, by the fact that the forms of words, 'It is whooping
cough', 'It isn't', always can at any stage in the dispute be used
to express an empirical dispute, since it is quite true that there
always remains some uncarried out test, with the consequence
that it is always possible to pretend that it was an empirical
issue one had in mind in raising the question.

The dispute is nearly always purely *a priori* when the question
asked is not particular, not, for example, 'Does this wire carry a

---

[1] Compare the seriousness with which people take 'But is there such a thing as
force or stresses and strains apart from our own sensations of strain?' and 'Is there
such a thing as sensation which I don't feel?' The seriousness with which people
take this is not unconnected with the seriousness on some occasions of questions of
the form 'Is there an invisible X?' But it has further sources which will be brought
out in the next instalment, where the point is taken up. But 'Are there fairies in the
trees' is different from 'Are their souls in bodies?'. 'Are there invisible twists in the
brain?' is different from 'Are there unconscious events in the mind?'

current?' but general, for example, 'Can we *ever* be sure that *any* wire carries a current?' Such a question usually arises not at all from the incompleteness of our researches into the habits of, e.g. wires, and so can be put in the form, 'Even if all the infinite number of tests for, e.g. a wire carrying a current had been carried out and found favourable to its carrying one, should we know that it carried one? Would it follow that it carried one?' In this form the *a priori* character of the general question has become apparent.

21.1. *The uses of 'Is this leprechaun-driven?'* Let us remember then (1) that the particular question 'Is there an invisible leprechaun within this watch?' may be purely empirical in that it is asked because, though from the watch's face the questioner thinks it's leprechaun-haunted and will sing if asked, he isn't sure; (2) that nevertheless the question may be asked *partly* because the questioner doesn't know what the watch is capable of but also *partly* because he isn't sure whether it is proper to call a watch leprechaun-haunted when it sings fairy songs all night but only when asked and never of itself. The more the question arises from the latter source the more *a priori* it is.

Now comes a second point. The field of uses of 'Is this watch leprechaun-driven?' has another dimension beside that running from the empirical to the *a priori*. For at any point on this scale the questions differ according to whether they arise because the questioner doesn't know the usage of the expressions involved in his question as well as he might of not because of this. Thus, suppose he asks because, though the usage of 'leprechaun-driven' is *in* fact fixed so that we don't call a watch 'leprechaun-driven' but 'parrot-driven' when it sings fairy songs only after it has just heard them performed, *the questioner doesn't know this*. Then we can put him right, tell him the answer to his question. Then our conversation with him will be a conversation in logic. But it may be that he doesn't know whether to call leprechaun-driven a watch which sings songs only when it has just heard them, not because there is a convention on this matter of which convention he is ignorant, but *because there is no convention on this matter*. There may be no customary procedure for such a case either because no such case has before arisen or because when such cases arise some people do one thing and some another. The more indefinite custom is, the less is the question a matter of logic and the more it calls for decision. There are two cases: (*a*) where the questioner asks the question as a logical question, that is, expecting us to be able to tell him the answer by improving what he thinks his defective knowledge of when it is 'the done thing' to call a watch leprechaun-driven; (*b*) where the questioner is amused and expects us to be puzzled as to how to help him because he knows he knows as much as anyone about when it is the done thing to call a watch leprechaun-driven.

Finally, we come to a queer case where the questioner knows what usage is and the usage is definitely for (or against) saying that a watch is leprechaun-driven. This is the case we have been considering. What in such a case induces the questioner to ask his question?

A man touches a wire, asking, 'Is there any current in this?' and as he touches it there's a blaze of sparks, a crackling, and a spasm crosses his face from the shock he gets. A man watching says, 'Is there a current?' but his question is a joke, an exclamation.

It's a joint joke because the speaker and hearer realize the 'inappropriateness' of the interrogative form.

21.2 *When a philosopher under the same circumstances doesn't laugh* but insists on seriousness *and says, 'Ah, but is there any current there? Of course it gives off sparks and so on but how do you know from this that there is a current there?' then what is he up to?* He is not issuing an empirical warning like 'True it looks like a log. But isn't it an alligator?' Nor a logical warning like 'He published abroad the scandalous story, but that wasn't libel, because the story was true'.

The philosopher who says 'Do we, even when we know that a wire gives all electrical symptoms, know that an invisible current runs in it?' is more like a man who when one says 'I'm afraid Brown is mad' says 'Aren't we all mad really?' This looks like an empirical warning such as the vet gives when having just examined a lot of horses he says 'They all look sound. But are they?' and pulls down his mouth in a knowing way. Nor is it a logical warning like 'These horses seem sound but, don't forget, you oughtn't to warrant any of them without a trial on hard

ground for navicular disease'. But 'Aren't we all mad really?'
and especially 'Aren't we all mad really, if you come to think of
it?' is often said without expecting anything different of people
from what all the rest of us expect. And it certainly isn't the case
that we oughtn't to call a person sane without trying the effects
of a week's solitary confinement on him. So no one ought to
say 'Are any of us sane? *Don't forget* you oughtn't to call a man
sane until you have tried solitary confinement on him'. On the
contrary, the person who says 'Aren't we all mad, if you come
to think of it?' is suggesting a logical reform. He wishes to draw
the line less sharply between the mad and the sane, like one who
says 'We are all sinners'. One who says 'We are all sinners'
('We all have an Œdipus complex') *may* say this because from
special experience he is confident that even those who best keep
the ten commandments in Kensington would react in other
places in such a way that we should all say 'They were sinners
at heart all the time'. I say he *may* say it because of this. But he
may say it not at all because of this. He may say it because
though he would in the ordinary way entirely agree with us as
to who is good and who is bad and on what they may be expected to do, nevertheless reflecting on the life of the pious Mr.
Jones and the wicked Mr. Vincent who ran off with Mrs. Jones,
he '*feels there isn't such a difference between them*' and feels disinclined
to give the one a white label and the other a black. He suggests a
new notation which shall make a difference between the difference between sheep and goats and the difference between saints
and sinners.

It is true that often these 'wise' generalizations, while they
arise partly by reflection in the way I have just reminded you of,
come partly out of experience, and when this is so then, while
partly they are recommending a notational reform, partly also
they are issuing an empirical and logical warning so that their
empirical and logical air is not entirely misleading.

Take the man who says 'Aren't we all mad really?' Surely,
often he is wishing to make our reactions, our confidences, more
continuous, so that we no longer have *no* confidence in the mad
and such great confidence in the unmad. He wishes to alter our
expectations of the mad and the sane as one who teaches us a
thing or two about doctors, clergymen and teachers. So isn't he

issuing an empirical warning? And as it is a warning about not taking certain appearances too unquestioningly, isn't it a logical warning as to the estimates we put on the evidences we get? But can it be both a logical and an empirical warning?

As to the last point. When a man says 'Bill isn't in the bedrooms and isn't in the sitting-room or the kitchen so he isn't in' then he is making an empirical statement and a logical one. And if another man says 'It doesn't follow he isn't in. He may be in the cellar' then he is holding up his hand in warning both logically and empirically.

As to whether a man who says 'Aren't we all mad really?' is issuing an empirical warning, there are many ways in which his question can be used. All can be described as uses in which the speaker wishes to draw the line less sharply between the mad and the sane. But this 'drawing the line less sharply' can be anything between a feeling, on reflecting over what we all know about our own hearts and our friends', that there's not such a difference between us and the mad and a real belief that everybody has now gone mad, that everybody is mad, though at the moment everyone is quiet. Of course in the last case there would be nothing misleading about bringing out this generalization with an instructive air. But no one uses it like this. People do, however, use it like 'We are all sinners' or 'We are all selfish', because, though they don't want to make the empirical generalization 'properly' expressed by 'We are *all* mad', they do want, because of their disillusioning experiences, to say that *some* or *many* people we think sane probably aren't.

But there is a more subtle way in which 'Aren't we all mad?' may reflect our eccentricity of expectation. A man may entirely agree with us as to who is mad and who is not, and yet his saying 'Aren't we all mad really?' reflect a difference in his expectations as well as attitude. Most people, if they find that one of their relatives has become very eccentric, will ask a doctor, 'Is he mad?' and if the doctor says 'No, he's not mad' then they are entirely relieved and say, 'No he's only a bit eccentric, the doctor says he's not mad'. ('The doctor says' they say, with pathetic faith. But does the doctor know as well as they do?) On the other hand, if the doctor says 'He's mad', they are plunged into despair, and suppose that now he must be hurried to a lunatic asylum. They look at him with scared and curious eyes. In contrast to this, the man who says 'We are all mad' (all are sinners) says to the doctor, 'You mean he's a bit "madder" than the rest of us or mad in more awkward ways'. And his saying this, though it may not reflect any difference in his bets as to who is mad and who isn't, may well reflect a difference in the bets he would make on the patient's recovery or on some sane person's doing this or that mad thing. His bets on various eccentricities in people will not show that sharp discontinuity between bets on eccentricities in the mad and bets on eccentricities in the sane, which the bets of ordinary people would show.

His expectations of eccentricity may be unusual in this way, although his devotion in ordinary life to the classification into sane and insane may be more stable than that of the rest of us. Most of us are apt if we find someone frightened into hysterics by the quack of a duck or unable to remember what happened five minutes ago, to exclaim, 'He's mad, you'd never have thought it but he's mad'. The man of more experience has had experience of eccentricities in the sane and realizes that since seven people out of ten are monsters they can't be.[1]

Of course to say 'We are all mad' is a way of expressing his unusual expectations of eccentricity which is very apt to mislead. For people are very apt to suppose that one who says this at least believes that many people who are thought sane aren't. The pear expert who says 'These pears look good, don't they? But really they're all rotten at the core' has expectations of every pear very different from the rest of us, who are taken in by them. But the expectations of one who says 'We're all mad really, deep down, only we keep it under' are not related to his words in the ordinary way, they are not as eccentric as they seem. It is true that such a remark seldom expresses no eccentricity of expectation, that case is a limiting case. But though usually when a man says 'We are all mad deep down' he's rather more prepared than the rest of us for poor Mr. Williams to brain his baby with its own bottle, usually he says what he says very largely because certain things we *all* know already but hurry over in our minds, can't so well be hurried over if we say 'We're all mad deep down', 'All sinners', 'All selfish'. And the more

[1] With acknowledgments to Henri de Montherlant.

he's playing this literary game and not a scientific game the more does his statement lead up the garden path those who take all statements in prose as prose.

In so far as one who says 'Aren't we all mad really?' realizes how far he's not correcting our ordinary confidences and conclusions, so far his anxious and interrogative air is a conscious joke; in so far as he doesn't realize this the anxious and interrogative air is an unconscious joke, as when people feel they can't find out whether a tomato is a fruit or a vegetable, though here the inappropriateness of the interrogative air arises in a rather different way. I am not saying that the question 'Aren't we all mad really?' is a joke. On the contrary, even the interrogative air is not a joke in so far as ordinary confidences are being questioned. But apart from this, the question has an importance of its own sort as we have seen. Still, it's something of a joke a man's saying, 'We're all mad really', and making us open our eyes in wonder and fear when really we ought to nod our heads in a knowing way and screw up our faces with a bit of a shudder or a grin. He isn't denying that we are not all mad. And if he's telling us that the sane aren't separated from the insane like sheep from goats, then we knew that before. Still, we must hand this to him, he does bring it home, especially as and when he 'supports' his statement.

And if a man says 'We never know that there's an electric current in a wire whatever impressive phenomena it exhibits. We always infer, guess its presence', then we must hand him this: He brings home the fact that we can never know of the presence of an invisible current in a wire in the way that we can know of the presence of petrol in a pipe, that is, not merely from the behaviour of the machine but also by cutting a section from the pipe and taking a look. In this way our knowledge of the presence of an invisible current resembles our knowledge of the presence of petrol before we have looked. But to say that we don't know, we only guess, that there's an invisible current in an electric wire, is something of a joke. For our knowing that there's an invisible current in a wire is very different from our knowing, our guessing that there's petrol in a pipe. In particular, the knowing that there's petrol in the pipe leaves open other hypotheses in a way in which the knowing that there's an invisible current in the wire does not, although, as we have seen, it does in its own way.

22. *And now to try to remember all at once this long description of the doubt* 'Surely from outward signs, however many and consistent, we cannot know a man's inward state, nor that his soul is still in his body, nor that it's not'. The Sceptic said: 'Sometimes I feel we never know what is going on in the mind of another. Sometimes I wonder whether other people aren't just automata. Do you ever have that feeling? After all, how do we know, even when a man has given every sign of being most religious all his life, that he wasn't secretly quite the reverse?'

I said: 'I know what you mean. But this doubt of ours is a queer one. To be plain, it's a philosophical doubt, and one never feels quite confident whether these are tremendously profound or quite silly. Now with this one, here we are pretending to doubt what the multitude unthinkingly assume. All the same, we expect nothing different from what they expect, all they look for we look for. What *are* we doubting?'

The Sceptic said: 'Yes, it's hardly a doubt, it's the contemplating of a possibility.'

I said: 'Well it's more than that with me. When I feel as if I can't be sure whether there are any feelings behind people's faces I feel as though a bit of the world which I had thought to be there though I couldn't see it, perhaps after all isn't there. And then, on the other hand, I feel a difficulty about saying that I am doing as much as the contemplating of a possibility. With the contemplating of any other possibility, such as Smith's being really colour blind though he passed the test against it, I am always contemplating what further investigation would reveal. But when I am contemplating the possibility of Smith's being colour blind although all investigation would give results to the contrary, then what am I doing?'

The Sceptic said: 'Surely you can *imagine* that Smith, though outwardly perfectly normal, sees the Union Jack in black, green and yellow instead of red, white and blue.'

I said: 'I know what you mean. But now it is our imagining that is queer. Other imagining that what we had thought to be so isn't really so consists in imagining further investigation producing disappointment. But in this imagining that things aren't what they seem we imagine no disappointments for ourselves. The image in this imagining doesn't guide to a copy of itself. When we imagine that there's a visible leprechaun in our watch we have a leprechaun-image which guides to a copy of itself, and whether what we imagined is so is determined by whether we find what we are guided to or not. But the image in imagining that Smith sees the Union Jack in black, green and yellow is an image of a black, green and yellow Union Jack which guides not to a sensation like itself but to Smith's painting the Union Jack in black, green and yellow when asked to paint what it looks like to him, and to his matching it with ebony, grass, and lemons instead of the usual pillarbox, snow, and sky; so when by the terms of the philosophical imagining the image isn't allowed to guide to these things, the question 'Is what we are imagining really so?' hasn't answers. Imagining that Smith acts quite normally but not because his inward state is that of seeing the Union Jack in red, white and blue but that of seeing it in black, green and yellow, is like imagining that a watch's behaviour is due not to an *invisible* leprechaun but to an *invisible* brownie, that light is not corpuscular but wave-like. Here are rival pictures, and if you like rival hypotheses, but the pictures play a part in the hypotheses which makes it a queer question to ask 'Which hypothesis is right' unless one *makes a story of* the facts to be explained better than does the other. When they do this equally well, the question 'Which is correct?' becomes inappropriate.

This is obscured by the fact that the question reaches this condition gradually. We often use 'There's an invisible X here', 'There's an invisible Y here' in such a way that the question 'Which is present?' is not a joke, and these uses are not sharply separated from the use in which such a question is a joke because it disguises the request 'Which fairy tale serves best to remind us of the clusters of phenomena in nature?' Indeed, we may say, if we like, that the question never becomes *merely* this.

The peculiarity of the question, 'Is there a leprechaun here or a brownie?' when 'leprechaun' and 'brownie' are so used that both are absolutely invisible and intangible and both have just the same effects on watches, comes out, if we imagine someone taught this use and then asked, 'Which will you have, a brownie-driven watch or a leprechaun-driven one?'

Whether we say of someone who asks of a textbook case of a leprechaun-driven watch '*Is* there an invisible leprechaun here?' that he is asking a joking question or making a joke, is a matter of choice, though the peculiarities of what he is doing are better brought out by saying that he is not asking a question. To say this removes confusion as to what he is doing, prevents abortive efforts to meet his demands, in the same way that to say of someone who asks 'Can one keep a promise unintentionally?' that he is not asking a question, prevents abortive efforts to satisfy him. And this is so although what makes the one not a question is different from what makes the other not a question.

The promise-question dissolves into 'Is it in a case exhibiting features $s_1 \ldots s_{n-m}$ but not $s_{n-m} \ldots s_n$ proper to speak of promise-keeping, where the usage of "promise-keeping" is not definite for such a case'. The dissolution of the latter and more characteristically philosophical doubt with regard to a textbook case of a leprechaun-haunted watch or, say, a wire with an electric current in it, 'Is there a current in this?' is more peculiar. It dissolves into 'Given that the history, present condition and future of this wire is just such as leads us all to speak of the presence of an invisible current in the wire, are we right in so speaking?' Here by hypothesis usage is definite. The consequence is that even in this form it is a puzzle to know what anyone who asks this question is up to. He appears to be asking in a doubtful voice 'Ought we to say that we know q from p?' in a case where he knows we all should say this. The only excuse he has is that we all feel some inclination to reform logic in the way he is suggesting. Looking at other cases of such astonishing temptations to departure from ordinary usage, such as 'We are all mad really', 'We never know but what we aren't suffering from illusions', we find that though these statements to some extent present us with the results of experience (the surprising eccentricities of the sane, the clever imitations at Tussaud's) they are often more a matter of *mentioning* certain matters which we know of but don't mention. These matters are not at all what is *literally* expressed by those daring departures from ordinary usage, whether in the form 'All S is P' or in the form 'No S is P', which are used for drawing attention to them. These 'wise' generalizations are thus extremely misleading to that sort of person who, however wildly one says 'Women are cats', 'Men are pigs', anticipates that one will support one's statement with statistics. These people will either think the philosopher quite absurd or they will be worried to death because while they cannot without qualm reject what the philosopher says they cannot accept consequences which it seems to them it must imply. They will ask 'Is he right?' with an anxious and interrogative air which would amuse the philosopher if he weren't himself half taken in by his own imitation of a scientist.

When a man says 'This car's possessed this morning', to reply 'Is she? By what?' is a sort of poor joke.

In the same way it's something of a joke, conscious or unconscious, to puzzle a busy scientist who speaks of some things as having invisible currents and of others as not, by asking him 'But are there any invisible currents?'

In the same way, in a country where it is the custom to say of watches which sing fairy songs and disappear on Midsummer Night that they are haunted by invisible leprechauns, it is something of a joke to say '*Are* there any invisible leprechauns? How do you know now that there is in this watch an invisible leprechaun?' Of course, in so far as the watch's behaviour, through leprechaun-like till now, is still in doubt, and in so far as there still lingers in the country a primitive idea about leprechauns so that the people of that country half expect to see one if they open a watch quickly, so far the interrogative air is appropriate and not a joke.

Likewise with 'Has his soul fled?' While we still wonder whether a specialist might revive him or still half expect to see his rha fly slowly at evening, the question is a question. But in these enlightened days no such thing is expected, so that when we know he'll never smile again then to ask 'Is he dead?' becomes a joke.

'Ah', it may be said, 'now here comes out a big difference. I see now why you say, "To ask 'Is there a current within?' 'Is there a leprechaun within or a brownie?' is to ask which fairy tale shall we choose to remind us of the facts". I see now how in the country you described it would be absurd to ask of a watch which sang fairy songs and disappeared on Midsummer Night, "Is there a leprechaun within it?" and equally absurd to ask this question of a watch which did nothing extraordinary. But it's different with "I know he won't speak or smile or give us any sign but still I can't help wondering whether he's lingering here or watching from another place". This expresses not a joke but an old hope.'

Other Minds II

'BUT THIS IS DIFFERENT'

Black. We can never really be certain what is going on in the mind of another. Even if a man, when given a gold watch, showed every sign of being delighted and never, before or afterwards, not even to his most intimate friends, gave us any ground to suppose he was anything but what he then appeared to be, it would still remain possible that he was not delighted. And by the same reasoning, even were parrots or monkeys to talk like people at a party it would remain possible that they neither thought nor felt, and there is nothing illogical in supposing that a friend's body should continue to nod, smile and talk just as before he went to sleep, although now his mind and soul are no longer in his body—the body keeps up the old habits—there is nothing logically absurd about this idea any more than there is anything logically absurd about the idea that though his body is still in death his mind is active, thinking and feeling in some other world.

White. You might as well say we can't be certain there aren't leprechauns in watches. You might as well say we can't be certain that any current runs in electric wires. You might as well say we can't be certain that there's any energy in live batteries, as say we can't be certain that there's any consciousness in live bodies.

Black. But this last is different. It is, of course, absurd to ask when a watch shows no pecularities whether it isn't perhaps leprechaun-guided. And it is also absurd to ask whether a battery contains a charge when it possesses just those pecularities which people describe by saying that it's charged. It is even absurd to ask whether a man is dead when his body continues to show no sign of life, and no one expects it to. Or rather, it is absurd to ask this if what you mean by 'dead' is 'no longer in the body, no longer driving it'. But it doesn't follow that the man doesn't exist anywhere, disembodied or in a new body. It is 'I shall be dead tomorrow' in this disembodied sense which provides 'a first-class puzzle for the positivists'.[1] For how could it be verified? I know indeed what it would be like to watch my own funeral—the men in tall silk hats, the flowers and the face beneath the glass-topped coffin. But 'Tomorrow I shall be no more' doesn't mean to me merely this account of what you'll see if you're at the cemetery in time. To prove that 'There's a current in this wire' means no more than 'This wire is connected to a battery at one end and rings bells at the other' is not to prove that 'There's a soul in this body' means no more than 'This body converses intelligently', much less is it to prove that 'The soul of this body exists somewhere' means no more than 'You can wake him if you shake him'.

White. We haven't proved anything at all. We haven't proved that it is absurd for the philosophical scientist to ask 'Is there a leprechaun in this watch?', 'Is there a current in this wire?' We have only reminded ourselves of the things everyone knows about the way these sentences work and described these things so as to make these 'questions' 'answerable'. There is a difference between these questions and 'Is there a soul in this body?' But, as so often happens, you are under-concerned about the cases which don't trouble you at the moment, and over-concerned about the one that is striking you at the moment. We have seen in what ways 'The watch shows all signs of being animated by an invisible leprechaun, but is it really?' *does* do something like registering a doubt; and we have seen how 'Is there a brownie or a leprechaun within?' *does* come near to opposing *two* hypotheses which are therefore not both identical with 'This watch sings fairy songs and disappears on Midsummer Night, etc.' The philosophical scientist who asks 'Are there leprechauns within the leprechaun-watches?', 'Are there entelechies in living things?', 'Are there currents in electric wires?', is not being merely absurd. True, it is queer to ask, 'Is there an invisible current in this wire?' when both (1) the wire shows all features which have been present wherever we have before applied the expression 'an invisible current runs through this

[1] Dr. A. C. Ewing, *Mind*, July 1937, p. 353.

wire', *and* (2) we can't explain what would more encourage us to believe that an invisible current is present. Certainly that is queer. At the same time, one can understand the scientist's feeling it difficult to say that the electrical symptoms the wire exhibits entail that an invisible current runs through it. It isn't a recognized principle of logic that if a thing gives off sparks, rings bells and drives trams then an invisible current runs through it. If you like, it *is* a logical principle that a wire giving such symptoms is 'electrically charged'. That expression you may well say just sums up the symptoms. But to say that a current runs through it—that is going further, and the philosophical scientist excusably expresses hesitation about saying that the symptoms entail the presence of a current. If he says he doubts whether even in cases where all the symptoms are present a current really runs, he is deciding against saying that the symptoms entail the current. No one has ever seen one and then, to take a different sort of consideration, if it is a current that flows it is a very knowing sort of current. For, unlike water or any sort of current, it knows before it enters a channel whether the channel is clear. It is as if when a wire is connected with a battery the wire becomes alive and willing to serve us in certain ways and apt to harm us in others.

But there is another point. I am astonished at your lack of sympathy with those who say that perhaps Smith is in his dead body though he will never move again.[1] To say this is, after all, no more absurd than to say that he is still somewhere. True, he is showing no sign of being in his body. But then he is showing no sign of being anywhere, anywhere in the world. If you think it is possible that he's still somewhere, isn't it possible that he's still in his body, and that if you mummify it he will play possum there for ever.

If Socrates is still alive, he is quite invisible. And when you die if you are still alive you will be quite invisible. And surely one of the places you may be in is your body. So after all is it absurd to say 'His body shows no signs of life and I know it isn't going to, but whether his soul is still in his body I don't know'? Surely it is no more absurd than saying that his body shows no sign of

[1] Rupert Brooke, *Doubts*. 'For if the soul be not in place, what has laid trouble in her face?'

life but perhaps he exists *somewhere*. Or, if you like, surely it is *more* absurd. I mean that there is no difference in principle. It is only a degree more absurd for me to say 'There are unicorns in Piccadilly' than it is for me to say 'There are unicorns some-where'. In both cases I can make excuses when we can't find the unicorns. I can say that there are unicorns in Piccadilly but that they are made of ectoplasm which can be seen only in infra-red rays and that ordinary matter such as buses and taxis goes right through it. It is only easier to make excuses for 'There are unicorns somewhere.' I just say 'Piccadilly is not the place for them'. You say, 'What about the Brighton Road?' I say, 'No, not the Brighton Road, but perhaps at the Pavilion.' If we also fail to find any at the Pavilion, and even in Ethiopia, then people will begin to lose interest in my statement that unicorns are still extant; and if people who haven't heard me say this before are astonished and interested, then those who have will warn them, saying, 'White's unicorns are *very* hard to find', or 'Yes, White's unicorns exist somewhere—in heaven you under-stand', or 'White's unicorns exist—at the point of infinity'.

Black. Ah! if all that is meant by 'in his body' is mere presence without action, then it *is* a serious question whether Smith is in his body. It's only when we use 'in his body' as most people use 'still in the body', meaning 'still shows all the usual signs of life', that it is absurd to ask, 'Is Smith in his body? His heart has ceased to beat, there is no sign of life and will be none, but is he still in the body?' In a use in which Smith's being in his body means that he is driving it such a question is absurd. But of course when no such activity is implied, then 'Does Smith exist, and is he still seeing out of his body or dreaming?' is a serious question, like 'Are people unconscious under chloroform or are they perhaps terribly conscious though they always quite forget it afterwards?' It all depends on what you mean by[1] 'Is Smith in his body?'

---

[1] This last remark is a heart-breaking one. It is a complication especially preva-lent in modern times. Again and again we have (1) philosophers who say '$s_1 \ldots s_n$ entail or are identical with Σ', and (2) philosophers who deny this. Sometimes we have (3) those who say 'There is a sense of "Σ" in which $s_1 \ldots s_n$ entail Σ and a sense in which they don't'. They are nearer a proper view of the dispute than those in (1) and (2). But just because of this it is harder to show what is wrong with their idea of it. Every question, *Does P entail Q?* (Is a tomato a fruit or a vegetable?), is a matter of what is meant by 'P' and 'Q' and that not merely in the way in which

White. But mightn't one just as well say that if all one means
by 'leprechaun haunted' is 'sings fairy songs, etc.,' *then* it is
absurd to ask 'This watch sings fairy songs, etc., but is it
leprechaun haunted?' but if one means more, then it is not
absurd.

Black. No, that is different. What we have seen in the leprechaun case is that 'There is an invisible leprechaun within this
watch' has a meaning different from 'This watch sings fairy
songs, etc.', but that this difference is such as to make the question 'This watch sings fairy songs, etc., but is it leprechaun
haunted or brownie haunted or not haunted at all but just
wonderful?' not a question as to which of several hypotheses is
correct but a request as to which of several mnemonic pictures
to employ. In this way, as you put it, the question 'Is there a
leprechaun within?' is not answered nor found to have two
answers. It vanishes. The anxious doubt becomes a cheerful indecision as we see the inappropriateness of the interrogative
form. But with an ambiguous question the interrogative form is
not inappropriate. Thus, in the case of 'Is Smith's soul in his
body?', the interrogative form is appropriate, it is only that
there should be two instead of one if conversation is to go for-
ward without confusion. In the ordinary somewhat loose use of
language we say when we know that a man will never move
again that his soul has left his body. And in this sense it is absurd
to ask 'Has his soul left his body?' when you know he will never
move again. But in this case, as opposed to the invisible leprechaun case, there is left another sense of 'Is his soul perhaps still
in his body?' which is a serious question. It is the question
whether his sensations and feelings are going on just the same

---

an empirical question *Is every P a Q?* is a matter of what is meant. For *Does P entail
Q* depends *only* on what is meant. But it doesn't *depend on* what is meant, it *is* a question of what is meant. Consequently, to answer *It depends on what you mean by 'P'* or
It depends on what you mean by 'Q' does nothing towards answering the question *Does
P entail Q?* It only reformulates it as *Does 'P's' meaning include the meaning of 'Q'?* or,
if you like, *Does 'P' stand for something which entails Q?* And if the answer given is *'P'
stands for one thing which entails Q and for another which doesn't*, then one must ask, *Have
you any reason for saying this except that some of us here and now wish to say that P entails Q
while some of us do not?* In cases of *philosophical* difficulty, e.g. *Does no sign of life entail
Smith is not in his body?*, the answer must be *That is my only reason*. But then the answer
to the question *Some of us are inclined to say that P entails Q, some that it doesn't.—Which
is right?* becomes *If 'P' and 'Q' were used as some of us are now inclined to use them then the
answer would be P does entail Q*, and if they were used as some others of us are inclined to use
them, then the answer would be *P does not entail Q*.

though now he can show no signs of them owing to a complete paralysis. The scientist who talks about a current running through an electric wire isn't serious about the current. He is of course, serious, sober, as contrasted with one who is telling a fancy 'In the clock on the stairs lives a hobgoblin', or one who says 'There's a demon in my watch'. But his sobriety arises solely from those purposes which his sentence serves, which could be as well served by a sentence which doesn't mention a current but employs some other convenient metaphor for reminding and warning us of the peculiar properties of this wire. And it is the same with 'The sea is angry' and 'Neptune is stirring up the sea'. People who say these things aren't serious. They know they are only 'making-a-story-of-the-facts', like your governess who, when the gate conveniently blew open before you, said 'A kind fairy opens the gate for you'. But one who, when Smith frowns, says 'Smith is angry', is serious, and is not merely 'making-a-story-of-the-facts' about Smith's behaviour. He is making a claim which goes beyond the behaviour, and may thus be in serious doubt when the behaviour is not in doubt. And 'Is it that Smith sees the Union Jack in red, white and blue or does he see it black, green and yellow?' are *two* serious alternatives.

White. Again, you do not sympathize enough with the cases which aren't striking *you now*. The primitive scientist who says 'Puck is in the churn', although he doesn't at all expect to see anything, is serious, like the Greeks who held there were spirits in the trees. Quite as serious as those who say 'God drives the world'. Would you call them serious? Would you call this question serious: 'Is the world controlled by a God who often forgets or by a Devil who sometimes relents?' Or would you say 'No, this is only a matter of what picture you employ to vent your attitude to the world like you vent your attitude to your watch'? And remember that very unprimitive, very sophisticated scientists say that, though of course they seriously believe that men think, they aren't serious when they say that dogs do, because they have discovered that dogs are really just complicated machines, so that when they say a dog has learned that a bell means meat they just mean that his saliva runs when the bell rings. These scientists don't expect anything different of dogs from what the rest of us expect. But they represent themselves as having lost their childish faith in dogs. Others again, moving in the opposite direction, say that they are convinced that flowers feel.

Black. Those who say that dogs don't think or feel, and those who say that flowers do are both serious. And even the modern theologian is serious. True, he is quite unlike the primitive believer in God, who believes that the floods have been sent by God, and thinks that if he prays before he sets about trying to save the sheep that will make a difference to the number of sheep he saves. The modern theologian knows that that is only an anthropomorphic superstition, and he no more expects sacrifice or prayer to make any difference to the number of sheep saved than does an atheist.

White. Perhaps the modern theologian has different expectations of the next world.

Black. Not the most modern ones. They regard hope of personal immortality as another childish feature of primitive belief But they seriously believe that something is going on now other than the processes of nature, namely, the supervising mental processes of a super-being. And this is what makes their question serious. This is what you either can't or won't understand.

There is, of course, some difficulty about drawing the line between serious psychological statements such as 'Smith is angry' and unserious ones such as 'The sea is angry', 'My motor-cycle is in a bad mood this morning', or (shall we add?) 'I suppose the flowers feel better for the sun'.

Nevertheless, just as 'A current runs through this wire' provides a picture only because it is in other cases a serious assertion that a current is running through a thing, so do 'The sea is angry', 'Neptune is angry', provide pictures only because 'The bull is angry', 'Smith is angry' are serious.

White. Steady. There's a difference here. There's not the same difference between a serious psychological statement and a non-serious one as there is between a serious physical statement and a non-serious one. I feel inclined to say 'Flowers feel pain when they are shrivelled by frost' doesn't involve any picture apart from a picture of shrivelling flowers. Now 'There is a leprechaun in the watch' does involve another picture besides the watch's singing songs, a picture of a leprechaun.

Black. Well, but don't you get an organic image of the pain the flowers feel?

White. Yes, only somehow this is different in a way we have already noticed.[1]

Suppose that from where we lie we can see hats and heads above a low hedge, moving smoothly along. Then if I say 'They are moving with the current' I speak seriously, because a picture[2] of liquid flowing is connected in the following way with what I aim to do by uttering my sentence: I aim to get you to expect to see a liquid corresponding to that picture. Suppose that we can see as we look at the blood in a vein little red bodies moving along but on no visible current. Then if I say 'They are moving on a current', someone may say 'It's an invisible one, then', thus drawing attention to a peculiarity in the connection between my words and pictures on the one hand and my claims on the other. When I say 'Yes, but not quite invisible' and hand him a stronger microscope which shows the red bodies floating on a clear liquid, then I draw attention to a likeness between (*a*) the connection between *my* words and pictures and *my* claims, and (*b*) the *ordinary* connection between the sentence 'They are on a current' and the claims made by one who utters it. Because of this likeness we may say that I am still seriously speaking of a current. We come to the case when I am not speaking seriously of a current. This is when I have in mind no means, not even eccentric means like microscopes, for seeing or feeling the current. When I am not speaking seriously, then it becomes absurd to speak of more direct evidence for my claim that a current is present, because my claim has come to include only the indirect signs of the presence of a current; I mean no more, I assert no more, and so my assertion cannot be supported by finding other signs. And by the same fact it is unshaken by their absence.

Now if this is what is meant by the distinction between serious and not serious statements then we must call *all* psychological

[1] P. 10

[2] Of course I need not have had such an image or picture when I spoke. In that case we must describe the difference between my speaking seriously of a current and speaking 'metaphorically', 'fictitiously', of a current in some other way. One might say that when I speak seriously, I aim to produce expectation in you which will be in fact the same as that of those who expect to see a liquid corresponding to the picture, in other words, expect to see a current.

statements not serious. For with all of them all the guiding pictures are not connected with the claims made in such a way as to allow us to speak of directly verifying the statement by finding the reality which fits the guiding picture.

Let us run over the way in which a sentence, e.g. 'There is a dagger in the air', may pass from a physical to a psychical use. Suppose Smith says 'There is a dagger in the air', then in the ordinary way I look up and expect a sensation to fit the image of a dagger which his sentence perhaps gave me. But maybe very queer things have been happening of late. One week everybody passing a certain place would get a wound showing the teeth marks of an animal. Another week everybody passing a certain place would get a wound such as a burning torch would make. Another week everybody passing a certain place would get a wound such as a dagger would make. It has become the custom to say in a horrified voice that there's a wolf's head, a burning torch, or a dagger at the place, according to which group of phenomena appears. Suppose now Smith says in the usual horrified voice, 'There's a dagger in the air'. I don't now expect a sensation of a dagger nor do I expect sensations of others saying they have a sensation of a dagger. Of course not. I know it to be an invisible dagger. But the word 'dagger' and the picture of a dagger guide me as to what to expect. I expect a different sort of wound when people say 'There's a dagger in the air' from what I expect when they say 'There's a torch in the air'.

Suppose now that Smith is an inmate of a mental hospital. Morning after morning he has some frightful hallucination. This morning he shouts, 'There's a dagger in the air'. I don't take this seriously in the sense that I expect to get a sensation of a dagger in the air nor a sensation of other people, dogs, cameras, or wire hoops saying 'There is a dagger in the air'. The sentence still gives me a picture of a dagger and not a torch, and this picture still guides me, but now it guides me only with regard to Smith. That is, it guides me only with regard to the sensations I shall get from looking at and listening to Smith and what I shall see and hear if I watch and listen to people who are watching and listening to Smith. This is what makes it a psychological, subjective statement. At least it makes it a psychological, subjective statement for me though not for Smith if Smith expects us all to see his dagger. As to whether his statement was objective because it was objective for him who made it or subjective because it was subjective for him who heard it, I leave it to you to decide. Let us say it was a false objective statement though it truly told us what Smith saw, or that it was false about the contents of the real physical world but true about the contents of Smith's mind. Suppose, lastly, that Smith knows very well that he is subject to hallucinations when he wakes, and only says to us 'There's a dagger in the air' because we are his doctors, and we like to know what form the hallucination takes each morning. Then, though the sound he makes is like that he made when he was making an objective statement with 'There's a dagger in the air', nevertheless what he is doing is like what is done by one who says 'It looks to me just as if there's a dagger in the air, but that's nothing to go by, I've been so queer of late'. Here again the sentence gives a guiding picture, but now no one expects to see anything to fit the picture, and no one, not even Smith, expects anyone to see anything to fit the guiding picture.

Black. I see what you are getting at. It is what you have been getting at all along. You want to say 'There's a dagger in the air' when used by Smith as a psychological statement, as a purely subjective statement, is only a way of telling us about what Smith will say he sees, about what he will draw if asked to draw what he sees, about what he will point to if asked to point to examples of the sort of thing he sees, in short, about what we may expect in the way of behaviour from Smith. You want to say that like 'There's a dagger in the air', used to predict a pattern of wound-sensations in oneself and others, and like 'There's an invisible leprechaun inside', used to predict a pattern of song and disappearance sensations, so is 'Smith sees an hallucinatory dagger' used to predict a pattern of sensations from Smith, a different sort of pattern, a psychological pattern, but for all that a pattern of what can be seen and heard. For it is used to predict what Smith will say he sees, what he will draw if asked to draw what he sees, what he will point to if asked to point to examples of what he sees. And you want to say that all psychological statements are unserious in that the guiding picture which goes with them, though it guides like the picture of the invisible

leprechaun, guides only in that way. You want to say that the
utterance of a psychological sentence doesn't ever lead one to
expect any sensation corresponding to the one it primarily
brings to mind. Thus, 'Smith sees the Tricolour in red, white
and blue' doesn't lead one to expect any sensation of red, white
and blue whether one looks up to the sky or into Smith's brain,
and 'Smith feels sick' doesn't lead one to expect a sensation of
sickness.

Nevertheless, somehow, you must allow, there is a difference
between a serious and a non-serious psychological statement.
Among physical and semi-physical statements there are (i) some
which would usually be called 'half-joking' or 'not serious', as
when the father says, 'The wolves are gaining', or someone
says, 'There must be a demon in this house, the way I lose
things'; there are (ii) others which have just now been called
unserious because of a certain likeness to the unserious ones—
such statements as 'There is a current in this wire'. These are
semi-serious, because though part of what you might expect
from 'There's a current in this wire is not to be expected', part
of it is to be expected, namely, what we should call a pattern of
reaction such as one would expect if one knew that really there
was a current running through it (or a leprechaun within); and
(iii) there are fully serious physical statements such as 'A slate
has fallen off the roof'. With psychological statements, too, there
are what would ordinarily be called non-serious ones as, for
example, 'A goblin lives in the clock on the stairs', 'My motor
cycle is very fickle'. The latter isn't quite unserious, it tells you
how irregular in response is the speaker's motor-cycle. And
there are, of course, serious psychological statements such as
'Evangeline is cross'. And then there are the semi-serious
psychological statements corresponding to the semi-serious
physical statements about invisible leprechauns and currents. I
refer to statements about unconscious feelings. When an analyst
tells you that Smith hates his mother and you protest that he
doesn't, that you have asked him, then the analyst smiles like
the scientist smiled when you looked with a magnifying glass for
the current in the wire. The analyst smiles and says, 'Not a conscious wish' (not a visible current).

White. This just confirms what I say. I may now put my

point in this way. Unlike goats and leprechauns, *all* feelings are invisible. The analyst's invisible feeling is called invisible, not because only indirect criteria are relevant to the truth of his statement, for that is true of any statement about a feeling, in the sense that one cannot feel with one's own senses whether Smith has a feeling,[1] but because some of the indirect criteria usually counted are not to be counted. Just as our seeing nothing when we look for a current in a wire is prevented from counting against the statement 'A current is now running through it', by the saving phrase 'an invisible current I mean of course', so is Smith's denial that he hates his mother prevented from counting against the analyst's statement that he does, by the saving phrase, 'an unconscious wish, of course'. But in the latter case it is not that direct criteria for the statement have been dropped; they never have been used. Or, if you like, since it is not that there are direct criteria which might have been used and have not, let us say that the distinction between direct and indirect criteria doesn't apply here, in other words, that we have not provided a use for the phrases, 'psychological statement directly verified', 'psychological statement only indirectly verified'.

When we went over the uses of 'There's a dagger in the air' we saw when this physical looking statement became psychological. It was when no dagger sensations or lack of them was relevant to it but only a pattern of sensations from Smith who uttered it and people looking at Smith. Now if this is all the claim it makes, it is absurd when you get these sensations to say 'Still I don't know whether it is true, still maybe it isn't true'.

Black. But this is just the point. *Is* that all the claim it makes? It makes, in addition to the claim that you and others will get a certain sensation on looking at Smith, the claim that Smith is having a certain sensation.

White. Isn't the meaning of a statement a matter of its effect on hearers? Now 'Smith sees the Union Jack in red, white and blue' puts a picture of a Union Jack into the heads of hearers, but if it is purely psychological and subjective it does not lead them to expect Union Jack sensations but only (1) sensations of Smith saying in all languages (mouth, pen and paint brush)

---

[1] Or should one say, 'We can imagine, of course, and in fact it has happened, that one person has felt with his own senses another's feeling'?

that he sees the Union Jack, and (2) sensations of people saying that Smith sees the Union Jack. This *is* its claiming that Smith is having a certain sensation, viz., a Union Jack sensation. 'Smith sees the Union Jack in red, white and blue' puts a picture of a Union Jack into a hearer's head. And for Jones to ask when he has these sensations from Smith and from people looking at Smith, 'Does Smith see the Union Jack?', is a joke. Jones is like one who, when it is well known how we use 'leprechaun haunted', nevertheless asks 'Is there really a leprechaun in this watch?' even after he has heard it sing and found it disappear on Midsummer Night. He relapses to a use in which there are not only outer but also inner signs of the presence of X, in this instance a leprechaun. It is like someone who, though he knows that by submicroscopic structure we mean a structure not visible by any microscope, nevertheless asks '*Has* this such and such a sub-microscopic structure? True, it shows the outward signs of this, but has it?' He asks a question which feels sensible because in other cases in which one speaks both of outward signs and inward explaining presence there is sense in saying 'The outward signs are here but shall we find the usual inward presence?' In other cases we have explained the different reactions of two like things by guessing at different things inside them and often these guesses have been correct but sometimes incorrect. But when the assertions, 'There's a dagger in the air', 'This stuff has such and such a structure', make no claim beyond those peculiarities of the air and the stuff which they are posited to explain, then having found these peculiarities, it would be absurd to ask, 'Is there a dagger in the air?', 'Has this stuff an *x* structure?'

Black. You keep saying the same thing in different words. The point is, 'Smith sees the Union Jack in red, white and blue, that's why he says he does, that's why he draws one when you ask him to draw what he sees', is a different sort of explanation from 'An electric current runs through it', 'There's a leprechaun within', 'It has such and such a sub-microscopic structure'.

I am quite prepared to allow, of course, that any matter of the meaning of a sentence must appear in the effects it has on its hearers or in the effects its speakers intended it to have on its hearers. I am prepared to go further and say that even when the effects on hearers of two sentences are different in a way which makes it incorrect to say they mean the same, nevertheless the difference is not such as to give sense to the question, 'Which is correct?', unless the two sentences lead to different expectations of sensation. Thus 'There is a leprechaun within', 'There is a brownie within', have different meanings, but, in the usages we have described, there was no sense in 'Shall I bring you a watch with a leprechaun inside or one with a brownie inside?' But what I insist upon is that 'Smith sees the Union Jack in red, white and blue and talks like the rest of us', and 'Smith sees the Union Jack in black, red and yellow, and calls colours by different names from the rest of us', *do* lead to different expectations. In other words, I insist that your account of the effects on a hearer of a psychological sentence was not adequate. Not only does 'Smith feels sick' raise in my mind a faint sensation of sickness which though I expect no copy of it, nevertheless serves to guide me in what I expect of Smith. It does something else as well. It leads me to expect *for* Smith a sensation of sickness, a sensation if you like corresponding to my faint sensation of sickness. And this is connected with another inadequacy of yours. You said, 'There isn't a difference between serious and unserious psychological statements in the way there is between serious and unserious physical statements, because no one ever expects a sensation to fit the principal picture that goes with "Smith feels sick", "Smith feels as if he sees the Union Jack" '. But it isn't true that *no* one does. Smith does. If Smith overhears 'We must take out Smith's teeth or he'll be colour-blind by tomorrow', this doesn't in Smith as it does in us merely produce a picture of frocks, faces, flags and landscapes all in grey, guiding us to expectations of his muddling his job as a signalman and being unable to tell the Belgian flag from the Tricolour. On the contrary Smith looks at the poppies in the corn and says 'No more of this, only this' and he looks at a colourless engraving, and so doing he expects. Not only has he pictures of things in grey, but he *expects with* these just as we *expect with* our pictures of Smith crashing the trains. The sentence, 'Smith will be colour-blind', in so far as it is positive, leads in Smith at least to an expectation of a sensation which copies the engraving and, in so far as it is negative, prevents expectation of a sensation

copying a coloured picture. It's serious for him. The description
of its influence on his expectation is not complete when we have
told how he expects to muddle the trains and the flags, for it
also affects his expectations in a way it affects no one else's. And
with these facts that 'Smith will be colour-blind' is serious for
him, and affects his expectations beyond behaviour goes the
fact that he can directly verify it, that the distinction between
directly verifying and indirectly verifying the statement has an
application for him. And as I said, you gave an inadequate
account of the effect on us of the statement, 'Smith will be
colour-blind tomorrow'. Not only does this statement lead us to
expect him to muddle the trains and the flags, it also leads us to
expect *for him* sensations corresponding to the engraving, although the only sensations it leads us to expect *for ourselves* are
sensations from his muddling the trains and flags and things.
And when tomorrow Smith crashes the trains, confuses the
flags, and fails with Holmgrens wools, and we still ask, 'Is he
colour-blind?', then we shall be wondering whether our expectation *for him* has been fulfilled.[1]

And this after all is only to be expected, in view of the fact that
'Smith will be colour-blind tomorrow' certainly means more
to Smith than any story, however complete, about his confusing
flags, crashing trains, etc. For if it is allowed that it thus means
more to Smith than any story about behaviour, it must be allowed
that it also means more to us, unless it is claimed that though
Smith speaks English, 'Smith will be colour-blind tomorrow'
has for him a different meaning from what it has for us.

White. You have brought out an incompleteness, a relevant
incompleteness, in my account of how the working of a sentence
passes from a physical to a purely psychical working. As you
say, 'Smith will be colour-blind tomorrow' means more to
Smith than that he will mishandle the jobs we entrust to him,
it is serious for Smith in another way, it gives further expectations besides the expectations of mishandling jobs.

Black. Yes. So even if we count as relevant to the meaning

[1] It may here be added, 'And when we wish we could know, we are wishing our
powers of knowing of mental states were increased so that we could know directly
the states of others as we know our own'; cf. our wishing that our powers of discriminating weight were increased so we could tell directly, as well as by the visual
clue of scales, whether feathers differ in weight.

for a person of a sentence only what expectations it gives and prevents in him we shall still have to say that there is a difference in meaning between, on the one hand, 'You will crash the trains, confuse the flags, and so on tomorrow because you will see everything in greys', and, on the other hand, 'You will see reds and greens and blues the same as ever tomorrow, but you will crash the trains and confuse the flags and fail in tests and say you see everything grey *just* as if you were colour-blind'. For these two sentences have different effects on the expectations *of the one to whom they are addressed*. So does 'You will be blind tomorrow' prevent expectation in the person to whom it is addressed in a way in which 'You will act just as if you were blind' does not. So does 'Tomorrow you will be no more'—the only pure negative—prevent expectation in the person to whom it is addressed in a way in which it does not in others, and in a way in which 'Tomorrow your body will lie still' does not. In general, the more a statement 'S is or will be P' is psychological, and even such a physiological statement as 'I shall be swimming tomorrow' is a bit psychological, the more does it raise or prevent expectations (for himself) in a hearer who is S, different from those it raises or prevents (for themselves) in hearers who are not S.

White. That's so. When a man who has recently had his tonsils out says to you, just as you are being wheeled off to have yours out, 'You'll be given chloroform, so you won't show any sign of feeling anything, but you will all the same, although many people forget all about it when they come round'. Then his saying that will have a different effect on you from what his saying 'You will be under chloroform, you'll feel nothing' would have had. The fears the latter would have soothed the former raises. Your expectations as you reach the theatre are very different from what they might have been.

Black. And so are the expectations of your friends. They expect you to lie quite still, but now they can't help fearing for you that you will be feeling it all the time. Not only your friends, but as you say, all those who speak English will understand what you understand by 'You'll feel everything just the same, although you will lie so quiet under the anæsthetic'. And since this certainly means something to you and alters your expectations

from what they were when you had been told that you would lie
still and feel nothing, it also means something to them, alters
their expectations. And this is so although their expectations of
what you'll *do* aren't altered. Likewise, 'Smith will be colour-
blind' plays on his hopes and fears, alters his expectations, in a
way in which 'Smith will confuse the flags, crash the trains, fail
in all tests, and never turn on people and say, "I was having you
on" ' does not. True, 'You'll be in tears in a minute' means as
much as 'You'll be unhappy in a minute'. But that's only because 'You'll be in tears in a minute' isn't really merely a
description of behaviour, but is really a semi-psychological statement. And if it were used merely as a description of behaviour
so that the speaker added, 'and there will be no tear gas about
nor onions near, nor pepper in your eyes', then, however much
information of this sort were added, it would never have the
same meaning as 'You will be unhappy in a minute'. A person
who hadn't ever been unhappy even if he understood all about
the onions and the gas couldn't understand 'You'll be unhappy'.
Some children know very well like doctors the symptoms of
being in love and use it of just the right people. But we say,
'They don't really understand, they don't fully understand.
They've never been in love'. Of course, when they shall have
been in love then they will understand, and it's just then that 'I
am sure Jack will fall in love with Joan' or 'I am sure you will
fall in love with Joan' comes to mean more to them than 'He will
call with flowers'. It is just then that 'Jack will fall in love' makes
a difference to their expectations in a way in which 'He will call
with flowers' does not, unless, of course, it does, because it has
become a hidden psychological statement. That is to say, when
they understand 'Jack will fall in love', 'Jack will be unhappy',
'Jack will see a dagger', then they understand what he understands by this, then it affects their expectations in the way in
which it affects his. Now, as I have admitted, only when 'love'
came to mean to Jack more than a motor in the moonlight did
he understand what love is and only when it does this too for the
other children, do they understand.[1] The point is, they don't

[1] This could be expressed by saying, 'Only when a motor in the moonlight came
to mean to him more than a motor in the moonlight did he come to understand
love, and only when it came to mean more to them too did they too come to understand love'.

understand 'He'll fall in love' until it means to them what it means to the person it is about when he understands 'You'll fall in love'. In other words, when they do understand then it means to them what it means to the person it is about. And as we have already seen that it means more to him than any story about behaviour, and does this because it leads in him to different expectations from those any prediction of behaviour leads to, it follows that when they understand 'He'll fall in love' it means to them also more than any story about behaviour, leads in them to different expectations. And your solicitous friend, if he knows English and understands 'You'll feel it all', will, like you, expect you to feel it all, however quiet you lie. In general, when other people understand a psychological statement such as 'Smith will see an hallucinatory dagger tomorrow', the statement means to them more, leads them to expect more, than any story about how Smith will look and what he'll do.

But now, since how Smith looks, what he does, and what he would do are the most that any of us ever really know about him, it follows that we don't ever really know what his state of mind is, and wouldn't know even if we were a great deal better informed about how he looks and so on than we ever are.

White. This conclusion is as shocking as the denial of the premisses which led to it. Never know that a child is pleased? never know that a man is worried? I'd sooner say that all that 'Smith is in pain' means to people who aren't Smith is that Smith is wounded or sick and groans. No doubt 'Smith will be in pain by tomorrow' has a different effect on a hearer from 'Smith will be complaining of pain by tomorrow', and a very different effect from 'This body (Smith's) will be complaining of pain by tomorrow'. But, after all, 'There's a leprechaun in this watch' has a different effect from 'This watch sings fairy songs and disappears on Midsummer Night', and 'Through this wire runs a current of power' has a different effect from 'This wire is attached to a battery at one end and a tram at the other and the tram moves'. Were we to allow this difference to make us say, 'The presence of the current is one thing, its effects another', then we should have people saying, 'When one reflects on what it is one really knows about electricity one has to confess that one doesn't ever really know that it takes the form of a current. All one

knows is that certain wires exhibit a regular pattern of electrical
phenomena'. At once others will say, 'Nonsense. To know the
latter is to know the former'. Now, what we saw in this case was
that this conflict between Sceptics and Phenomenalists is removed not by proving the one wrong and the other right, but by
investigating certain of the causes of each one's saying what he
does. And what we found was that a careful description of those
differences between the use of 'There's a current in this wire'
and 'If this wire is attached to a tram, a bell or a light they will
go', which led the Sceptic to say, 'The current is one thing, its
manifestations another; we know only the manifestations'—a
careful description of these differences leaves us quite willing to
say of 'This wire rings a bell, drives a tram, etc., but is there an
invisible current in it?' that it is not a real question. At the same
time, a careful description of those likenesses between the use of
'There's a current in this wire' and 'If this wire is connected to
a bell, etc.', which led the Phenomenalist to say, 'To carry a
current just is to exhibit a certain stimulus-reaction pattern',
leaves us willing to say that it is not a merely verbal question.
The two careful descriptions are the same. For a careful description of the likenesses involves, e.g. noting their differences from
the likeness between a sentence in one language and its translation in another, and it involves, e.g. noticing how there are
circumstances in which it is conventional to answer 'Is there a
current in this wire?' with 'I don't know', when it is not conventional to answer in this way the question 'Does the wire give the
electrical reactions?' The circumstances are those in which the
wire responds in some typical electrical ways and fails to respond in others. And a careful description of the differences will
involve these points, but if it's careful it will involve also explaining that the differences are quite unlike the differences
between 'A current of water runs in this pipe' and 'The events
at either end of this pipe exhibit a hydraulic stimulus reaction
pattern'. It will emphasize the likeness of the question, 'Is there
a current in this wire?', asked when the wire gives all signs of
such a current, to the question, 'I suppose the poor old average
man takes shelter when the siren goes. But why should he, for he
can hardly be killed can he?' And isn't this the right procedure
in the controversy 'Surely consciousness is something more than

its bodily manifestations? And yet is it?'? However often it is proved that 'Smith will be colour-blind' means more than that he will crash the trains, etc., and that it means the same to the rest of us as it does to Smith, people will return to the assertion of the paradoxical opposites of these conclusions. Every time I take his pieces by the rules of chess he replaces them on the board. Maybe it's not chess he's playing. And why not? Do we want everlastingly to be reminded of what we do say? Do we want everlastingly forced upon us that particular grouping of the infinity of individuals which results from the use of the most usual linguistic machine? So many of us welcome philosophical paradoxes because in them we find what we 'have often thought but ne'er so well expressed'.

Philosophy has been described by Wittgenstein as descriptive, and Stevenson and Wisdom do something towards elaborating this in *Mind*, 187 and 188. (Note here the Idiosyncracy Platitude, 'The only *correct* answer to a metaphysical question, "What is an X?" is "An X" '.) This comparison of 'What is a philosopher?', 'What is an art critic?' to 'What is a reptile?', 'What is love?' is first rate. But the last questions you will notice are best answered by the poets. And they are allowed poetic licence. They don't rely wholly on that. That technique is blended with the detailed description of the concrete occasion.[1] But they don't hesitate to say that love is what it's not, a disease, a religion, a moment of immortality.[2] And, saying what they say, we can feel why they say what they say. And that's enough. The poetry of love, of God, of woman, is not an incorrect reply to a question, nor even an incomplete reply, though it's never finished.

Saying what they say, we can feel why they say it. That's how to settle the dispute 'In love does the individual die or is he born into a new life?' That is how we settled the disputes about the average man, the invisible leprechaun, the invisible current and the wind. These conflicts were all of the form: 'It is something other than its manifestations, we know only these, so we can't know its nature or existence', versus 'We know its existence and nature—east or west, positive or negative, irritable or amiable,

---

[1] 'Therefore the love which us doth bind', Marvell, *Definition of Love*; 'Once did my thoughts both ebb and flow', Anon., *The Heritage of Poetry*, p. 80.
[2] R. Browning, *The Spell*. 'O moment, one and infinite.'

still courageous or not—we know only its manifestations, so it must be these.'[1] They were dissolved by entering into them. Surely the conflict: 'Consciousness is other than its bodily manifestations—"Smith will be colour-blind" means more than "Smith will fail in colour tests"—in others we know nothing but these manifestations, so we can't know its nature or existence in others' versus 'We know that Bobby feels sick and therefore of the nature and existence of consciousness, in others we know only its manifestations, so it must in others at least be nothing but its manifestations', can be dissolved in the same way? Can't we come to see that though 'He has a picture in his head' differs in meaning from 'He acts just as if he had a picture in his head' this difference is so different from the difference between 'He has a stone in his bladder' and 'He acts as though he has a stone in his bladder', that though the latter difference prevents knowledge of the symptoms giving knowledge of the cause the former difference does not? In this way we should come to see that though knowledge of a picture in Smith's mind is not like knowledge that a picture is in a room when we have looked, it is also not like 'knowledge' that a picture is in a room when we haven't looked but might have. In this way we should come to see how 'Smith gives all signs of having a mental picture in his head but has he?' is a mock question which is the first move in the game of describing the peculiar use of 'mental picture' as opposed to the use of 'valuable picture', just as 'This gives all signs of carrying an invisible current but does it?' is a mock question which is the first move in the game of describing the peculiar use of 'invisible current' as opposed to 'swift current'.

Black. But, for the seventy-seventh time, these cases are different. In the case of the current and also in the case of the leprechaun we could say that the difference in meaning between 'There's a current in this wire' and 'This wire gives all signs of carrying a current' is such as to make the question 'This wire gives all signs of carrying a current but is there one, there's none to be seen?' a mock question, because we could say that the dispute, 'This wire carries an invisible current', 'No. It gives all signs of carrying a current but it doesn't', is not a factual dispute when the disputants are agreed upon *all* the signs. And we

---

[1] W. E. Johnson, *Logic*, Part II, p. 81.

could say this because we could say that when the disputants
agreed utterly upon literally all the signs past, present and to
come, then the dispute reflected no difference in expectation but
only a difference in notation and mnemonic picture.

Now, what we have just recalled is (1) that 'Smith will be
colour-blind tomorrow' means more to Smith than 'Tomorrow
Smith will give all signs of being colour-blind', and that this
difference in meaning is a difference in the expectations the two
sentences lead to; (2) that 'Smith will be colour-blind tomorrow'
means more to us than 'Tomorrow Smith will give all signs of
being colour-blind'. And that this difference in meaning is a
difference in expectation. We noticed that we say that children
don't fully understand a statement to the effect that another
person has a certain feeling until they have felt that feeling
themselves and thus would know what to expect if told that they
were going to feel that way tomorrow and thus know what to
expect for a man who is told that he will feel that way tomorrow.
Consequently, the dispute as to whether tomorrow behind a
face and behaviour, e.g. smiles and clever talk, there will or will
not be a mental process, is a real question; because one who
says there will be and one who says there will not be have different expectations. And this is the mark of what even you deign to
call serious, genuine, real questions. Now, the trouble is that the
only expectations about the fulfilment of which the disputants
will be able to make sure tomorrow are the expectations of the
smiles and clever talk, of the sights and sounds, they *both* expect.
That is, they will not know whether what further the one expected and the other did not, did or did not come about. One
can never really know what is going on in the minds of others.

Other Minds III

White. But to me this conclusion, that one can never really know what is going on in the minds of others, is as objectionable as denying the premisses which brought us to it. Indeed, I would rather say that 'Smith will be blind in a few days' means more to him than it does to us, I would rather deny that it means the same to us as it does to him, than say that we can never know that he's blind or know that he sees. If I were to say 'We never know what is going on in the minds of others' I shouldn't be able to face the gibes of Professor G. E. Moore— 'What, so you don't know that I'm thinking about philosophy now as we sit here talking?' And I shouldn't face these gibes because I feel inclined to make them myself, they are echoed by my own linguistic super-ego.

Black. If you were to say that 'Smith will be blind in a few days' means no more than something about the behaviour of his body or to say that at any rate certain behaviour is all it leads us to expect you would come into conflict with Professor Moore again. For it just isn't true that that is all it leads us to expect, as we have noticed with some care.

White. True. And now it occurs to me to ask: Why shouldn't we stick entirely to the truth? Why shouldn't we say that 'Bobby will feel sick' doesn't mean the same as 'Bobby will sit silent, turn yellow and bring up his breakfast' *and* that nevertheless we sometimes know that Bobby feels sick? But no, an uneasiness remains. However often it is proved that psychological statements about others don't mean the same as the bodily stories on which they are based, and however often it is proved that nevertheless we sometimes know psychological statements about others to be true, people constantly advance the paradoxical opposites of these. For the proofs of the proper statements suppress but don't remove the inclinations to make the improper statements. Indeed, can't we define a philosophical discussion as a discussion as to whether any of us know what all of us know we all know?

Black. No. For some philosophical discussions are about how we come to know what we all know, for example how we come to know that $3+1$ makes 4. Indeed, the uneasiness about our knowledge even of matters of fact sometimes shows itself in this way. Once I said to Moore, that great apostle of propriety, 'What bothers you about statements about the minds of others? You are satisfied that they don't mean the same as any stories, however complete, about their bodies; you are satisfied of course that sometimes you know such statements to be true. Is it then only the folly of others that bothers you? You yourself surely find nothing puzzling about the matter?' He replied that of course sometimes he knew statements about the minds of others to be correct, but that what bothered him was that he didn't know *how* he knew them to be correct.

White. You should have replied, using the Hume[1]-Moore technique, 'Not know how you know statements about the minds of others! What, don't know how you know I'm thinking about philosophy? You pour scorn on philosophers who say we don't know things we all know we know. But you yourself are doing this with regard to our knowledge of the knowledge'.

Black. Moore would have replied, 'Of course I know that it's somehow from your expression and the things you say that I know you are thinking about philosophy. But I don't know how I get from my knowledge of your expression and what you say to my knowledge of what you are thinking about or even my knowledge that you are thinking'.

White. You might then have replied, 'You might as well say that you don't know how you get from knowledge of how things have happened in the past to knowledge of how they will happen in the future'. There are, as you will remember, people who say this kind of thing. Indeed, there are people who say this kind of thing in connection with knowledge of mental events. Such people say, 'To know a man's mental state involves at any

---

[1] Hume's remark is to the effect that while a philosophy keeps 'wholly in generals' it may include any absurdity, but when brought to particular cases, . . . I cannot find the passage.

rate knowing more than what he is doing at the moment, it involves knowing also what he would do if this or that were now to happen. Now we can know what a man has done and is doing, but (1) we can't know what he would do, or (2) if we do it's very obscure how we do unless (3) when we talk of what he would do this is only a way of describing the sequences we have already observed in his past behaviour, and what he is doing now'. This, in characteristic threefold form, is a case of the inductive metaphysical puzzles, and just as this difficulty is met by talk in accordance with the principle 'Every sort of statement has its own sort of logic' so might we meet the difficulty 'How from outward signs do we learn of inward states?' But the point I wish to make at the moment is that the cry 'Don't know how we know', 'Don't know how from Y's we know X's' is an expression of the same uneasiness as finds expression in the desperate expedients of Scepticism, Phenomenalism and Intuitionism. When an animal finds it can't jump out of an enclosure nor break out and has not yet fallen into despondency, then it will stand alert but motionless.[1] But this too is an expression of its uneasiness.

Faced with someone who says 'Our only basis for knowledge of X's is our knowledge of Y's, but how do we make the step?' the Sceptics reply 'We don't'; the Phenomenalists reply 'There is no step'; the Intuitionists reply 'Knowledge of Y's is *not* our only basis for our knowledge of X's, there is another mode of knowledge'. To say 'None of these answers will do. There is a step, and we take it, but goodness knows how' is not an alternative answer, it is a repetition of the complaint.[2]

We want assurance of a father in heaven, of a world beyond the stars. But how to get it from our vast but ambiguous information about the habits of animals and the properties of materials? Perhaps it can't be got. Or perhaps the fatherhood of God is the brotherhood of men. This is something more imaginable and ascertainable. But it isn't the same thing. And it hardly

[1] This connects with Wittgenstein's man who strives to get out by the window, by the chimney, but doesn't notice the door behind him.
[2] This would be apparent if Phenomenalism, Scepticism and Intuitionism were always properly introduced as moves made after other moves. The value of a move cannot be judged without knowing what moves have been made and what are intended.

fills the bill. It provides for life maybe. But not for death. Was then the old assurance an illusion? Since it cannot be reduced to and cannot be inferred from what we learn by our five senses, must it be a myth like Charon and the Styx? Or is there another equally sure but less obvious mode of knowing which serves us here, the inner light, the knowledge that comes by faith, a knowledge where nature and beauty and kindness may play a part in providing a setting[1] in which this knowledge may come to us, though they do not provide premises from which it can be obtained as an inference?

It is no answer to reply to all this 'It is very true that what has always been meant by the existence of God is something more than the brotherliness of men or the beauty of the world, and I don't see how we may pass by any known process of argument from such facts or any other facts of nature to the existence of God, and I can't find in myself any special mode of knowing that God exists. And yet somehow we know that he does'. That states the dilemma, but it doesn't describe a way out.

Gray. But it suggests a way out of the difficulty about how we know the mental condition of others. The words 'process of argument' suggest an alternative which neither you nor Black have mentioned in connection with the step from patterns of behaviour to the existence and nature of mental states. I agree with you, White, that we cannot say that we never know when someone is feeling sad or happy or sick, although, of course, it's easy to make mistakes about these things, and I agree with Black that what we know when we know someone is sad is not merely something about how he would answer if we spoke to him. I agree with what you have now both agreed to, namely, that when we expect a man to go colour-blind then we don't expect only what we shall see. Like the man himself, we also expect him to see things differently in a way with which we are quite familiar from ourselves having seen things under a full moon and so on. And don't think I am going to say that our knowledge of other minds is gained by some special means, a sort of intuition or unconscious telepathy. The only sense in which I understand telepathy is that in which a man may guess from his

---

[1] Cf. Broad, *Five Types of Ethical Theory*, p. 110: 'Emotions . . . furnish the necessary occasions on which the intellect intuites certain ethical relations.'

own sensations (his images or what he finds his hand drawing) at what another man will report as his sensations. What I want to know is, why we shouldn't say what it seems to me we do say, namely, that how a man looks and what he does, though it doesn't constitute his state of mind, provides good evidence from which we may infer what his state of mind is. It is true that we cannot absolutely *prove* conclusions about a man's state of mind from premises about his behaviour, but such premises may *render probable* conclusions about his state of mind, and in certain cases, in many cases, this probability is very high.

White. But such an account of our uneasiness at saying that we don't know what is going on in the minds of others fails to give us enough; for what we say and can't comfortably give up saying is that we sometimes, indeed often, *know* what a man is thinking about and how he is feeling.

Gray. Precisely, we do use 'know' thus loosely. Conclusions about a man's state of mind cannot be proved demonstratively from premises about his behaviour, but they can by such premises be rendered very probable, we may even say proved in a loose but colloquial sense. We do, in fact, so use 'know' that we speak of knowing Q on the basis of our knowledge of P even when P merely renders very probable Q. And this is why we feel uncomfortable about saying that we don't know what is going on in the minds of others. For, of course, we often have knowledge which renders very probable conclusions about what is going on in the minds of others.

White. There are, it is true, cases in which we say 'I know that Q because I know that P' where we should be prepared to substitute 'I have the best of reasons for believing that Q because I know that P' or 'It is practically certain that Q since P'. We say such things as 'I know he's in because his hat's in the hall' when we should be prepared to say instead 'I have the best of reasons for believing that he's in' or 'It's practically certain that he's in' or 'I've noticed something which makes it extremely probable that he's in'. But there are cases where we should not be prepared to substitute for 'I know there are two loaves left, I've just looked' 'It's extremely probable there are two loaves left, I've just looked'.

Gray. I admit that the higher—the highest degrees of probability we do not usually express in terms of probability at all. The consequence is that to speak in terms of even a very, very high degree of probability suggests that the speaker has some doubt and would not offer more than 1000 to 1 against being wrong. And the consequence of this is that where the speaker feels not even such doubt it is unconventional for him to speak of probability. But there is no difference in kind between those cases of very high probability which we speak of as knowledge and cases where we quote a price.

White. We do sometimes describe the higher degrees of probability as knowledge. But do we *seriously*? We say 'I don't think it very, very probable that he'll win, I *know* he'll win'. But then you must remember that at this others smile a little and say 'Too many cast-iron certainties have come unstuck when the flags went down'.

Gray. A scientist may say 'I don't think it very, very probable that if you put some of that in there'll be an explosion, I know there will be'; a doctor may say 'I don't think it very, very probable that if you give him a double dose of that he'll die, I know he will'. Can you say they are not colloquially right to speak of knowing here? And yet, after all, what is a doctor but a high-class professional backer?

White. Yes, but I must insist that there's a big difference between the doctor and the housewife who knows that there are two loaves left in the larder, or the mother who knows her child is pleased.[1] When the doctor says 'From the state of his heart I know that a double dose of that stuff would be fatal' or 'From his general condition I know he can't live till morning' there is something we can do which we should call 'making sure whether the doctor is right'. For example, we might say to the doctor, 'You never know till you try', and give the patient the double dose, and then, when he dies, say '*Now* I know that what you said was right'. But there's no way of making sure whether our eyes are right. When we stand with the housewife before the loaves in the larder there is no more to be done which we should call really making sure whether there are two loaves left. We

---

[1] I feel inclined to say I know there's a loaf before me better than any doctor knows how his patient will respond to this or that treatment, but that I can't as well see how I know nor see how I know as well.

can, of course, feel with our hands and sniff with our noses, but that's only doing more of the same sort of thing as looking. When a man predicts an explosion or death, then from one thing he predicts another on the basis of experience—again and again such a condition of the heart has been followed by death. If someone questions the doctor's prediction of collapse, it is only necessary to wait to see whether the association between the heart's present condition and collapse is or is not maintained in the case in question.

And it is this which gives point to saying to the doctor 'You don't know he'll collapse, it's only that it's very probable on your information'. The point of saying 'It's not more than probable' and the justification for saying 'It is probable' are as follows: the point of saying 'It's only probable' is to contrast the sort of knowledge which the doctor has with the superior knowledge of one who waits and sees the collapse. To take another example, one might say 'You don't even know that the valves of his heart are leaking', in order to contrast the doctor who believes they are leaking, on the basis of what he can hear, with the doctor who believes they were on the basis of what he can see at the post-mortem.

The justification for saying that experience gives a high probability to the doctor's belief that the patient will collapse is the frequency with which a heart with leaking valves has led to collapse.

Now the statement 'The housewife doesn't know, though it is probable on her data, that there's bread in the larder' differs in two respects from 'The doctor doesn't know, though it's probable on his data, that the patient will collapse'. The former differs from the latter in that (1) it lacks the point in what it denies which the latter has, and in that (2) the probability it claims, if it exists, has a different sort of justification. It lacks the point in what it denies, for, as we have just reminded ourselves, there is no way of finding out whether there are two loaves in the larder superior to that of going and having a good look, there is no other process suitable for this purpose which it is proper to dignify with the name of 'coming to know' in opposition to the mere 'concluding from the testimony of' our senses which happens in seeing.

And the statement lacks the justification it should have for what it asserts. For our experience has not proved our senses reliable witnesses like leaking valves. True, our senses mostly agree among themselves. But so they would if they were lying, if they had any sense, so that proves nothing. True, when they all agree we have never found them all wrong, indeed, one can't even imagine doing such a thing. But in the very same way one cannot even imagine finding them all right. *A fortiori* we have not, in fact, done so. We have not often found that when they all agree they are right, as we have mostly with human witnesses. And if we have never found a B associated with an A, not even with the most striking A's, then how can the presence of an A here and now, in the larder say, support by analogy the presence of a B?

Gray. Like this: many diseases whose causal story, progress and disappearance follow a certain pattern have been found to be associated with germs in the blood stream in the sense that when a sample of the patient's blood has been taken and carefully examined under the microscope small creatures have been seen swimming about in it. By 'a certain pattern of causal story' I mean this sort of thing: These diseases are catching but less catching if the people who have them are careful, and still less catching if the people who haven't them are careful too and wear muslin masks and gargle every night and so on. And by 'a certain pattern of progress and disappearance' I mean that the temperature of sufferers from these diseases rises and their other symptoms increase until a climax and then—and so on. Of course, the period of incubation and infection varies, but there is a likeness in the way these diseases come and the way they go, and what makes them worse and what makes them better. Colds and influenza and measles are diseases whose causal story, progress and disappearance is of this pattern. And surely it is on this account that it is reasonable to suppose that colds and influenza and measles are due to germs. And this, notice, is reasonable, although the most careful microscopic examination of persons suffering from these diseases fails to reveal any associated germs.[1] And surely it would remain reasonable, even though *every*one should give up *all* hope of ever making a microscope

---

[1] In fact there is *a* visible influenza bacillus.

which would reveal them. And isn't this so because in analogous cases we have found germs?

White. But this is different. As you say, it is reasonable because in *analogous* cases we have found germs, that is to say, it is reasonable because though we have never found a measle germ associated with measle-symptoms we have in cases with like symptoms found, not indeed measle germs, but things of the same sort—we have in other cases found germs, though not measle germs. But we have not in other cases found things which though not physical objects are of the same sort. It is nonsense to talk of doing such a thing, because a thing of the same sort would be a physical object. Physical objects aren't a species of object in the way that measle germs, if they exist, are a species of germ. And another aspect of this is that even if people were to have no idea as to what would lead to the seeing of a measle germ and were to have no expectation of seeing one they nevertheless could explain what it would be like to see one. But not only does no one expect to come on anything more once he has seen, smelt, touched and tasted a loaf, he also could not explain what it would be like to do so. It is, indeed quite nonsense to talk about his 'finding a loaf'.

Gray. But you yourself have explained how invisible wolves are not a species of wolf like timber wolves are. And even wolves which though visible were visible only after carrying out a certain procedure in magic would not be a species of wolf in the way that timber wolves are. For the grammar of 'magic wolf' is different from the grammar of 'curly wolf' and 'timber wolf'. And, of course, in the same way, the grammar of 'microscopic wolf' is different, since the microscope is only a kind of magic. And the grammar of 'sub-microscopic wolf' is different again from the grammar of 'microscopic wolf'. Indeed, the difference here is very marked indeed. For, as we have seen, a dispute as to whether there is a magic or a microscopic wolf in a wood where the wolfhounds give tongue though no wolf is to be seen by the naked eye is what you would call a betting issue. But the dispute as to whether there are sub-microscopic wolves when it is already agreed that the wolfhounds are giving tongue is no more a betting issue than is 'There will come a day when there will be no more war'. And so I want to say that no one has ever observed a thing of the same sort as a sub-microscopic germ. And yet I must insist that our experience justifies by an argument by analogy our belief in the existence of sub-microscopic germs.

White. What this shows is not that we know by analogy of the existence of physical objects, but that we don't know by analogy of the existence of things which we have found to be invisible. It is true that analogy may put into our heads the idea that measles is due to a germ, that there is something the presence of which is responsible for the multitude of symptoms, and, further, this idea at first has a certain plausibility, probability, because of the analogy of the symptoms with other groups of symptoms which have been found to be due to something in the blood. But the idea which is probable is the idea that there is a *visible* thing; *that* is what analogy suggests. When we have looked and found there isn't any such thing, then that idea can no longer be said to be probable, but is on the contrary known to be false, the analogy is known to have broken down.

Gray. Yes, *that* idea is no longer probable. What is then probable is that there is an invisible germ. Surely you are not going to say that measles is not due to an invisible germ, or that this conviction of yours is unjustified, or that the ground for it is not the analogy between the symptoms of measles and the symptoms of diseases which have been found to be due to germs? The existence of the invisible measle germs is probable by argument by analogy, though, of course, not every one who reasonably believes in it sets out his reasons in such a way that this is quite apparent. The presence of the invisible measle germs can be proved, Dr. Pantin the zoologist says. At the same time, he is perfectly aware that the reactions of the measle patient's blood to certain tests is no more a *direct* proof or verification of the existence of the germs than is the pattern of other symptoms the patient exhibits. We cannot know directly of the presence of the invisible germs, but we know of it indirectly by an argument by analogy with cases where our senses do not fail us so soon.

White. No doubt measles is due to an invisible germ. And no doubt what justifies us in saying this is the likeness of the symptoms of measles to the symptoms of diseases which have been found to be due to visible germs. No doubt that is the conventional way of describing the justification. What I want to insist upon is that 'Analogy justifies belief in invisible germs' is only another way of saying 'Until we looked it was probable by analogy that there were germs (visible) in the blood of patients suffering from measles but when we looked we found none'.

I own I ought not to have said that there is no justification for the belief that measles is due to invisible germs from the analogy of its symptoms with symptoms of diseases due to visible germs. I should have insisted only on the idiosyncrasy of the analogy. To say that analogy does not justify belief in invisible germs is to be like those who have said 'Even if a thousand people of all sorts have got better from anaemia after taking raw liver it's nothing but a *post hoc ergo propter hoc* to argue that raw liver cures anaemia. The evidence doesn't really render the conclusion probable'. When such a thing is said we are revolted. But I want to insist that a little sophistical reasoning soon makes it attractive, soon shows that it's 'really quite right'. Consider: The evidence surely couldn't make the conclusion probable, more likely than not, if that conclusion were too improbable to start with. No doubt the thousand cases eliminate certain alternative explanations which would not have been eliminated by only a hundred cases. But that doesn't tell us how many alternative explanations remain. And without knowing that, how can we be confident that the suggested explanation is the right one? At the same time, the fact remains that the thousand various and carefully studied cases are just what we do call good evidence for such a conclusion. Such evidence has made it more than probable that raw liver is the thing for anaemia. It is as absurd to say that the evidence ought not to have led to *some* confidence in this conclusion as it is to say that the information 'Smith has twice as many goats as Jones and Jones has as many goats as fingers' ought not to lead to *equal* confidence in the conclusion 'Smith has twenty goats'. Or shall we say that it is as unconventional but not as absurd? For the evidence couldn't be said to 'increase the probability of the conclusion' if we meant by this 'have the logical relations to it' which hold in the typical case of increasing probability, where the increase can be *calculated*; and if the evidence can't be said to 'increase the probability' can it be said to 'justify increased confidence'? Thus, although it's a tiresome eccentricity to say that high-class scientific evidence isn't high-class, I like the eccentricity. For it forces us to face our conflicting inclinations, and in avoiding it we begin to see that there are more logics than are dreamt of in the textbooks. And though when I said 'The analogy between measles and germ-caused diseases does not give ground for supposing that measles is due to invisible germs' this was a tiresome eccentricity, it too will force us to grasp how unlike this ground by analogy is to the ground by analogy for expecting a visible germ which we haven't yet seen, and how like this *association of X's visible or, if not, invisible with Y's* is to the *break-down of the association of X's with Y's*. And grasping the idiosyncrasy of the logic of the argument to invisible X's we shall see how it is that to reply to 'How do I know there are invisible X's?' with the response 'By analogy' is to reply 'In the way you do'.

By all means let us say, then, that analogy with cases of visible germs establishes the existence in other cases of invisible germs. But remember that analogy with visible currents establishes invisible currents. And that a leprechaun is a sort of germ. The singing of songs and the mischievous tricks of a grandfather clock are good evidence for the presence in it of a leprechaun, because often with grandfather clocks when we have observed the former we have found the latter. And when a watch shows analogous symptoms we have good evidence by analogy for the presence of a little leprechaun in it, at least until we have found there isn't one. And by all means let us *still* say that we have good evidence by analogy, even when we have looked and found there isn't one. Call it good evidence if you like, call it argument by analogy proving the existence of things it is beyond our senses to detect, but notice that is is uncommonly like those cases where we say 'But it was found that there the analogy breaks down'.[1] 'Amongst the larger termites we find societies in which there are workers, nurses and soldiers who guard the queen. Analogy would suggest a king. But observation shows that this is not so.' Or shall we say that the drone is a king but that when he comes to the throne he is deposed at once?

But take no notice of my gibes. You are doing the done thing. The way in which phenomena at one end of an electrically

---

[1] 'It was found that that feature of the positive analogy of the hitherto examined instances, viz. being clocks and not watches, was after all not irrelevant.'

charged wire are connected with phenomena at the other end reminds us of the way phenomena at one end of a pipe carrying water are connected with the phenomena at the other end—an electrical system reminds us in many ways of an hydraulic system. And this resemblance provides evidence by analogy for there being a current of something running through the wires of the electrical system; it is analogy between what we now experience from the wires and what we have experienced from pipes which makes us think there must be a current of something in the wires. Experience then supports this idea. But doesn't it also refute it, when we look and find no current of anything in the wires? Not at all. Don't let this gibe put you off. What we in fact choose to say is that experience supports the theory, though it shows the current to be very disappointingly unlike the current in pipes. That is what we say. You are quite right. Only remember that we say that you and I have the same father because there are *not* two fathers, the one yours and the other mine, and also say that you and I have the same picture because there *are* two pictures, the one yours and the other mine, and they are just alike. This is the sort of thing which is apt to make a furniture remover say that really you and I have not the same picture. He says this because, though the situation resembles in important respects the situation in which there is only one picture between the two of us, it also differs from that situation. And the way it differs is just the way that is important to the furniture remover in guessing how large a van will be needed to remove our effects. Like the furniture remover, when I am concerned with removing the difficulty 'How do we ever know from our sensations of the existence of material things?' I am inclined to contradict one who answers 'By analogy'. For the analogy differs from other analogies in exactly the way which produces the original difficulty with regard to the knowing. The only analogies it doesn't thus differ from are other arguments by analogy to invisible things where the same difficulties are felt. It isn't that we don't know of the existence of invisible things, but that we do and that there's something queer about the knowing. And again it isn't that we don't know of their existence by analogy, but that we do and that there's something queer about the analogy. Something very queer. This is what you called the peculiar grammar of the expression 'invisible things'. When you insisted on recalling that peculiar grammar you were insisting on my point. For the peculiar grammar of that expression is the peculiar logic of invisible things. And that peculiar logic is what I am insisting upon. And I insist upon the idiosyncrasy of the logic of invisible things and of chairs and tables and of minds because this is another way of insisting upon the idiosyncrasy of the relationship between the phenomena in which these things manifest themselves to us and these things themselves, between the basis of our knowledge of these things and these things, and this is a way of grasping the nature of these things.[1] One way of getting a better grasp of a new machine is to see how far it resembles a gyro-tiller, or if it is a gyro-tiller how far it differs from all the old ones. To examine how far in these cases the step from the signs to what they signify is argument by analogy and, granting that it is, how far it differs from the step by analogy from the likeness of two animals, and the presence of teeth in one, to the presence of teeth in the other, or the step from the likeness of a new, enormous animal to familiar animals with teeth, to the conclusion that in the mouth of the new animal are teeth bigger than any we have ever seen—to examine all this is to answer the questions 'How do we know that there are any invisible germs?', 'How can we justify our confidence that there is anything beyond our sensations?', 'What justification is there for our confidence that thoughts and feelings prompt the behaviour of others?' Metaphysics comes from obsessional qualms about the use of 'justify', a Pharisaism in Logic instead of in Morals or Art.

---

[1] (i) The verification principle follows from the doctrine that all necessary propositions are analytic and (ii) the doctrine from the principle. As to (i): (a) all propositions of the form P has R to Q, where R is a logical relation, are necessary, whether of the form P entails Q or of the form P is entailed by Q or of the form P lends probability to Q or of the form P is lent probability by Q. Call these propositions the logic of P. (Of course, 'The murmur makes a leaking valve probable' is not a necessary proposition. It is not a logical proposition. You don't get a logical proposition till you add the rest of the data.) Now (b) if Q is involved in the meaning of P then P entails Q. From (b) we have (β) if Q is involved in the meaning of P it is included in the logic of P. From (a) with the doctrine that all necessary propositions are analytic we have (α) that everything included in the logic of P is involved in the meaning of P. From (β) and (α) we have the verification principle that if two statements have the same logic they have the same meaning, and that if two statements have different meanings they have different logics, with the useful corollary that every different sort of statement has a different sort of logic.

Let me put the thing in another way. People sometimes ask 'How do I know of the existence of sensations of pain and hunger and so on in others?' and receive the answer 'By analogy' and are satisfied. And people might ask 'How do we know of the existence of invisible germs?' and receive the answer 'By analogy' and be satisfied. Now here is a point of great interest, because people sometimes say to me 'You don't seem to bother about what is true in philosophy. You only concern yourself with stopping people from complaining. Your object, you say, is to satisfy them'. Well now, here I am going to say that people oughtn't to be satisfied with the answer 'By analogy', not even if it satisfies lots of people, any more than they ought to be satisfied with *The Way of an Eagle*, by Ethel M. Dell, although it sold 50,000 copies. Of course, *The Way of an Eagle* didn't sell like it did for nothing. Nor is it for nothing that the answer 'By analogy' appeals so much. It gives satisfaction. But the satisfaction is unstable. It too readily gives way to new dissatisfaction, especially if someone taps, like you did, on the weak place in the answer, and says 'But invisible germs aren't the same sort of thing as visible germs in the way that larger teeth are the same sort of thing as smaller teeth'. It is true we may argue by analogy to the existence of things of a sort different from any we have seen. When we see a new enormous animal we expect bigger teeth than we have ever seen, and when we see a new tiny animal we expect tinier teeth than we have ever seen, both by analogy with animals and teeth we have seen. But now that this argument is set down beside the one about the germs is clear that it is different. It's especially clear when we notice that before we have looked and found no germs *then* the position is like that which we describe as knowing by analogy that this animal will have big teeth. But after we have looked, *then* the position is very different, and to describe it also as knowing by analogy that there are germs seems too near to saying that when we find that the enormous animal has no teeth, what we find is that it has invisible teeth. In other words, looking at the arguments side by side people may begin to say 'But is this argument for the germs argument by analogy?' They are like people who . . .

Gray. Forgive my interrupting. But do you wish to say the answer 'By analogy' is correct, or do you not?

White. The matter as to whether in the special context described it is a correct answer I leave to you. When Shelley wrote 'Bird thou never wert' was what he said incorrect?—in view of the fact that on the outside of the book was written 'Poems' was what he said incorrect? In view of the fact that he said that the skylark is not a bird, when of course it is, was what he said correct? Whether or no it is correct to say to the furniture remover that you and I have the same picture is as maybe, but it is certainly either misleading or tiresome. And to reply to 'How do we know from outward signs inward states?', 'How do we know from the effects of the external world on us what it is really like?', 'How do we know from visible signs that a patient has invisible germs in his blood?'—to reply to these questions with the answer 'By analogy' is very apt to be bogusly soothing and thus misleading.

It wouldn't be so misleading if it weren't correct, just as it wouldn't be so misleading to say that 'There is an electric current flowing in this wire' means more than 'This wire gives off sparks, etc.' if it weren't correct. It wouldn't be so misleading to say that the hypotheses of a brownie and of a leprechaun are different hypotheses if it weren't correct. Suppose a man sees a coyote for the first time. 'Now', he says, 'is this a wolf or a fox?'—with a sort of chuckle he asks this, because he fancies he is asking a riddle. Your answer 'It's neither. It's a coyote' wouldn't be so misleading, so inappropriate, if it weren't correct. How inappropriate your answer is depends on how much the man who asked 'What's this now? Is it a wolf or a fox?' was putting a riddle instead of asking a question of logic, viz. 'What is this animal called?' Now the man who asked the question chuckled, and that was because he thought he was putting you in a certain kind of difficulty. You prick the bubble with which he proposed to play. Maybe he now becomes confused, or maybe he becomes irritated. Maybe he doesn't notice that he might now ask 'And are coyotes foxes or wolves?' And if he did wouldn't you answer 'They are neither' and answer correctly? And probably he wouldn't even then realize that you aren't playing his game. You see he's playing his game with pieces habitually used to play the game you are playing, and that prevents his realizing properly that though he's using those pieces he's playing

a different game. So he's misled into an unwilling silence. Or
maybe he finds your answer tiresome. You don't see his point,
he says, but alas, he finds some difficulty in explaining what it is.

But there's another reason why the answer 'By analogy' appears good. If it were entirely clear what questions they are
which are asked by one who asks 'How do we know of the existence of invisible things?', 'How do we know of the existence of
trees and water?', 'How do we know of the existence of thoughts
and feelings?', then the answer 'By analogy' wouldn't be so
attractive, and thus less of a trump-card in the hand of the Devil.
But the questions are not clear. When someone asked me 'How
do we know what we know in memory?' I replied 'By experience'. And if asked 'How do we know what we know in perception?' I might likewise reply 'By experience'. How does your
dog know when he hears your voice that you are in the hall? By
experience, by analogy; for he knows your voice, he has learned
—at first he didn't know—that that voice is associated with you.
It's only when someone asks the absurd question 'How does he
know it's you when he's seen you, smelt you, pawed you, licked
you, and chewed your gloves?' that the answer 'From experience, by analogy' becomes absurd. It is true that the queerness of the last question begins in the first, that the queerness of
the last answer begins in the first. But it only begins. It would
be absurd to deny that it was from past experience that when
you smelt burnt almonds this afternoon you expected prussic
acid or, possibly, burnt almonds. In the past that sort of smell
has been associated with prussic acid and burnt almonds, very
like the chattering of the jay birds has been associated with the
presence of a fox. Very like, fatally like. And yet it is easy to
see that there is something queer about saying that having
smelt Eau de Cologne one argues by analogy that the stuff in
the bottle is Eau de Cologne.[1] This same queerness begins in 'It

---

[1] We are apt to assume that what holds for chairs and tables in the philosophy of
the external world holds for all physical things. But even within the category of
physical objects there are differences in logic. This isn't anything new. Everyone
knows that 'having legs' is relevant to 'is a chair' in a way in which it is not to
'is a cushion'. But there is a point in bringing together under one name all differences in what counts for and against a statement, and there is a point in drawing
the line between differences in logic (form of argument) and differences in definition
(content of argument) in various eccentric places between the ordinary and the
limit which gives every statement a different logic.

smells like cheese, but *is* it cheese?' But though it begins here it doesn't reach a maximum until we have such a question as 'To all of us it looked as if there were cheese in the larder, and it felt, smelt and tasted as if there were, and I am sure that no one else would have detected anything to the contrary, and I am sure that no one ever will detect anything to the contrary, but can we be sure that there really was cheese there as opposed to being sure that everything will go on seeming just as if there were?' And it is not until we reach this very queer question that the answer 'By analogy' is so very queer.

Gray. What do you mean, 'queer'? And you have been explaining why the answer looks good, but to prove it misleading, meretricious, pretentious, it is necessary to show too how it's bad.

White. Well, that's what I've been trying to do ever since I began talking about the queerness of putting 'probably' before 'There is bread in the larder' and before 'Smith feels sick'.

Gray. But if the question is 'How do I get from these signs to this conclusion?', and the answer given is 'By analogy', and you allow that that answer is correct, isn't that the end of the matter? Surely the only question is '*Is* it correct?'? But you seem to think that its being correct doesn't prevent its being a bad answer, bad, I suppose, in that it's what you call misleading. But *how* is it misleading?

White. That's what I've been trying to explain. You say 'It's correct, surely that's the end of the matter'. You have already forgotten the man who asks 'Is this a wolf or a fox?' My points are (1) that whether it's correct or not is not the point and then (2) that it's misleading. Allow me to take two other examples of my sort of procedure in philosophy. You remember how it was said that 'There's a leprechaun in this watch', even in the special usage we described, would not mean the same as 'This watch sings fairy songs on being politely asked, especially when the moon is full, etc.', and you remember, too, that correct as this statement is it is most subversive, because it prevents our noticing the difference between the relation between the use of 'There are here all signs of a leprechaun' and the use of 'There is here a leprechaun' on the one hand and the relation between the use of 'There are here all signs of malaria germs' and the use of 'There are here malaria germs' on the other. It is bad to prevent our noticing this because it includes preventing our noticing the difference between the question 'There are, it is true, all signs of leprechauns (measle germs) in these watches, but I wonder are there really any?' and the question 'There are all signs of malaria germs in these people, but I wonder are there any (or is it Malta fever)?' And this is bad because to prevent our noticing the difference between these questions is to leave us to try to deal with the leprechaun question by the same technique as is available for the malaria question, viz. further investigation. And when this technique proves impossible with the leprechaun question we feel as we feel when we haven't a microscope and so can't employ this technique on the malaria question. The only differ- ence, it then seems to us, is that the former feeling is hopeless, while the latter is not, because we can save up to buy a micro- scope. We don't see the inappropriateness of feeling the same feeling with regard to the leprechaun question because saying, as we have said, that to assert the existence of a leprechaun is to assert something more than and different from the presence of the signs of its existence we then treat the relationship between these two assertions as like that between typical cases in which we say of one assertion that it is different from and involves more than another, as in ' " She's half sister to Royal Minstrel" means more than "One of their parents is the same", it means "Their dam is the same" '. Take the thing the other way round. To say 'The sentence "There are measle germs here" means something different from what the sentence "This measle patient gives every germ-reaction" means' is bad because it's un- duly worrying. You remember it was said—to stop the worry it was said—' "He has the measle germ" just means "He gives and will give all the measle-reactions" '. Now this was incorrect. But that again is not the point. The point is that this answer is too soothing. Or rather not too soothing—nothing could be that, everything's absolutely all right in metaphysics—but it's too slickly soothing. It's soothing without requiring of us that act of courage, that flinging away of our battery of crutches, which is required in order to realize that everything's all right. This phenomenalist answer soothes without demanding this change of heart only by soothing deceptively and saying that this alarming hippopotamus is only a horse that lives in rivers. It's true that the hippopotamus is quite O.K. and not at all carnivorous and won't hurt anyone who treats him right—that is, treats him like a hippopotamus has to be treated; but it's a mistake to soothe people about him by telling them that he's a horse because, though that may soothe them for the moment, they will soon find that to treat him like a horse is not satisfactory. Or if you do tell them that he's a horse, then you must at once explain just how this is misleading, whether because, though it's correct that he is a horse, he differs from all other horses in the following respects relevant to their attitude to him, or because, though like a horse, he isn't one, and differs from them in the following respects relevant to their attitude to him.

Now the answer 'By analogy' is another deceptive soother. It happens (1) that it is not incorrect and (2) that the case where it is so very deceptive is, as we have noticed, not sharply separated from cases where it is but little deceptive. But these things only make it the more dangerous, like the hippopotamus's being properly called a river-horse and eating grass. You will remember it was the same with the statement ' "There are all signs of an electric current" does not mean the same as "There is an electric current here" '. This statement is (1) quite correct and (2) only thoroughly misleading when 'all signs' is eccentrically taken to mean quite literally *all* signs, i.e. to as to leave none behind. Indeed, these issues 'Is the step from *There are here all signs of germs* (*of bread*) (*of pain*) to *There are here germs* (*bread*) (*pain*) argument by analogy?' reflect the issues 'Does "There are here all signs of measle germs (bread) (pain)" mean the same as "There are here measle germs (bread) (pain)"?' In short, the "Is it analogy?" controversies reflect the 'Do they mean the same?" controversies.

Black. Yes, and may I point out that the reflection doesn't fail to reproduce the *difference* between the germ, the bread and the pain issues?

White. Certainly, certainly, but give me a chance. That indeed, as we found, is where the rub is. But we are coming back to that. At the moment the point is to explain why it's misleading to say that we know by analogy that there's bread in the larder and even (for these two are different, too, as no doubt you

would wisely point out) misleading to say that we know by
analogy that there are invisible germs in a man's blood. And
what I am first saying about how it is misleading is that it mis-
leads like 'They mean the same' and also like 'They don't mean
the same'', in some ways like the one and in some ways like the
other. And what I want to say further is that in these cases of
germs, bread and pain, and in other philosophical cases, the
features of the relationships between the signs and the signified
which lead to the controversies as to whether the signified is
constituted by the signs are the very features which lead to the
controversies as to whether the steps from the signs to the signified are arguments by analogy.

Gray. Still you won't say what these features are.

White. I have. If you still ask 'What are they?' I shall say
what we've said already. Someone said 'How about this step from
our sensations to the real physical things which cause them? How
about this step from behaviour to the inward states, the thoughts
and feelings behind it? Is it all right? Some say that there is no
step, some that there is a step but that it is quite unjustified'.
Gray replied, 'There is a step and it's justified'. Black said,
'How?' Gray said 'By experience. By induction and analogy.
You know, it's like the step from the chattering of the jays to the
passing of a fox, from presystolic murmur to leaking valves,
from leaking valves to death tomorrow'. Black said 'Not quite
like that surely. For these arguments depend on premises reporting experience. We say 'Whenever I've heard the jays like
that it wasn't long before hounds . . .'' We say "When there's
that murmur it's always found that the valves have been leaking". But we can't say "Whenever I've seen, smelt and tasted
bread I've soon found bread". For if we say (1) that "finding
bread" is something different from getting the sight, smell and
taste of it, then we have never found bread, and if we say (2) that
it is the same, then we can't say that we have often *first* got the
smell and taste and sight of it and *then* found it. Whichever we
say we can't represent the step from sensations of bread to bread
as like that from the chattering of the jays to the passing of a fox.
For if we say (2) the step is an immediate inference, and if we
say (1) it is an argument by analogy with a false, if not unintelligible, major premise'. Gray said 'Well yes, there is some differ-

ence'. '*Some* difference!' we said. 'There's all the difference. The bread case differs from ordinary, orthodox, thoroughly accepted cases of analogy in just those ways which leave us where we were, because they leave us saying "On the one hand it looks as if there is no justification for this step because there's never been a time when we have observed besides the signs the signified, while on the other hand it looks as if the step is only too well justified for us to speak of justification, because it's so well justified that there is no step".' That is, the bread case differs from the steps from the chattering of the jays to the passing of a fox, from presystolic murmur to leaking valves, in such a way that we can say that it's the same sort of step only by insisting that it's the same sort of step although it differs either in that its premise reporting experience of association between signs and signified is quite false, even if it's intelligible, or in that that premise does not really report experience but is a logical principle, so that to put 'probably' between the premisses and the conclusion is absurd. In this way it comes out that we are back to where we started from. We started from a hesitancy as to whether to accept the paradox that we don't really know that there is bread in the larder or to accept the paradox that there is bread in the larder means no more than that it will always seem as if there is now bread in the larder. What we now see is that to describe the situation—the relation between our knowledge of what we can see, smell and taste and our assertion that there is bread in the larder—by the name of 'argument by analogy' doesn't alter its features. These features made us hesitate to say that we can see, smell and taste bread and not know that there is bread there, and also made us hesitate to say that there is bread there means no more than that it will always seem to everyone as if there is now bread there. These same features now make us hesitate whether to say that the argument by analogy by which we step from signs of bread to bread is founded upon a falsely favourable report of our experience, or to say that it is an argument in which the conclusion that there is bread is no more than a redescription of the premiss that there is sight, smell and taste of bread. The avenger of blood hesitates when he sees the man who killed his father playing with his children and mutters 'Can it be right to kill this man?' We say 'But it's your filial blood-bond'. But the avenger of blood, even if he doesn't question that it's his 'filial-blood-bond' (well-known phrase in the tribe), will still—if he doesn't think by labels he will still be uneasy and say 'But is it always right to do what is the keeping of my filial blood-bond?' Likewise the philosopher who, suddenly questioning himself and others, says 'But is it right, this step from sights, smells and tastes of ours to bread?' 'It's the right argument by analogy' we say. But if he doesn't think by labels—'a rose by any other name' smells just as sweet, or not, as the case may be—if he doesn't think by labels, then he will ask, 'Well, but then is this sort of argument by analogy all right?'

Gray. Yes, yes, I remember. But then I admitted that it's not *that* sort of justification by experience which the justification of our confidence in the existence of bread is like. What it is like is the sort of argument by analogy from A to B which is based on the association not of A with B but of something like A with something like B. It is like the justification of our belief in measle germs which we have never seen, from our experience in other diseases of the association of a pattern of symptoms like that a measle patient exhibits with visible germs.

White. It's not like our expectation of measle germs (in fact invisible) while we still expect them to be visible. While we still haven't looked with the microscope our justification for our confidence in the existence of measle germs differs from our confidence in the existence of bread in the following way: while we still haven't looked, and are thus still expecting visible, though perhaps oddly shaped, germs, we can well understand someone who says 'Probably there are germs there, but perhaps you will find there are none'. Now in the case of the bread we cannot understand what it would be like *to find* that what all the evidence suggests is so is after all not so. I do not say that we cannot understand, that it's meaningless to suggest, that what all the evidence suggests is so is in fact not so. What I am claiming here is that in the bread case we don't understand the suggestion that we might *find* that what all the evidence suggests is so is not so. This proves it unlike the justification of the belief in visible germs. But of course this very feature makes it like the justification by analogical extrapolation of our belief in *invisible* germs. For in the case of invisible germs it is once more impossible to understand the suggestion that we might *find* that what all the evidence suggests is so is not so.

Gray. There you are. My answer 'By analogy' was quite right. It amounted to the answer 'You are troubled about the step from signs of bread to bread. Don't be troubled. It's a species of argument by analogy. Not of the familiar species, "This dog's like the one that bites, so probably he bites too", but of the species by which we establish the existence of germs we cannot see and do not expect to see'.

White. Undoubtedly that is the species. Now arguments of that species, as we have just seen, are different from other analogical extrapolations, i.e. arguments of the form

(i) *Here is a pattern of phenomena $A(a_1 \ldots a_n)$.*

(ii) *Similar patterns A' $(a'_1 \ldots a'_n)$, A'' $(a''_1 \ldots a''_n)$, etc., have been found to be due to things B', B'', etc.*

(iii) *We may then expect here that the phenomena $A(a_1 \ldots a_n)$ are due to the presence of a thing B.*

They are different in that in them B differs from B' and from B'' not merely in a way in which B' and B'' differ from one another but in that the finding of B here could include nothing not included in the finding of $A(a_1 \ldots a_n)$. For arguments of this species have this in common: that the thing whose existence they establish is known only by its effects. The consequence is that we cannot say of these arguments that however good the evidence in them we can always understand the suggestion that we may nevertheless find their conclusions false or find them true. On the contrary, when the evidence is supposed so good as to include all the effects of B we cannot understand the suggestion that we should find that B doesn't exist. If B is known only by its effects, then the nearer does a set of phenomena come to including all those effects the nearer does an argument from those phenomena to B come to being an immediate inference. And when the phenomena include *all* the effects, all the signs, i.e. when the argument is like the bread argument, a perfect member of the species which interests us, then the argument becomes quite an immediate inference. It involves, if you like, an empirical generalization, e.g. in the germ case the generalization 'In other diseases such symptoms have been associated with germs', and the conclusion, if you like, means more than the statement that $a_1 \ldots a_n$ are present, it means also, if you like, that such phenomena are usually found associated with B's, e.g. germs; but the fact remains that the conclusion is no more than a way of redescribing the evidence. This comes out in the fact that the evidence is of a sort which we might well choose to describe by saying that though patterns of phenomena like $a_1 \ldots a_n$ have been hitherto associated with B's the present case shows that this association breaks down. This comes out, in the case that primarily is interesting us, in the fact that if someone says 'I know by analogy, from the association of groans from my body and pain, that behind the groans of others is pain' then we feel inclined to say 'You might as well say that you know from the groans of other bodies unaccompanied by pain that the generalization which holds so well for your own body fails for others'. Now it isn't that we don't know which conclusion is correct, but that we have to choose which way to describe the facts.

Black. But this is different. We have never experienced bread apart from the sight, smell and taste of it, and it's impossible to experience invisible germs except through their effects. But in the case of pain we have in our own case found certain behaviour associated with something else—a sensation of pain

White. Yes, and each of us also finds many instances of such behaviour without pain, so each of us had better conclude, as I have just suggested, that though when *his* body shows these symptoms pain is to be expected, when other bodies show these symptoms it is not. And that is what we in fact do, we do not expect pain when we see a wound in the side of another.

Black. We don't expect pain for ourselves, but we do for him.

White. We are back to where we were. There is a difference between the relation between the members of the pair 'There are all the symptoms of germs, and there will be' and 'There is an invisible germ here' and on the other hand the relation between the members of the pair 'There will be all symptoms of pain here' and 'There will be pain here.' This difference is one which one may fairly describe by saying that in the latter case one who expects that there will be pain expects something different from one who expects nothing but symptoms of pain, while in the former case, though there is a difference between one who says 'There will be invisible germs in his blood' and one who says 'There will be all symptoms of germs in his blood, but no germs', this difference is not one in their expectations. They both expect the same.

Gray. The difference between the pairs isn't as sharp and absolute as you two make out. For on the one hand someone might say, 'One who expects invisible germs expects something different from one who merely expects all symptoms of germs; this isn't merely a difference in the pictures with which they work, like the difference between one who says "The sun is going down" and one who says "The earth is turning from the sun" '. And then on the opposite side someone might say 'Whether one says "He will be in pain" or says "He'll still complain" one's expectations are the same, only one's feelings are different'.

White. The fact remains that there *is* a difference. There *is* much *more* inclination to say that when I expect that Smith will be in pain I really expect another fact besides the symptoms of pain than there is to say that when I expect invisible germs I expect another fact besides the symptoms of them. And this difference now comes out in the inclination to say that while the inference to germs isn't really an argument by analogy, but only a 'summing up, redescription of the evidence', the inference to mental states in others is a real inference, is a problematic inference, is an inference based on analogous experience in other cases.

Black. As you say, there is a difference between the differences. There is a difference between one who expects that Smith will have invisible germs in his blood and one who expects merely that he will show all signs of such germs. But this we have seen through, we know what sort of difference in expectation this is. Again, there is a difference between one who expects that there will be a loaf in the larder and one who expects merely that all our sensations will be such as they would be if there were a loaf in the larder. But this difference is very like the difference between the man who expects invisible germs and the man who expects merely all symptoms of invisible germs. On the other hand, between the man who expects that Smith will be colour-blind tomorrow and the man who expects merely that he will give all signs of being colour-blind there is a real difference in what they expect, and there is a real difference in what they expect between a man who believes that tomorrow Smith will be in pain and one who believes merely that Smith will give all signs of being in pain.

Gray. And this difference in the relations between the signs and the signified now comes out anew in the fact that, while to find visible germs associated with a pattern of symptoms is not to find something analogous to invisible germs, to find oneself in pain is to find something analogous to pain in others. So that even when we say that the argument to invisible germs is not a genuine argument, much less a genuine argument by analogy, we may yet insist that the argument to pain is a genuine argument by analogy.

Other Minds IV

Gray. Now where were we? It began by Black saying 'Apart from the fact that from a man's present behaviour we can never know whether his future behaviour will confirm our diagnosis of his mental condition there is unfortunately the further fact that we can never know from a man's behaviour, however complete and consistent it may be, what his inward state is nor whether any inward state exists, that is whether in a body we observe from its cradle to its coffin there is any mind or soul at all'.

White. And I said, 'You-might-as-well-say, "Apart from the fact that from the present behaviour of a watch we can never know its future behaviour there is unfortunately the further fact that we can never from any story about its behaviour, however complete as well as consistent, know whether that behaviour was due to an invisible leprechaun or not". You-might-as-well-say, "Apart from the fact that from the present symptoms of a patient we can never know his future symptoms—the prognosis is for ever problematic—there is unfortunately the further fact that however complete the history of the case from the cradle through the clinic to the grave we can never really know whether his symptoms were due to germs or not, when those germs if they exist are invisible—the diagnosis is for ever problematic." '

Black. And I said, 'But-this-is-different. If two doctors agree as to what symptoms a man does, will and would exhibit, as to, for example, what would happen if he were given this drug and what if that, then even if the one says "There are germs in his blood though we can't see them", and the other says "There are not, though his symptoms are like they would be if there were", still there is no real difference of opinion between these doctors. For there is no difference in what they expect. In contrast to this there is a great difference between (*a*) what a man expects if you tell him that he will be colour-blind tomorrow but will avoid all mistakes because he will see printed on everything the name of its colour though he will never be able to tell people this, and (*b*) what a man expects if you tell him that he will be all right tomorrow and see things in colours as well as appear to do so. The one has for him a very different meaning from what the other has.' And I insisted (1) that when your hearer is the person about whom you are speaking then a statement about how he will feel has for him a very different meaning from what the corresponding statement about how he and his environment will look has. Thus it makes no difference to us whether Smith has his stitches out under an anaesthetic or not, nor whether he's shot at dawn and joins the choirs invisible or shot at dawn and joins the devils in hell. But it does to him. And then I insisted that though it in some sense makes no difference to us whether Smith has an anaesthetic or is very self-controlled, if it makes a difference to him whether he is told that he will have an anaesthetic or told that he won't, it must also make a difference to all who speak the same language. For to all who speak the same language the predictions must have the same meaning as they have to Smith. And this isn't a mere inevitable conclusion from a proof we can't pick a hole in—it is a fact that in some sense we *do* mean something different by 'Smith will lie still but feel everything' from what we mean by 'Smith will lie still and feel nothing'. And we *expect* something different.

White. In some sense we do, in some ways we do, somehow we do. But how? That is the crux of this affair. And somehow we know our own pain in a way we don't know the pain of others. But how? Is it in a way that gives sense to talk of knowing in the same way the pain of others? That is the epistemological aspect of the crux of this affair.

Black. What do you mean '*How* do we mean something more?' We make a further claim. We make a claim about the state of Smith's mind while his body lies still. And one who says that Smith's soul is still there, that Smith is conscious, that Smith is in pain, differs *seriously* from one who says that when Smith is under chloroform he isn't conscious at all. The difference is serious although the issue cannot be decided. For the disputants can only wait and see what happens and that won't decide the issue. For either Smith will lie still and then when he comes round say that he felt everything and describe the operation, and that won't decide the issue because, though it's odd, it may be that after chloroform people wake with memories just like those they would have had[1] had they been conscious. Or Smith will lie still and say he felt nothing. But maybe he's forgotten. Or Smith will lie still and say he felt nothing while he writes that he felt bad. And that won't decide the issue.

Gray. And I said 'It's true we cannot decide about whether people feel when they are under chloroform, but that doesn't mean that we *never* know what is going on in the minds of others. It is true, if you like, that we cannot even *prove* that a man is in pain but sometimes what we observe is such very good evidence for his being in pain that it would be absurd to say that we don't know that he is in pain just as it would be absurd to say that a doctor doesn't know that the valves of a patient's heart are leaking even when there are conclusive signs that it is.'

White. And I said. 'On what occasions have we in the past first found the signs of pain in others and then found the pain?'

Gray. And I said, 'Never. But that doesn't stop me saying that we sometimes know by analogy that a man is in pain. You might as well say we don't know by analogy of the existence of measle germs because there's never been a time at which we have seen them. But of course we do know of their existence, and by an argument by analogy with other cases in which, though we haven't found measle germs, we have found other germs associated with symptoms rather like those of a measle patient.'

White. And I said, 'Yes, but *what* an argument by analogy. For amongst the premisses leading to the conclusion "There are invisible measle germs" is the premiss that no germs are to be seen, and the consequence is that people very naturally are apt suddenly to have qualms about whether this argument justifies its conclusion in just the very way they have qualms about whether the argument for souls justifies its conclusion.' They are apt to say 'Mightn't we just as well say that this shows that the analogy breaks down, that these symptoms sometimes occur without germs?' just as they are apt to say 'Mightn't one just as

[1] The chloroform question came from trying to find a question analogous to 'Can a man still exist when his body has disintegrated? When his body lies still?' But it will be seen that at this point it meets Wittgenstein's question, 'Do we dream or wake with memories of what never was?'

well say that observation of other bodies shows that the association between groans and pain which holds so well of one's own body breaks down for others?' And they are very right to feel the same qualms, for the arguments are very like, as you yourself insist. And the only way to restore confidence to the step from symptoms to germs is not to say that the sceptic has overlooked certain evidence, for he hasn't, nor to say that he has not made the best of the evidence he has, for the cleverest calculators, the slickest logicians can do no better with it, but to say that there is no step. The only way to restore confidence in the passage of thought from symptoms to germs is to say this: Were we to know that *all* the effects of invisible germs were to be found in a patient then we could not conceive of finding that after all there were no germs in him. Therefore the inference from the effects to the germs vanishes towards immediate inference as the effects known to be present come to include more and more nearly *all* the effects of invisible germs. The inference vanishes into immediate inference, the argument into redescription. The sceptic about the invisible germs mistakes their logical type, i.e. mistakes the grammar of 'invisible germ', i.e. the logic of statements about invisible germs, i.e. the justification-syntax of sentences involving the expression 'invisible germs'. Likewise the sceptic about the soul invisible, intangible, illuding the five senses, mistakes the grammar of 'souls'. He becomes sceptical about the step from the signs of souls to souls. You are right to say that he's wrong to be sceptical about the step. But it's not for the reason your words suggest that he is wrong. He is not wrong because though he can't *prove* the existence of souls he can be sure they exist in the way that even before one has tried one's microscope one may be sure that there are malaria germs in a man because on other occasions one has seen these germs associated with the symptoms the man is now exhibiting. The sceptic about souls is wrong like the sceptic about invisible germs because he remains sceptical when an inference which is constantly approaching an immediate inference has become one, when an argument which is constantly approaching a redescription has become one, when although we make all the motions of taking a step there is no step we take.

Gray. And I said, 'But-this-is-different. We do know what

observing pain is apart from observing its effects.' It is of course
absurd to talk of finding, apart from its effects, a germ *defined* as
invisible, intangible, etc., and so when all the effects to be
expected are present it is absurd to ask, 'But are there invisible
germs here?' But it by no means follows that it is absurd to talk
of finding, apart from their effects, germs in fact invisible, that is
germs which are always in fact detected by their effects. Now
bread and the mental states of others are not *defined* as detectable
only by their effects, although they are in fact always detected
through their effects. Consequently you, White, have not shown
that the step from the effects of bread to bread and from the
symptoms of pain to pain are not really steps but are immediate
inferences or redescriptions. For bread and the mental states of
others are like germs hitherto in fact invisible, not like germs
defined as invisible.

Brown. Before you press this point about the difference
between, on the one hand, the arguments from the signs of germs
in fact invisible to the germs and, on the other hand, arguments
from the signs of germs defined as invisible to the germs, and
declare that if the former is like the latter it is no argument but
only a redescription, so that the question, 'Here are all the
signs of measle germs but are there measle germs?' is not a
question, I should like to dispute an assumption involved in this.
It seems to me that you and Black admit more than you need
when you allow White to step from the statement that since one
cannot conceive of *finding* an invisible germ apart from observing
its effects it therefore *is* its effects so that the argument to in-
invisible germs is not an argument. Undoubtedly one cannot
conceive of finding all the effects of invisible germs and then
finding that there are none; but this does not prove that one
cannot conceive of finding all the effects of invisible germs and
there *being* none. You all assume that when we can't find out
whether S is P then it is senseless to ask whether S is P.

Black. So it is. If you know what it is for S to be P then you
know what it is to know that S is P, for it is to know that what
must be so for S to be P is so. And if you understand the question,
'Is S P?' you know what it is for S to be P. Indeed, 'S is P' in an
interrogative tone, 'Is S P?' and 'Do you know whether S is P?'
all mean the same thing as near as makes no difference.

Gray. Exactly. Of course when Brown puts the assumption in the words, 'When we can't find out whether S is P then it's senseless to ask whether S is P', then that seems wrong because these words may well express a falsehood. For there certainly are cases where we say 'We can't find out whether S is P', where, nevertheless, we would not say that the question 'Is S P?' is senseless. To begin with the simple case where 'can't' refers to physical difficulty, e.g. expense. We say 'I do wish I knew whether he buried the papers or burnt them. But I can't find out now because he's gone to Borneo.' This is a case where a man says he can't find out whether S is P and yet would insist that the question whether S is P is a meaningful one. There is however a very great difference between this case in which someone laments his ignorance of something he can't find out and other cases, for example, the case of someone who says 'I do wish I knew whether he buried or burnt the papers. But I can't find out now because he's gone to Heaven.' This is very different. One *could* go to Borneo but not to Heaven. Because of this the latter lament is less of a lament. In other words, Black and I, and presumably White also, want to maintain that the harder it is given H to find out that S is not P the more improbable does it become, given H, that S is not P. By 'the harder' I don't mean 'the greater the expense'. What I mean is that the less *possible* it becomes given H to find that S is not P the less possible does it become given H that S is not P, and that when it's impossible given H to find that S is not P then it's impossible given H that S is not P. For if there is a possibility which if realized would make S not P then we have only to find it realized to find that S is not P. In other words the less 'find that S is not P' stands for, i.e. the fewer situations it describes such that to find one of them would be to find that S is not P, the less does 'S is not P' stand for, so that when given H 'find that S is not P' describes no situation then given H 'S is not P' describes no situation. And surely there is nothing surprising about this? Surely when I ask 'Did he burn or bury them?' this amounts to 'I wish I knew whether he burned or buried them'. But then if this last is senseless so is the question to which it is equivalent.

White. Well, but there are cases where we would say or feel inclined to say it's a question whether S is P when we haven't an idea of what could be done to answer it. For example, some people would say that it is senseless to talk of now really finding out what happened in the past or whether there has been any past, but that doesn't mean that we can't understand the suggestion that though all the evidence now suggests and will suggest that Charles I was executed someone in fact took his place and he escaped to live quietly in Savernake Forest for the rest of his days. He used to keep bees. Even when there is no process left which we would call finding out whether a man burned or buried certain papers we can understand the suggestion that he burned them and the suggestion that he buried them. We can imagine both alternatives, can consider both hypotheses.

Black. But we are up to this now. We realize that there is imagining and imagining, that there are alternatives and alternatives, understanding and understanding, meaningfulness and meaningfulness. So we realize that the point is 'Can the question "Is S P?" be anything but a "joke" question when there is nothing which if it did happen we would call finding the answer?'

Gray. What's all this about meanings and meanings? What I allow to White, and I believe you agree with me, is this: If it is *logically* impossible to find out whether S is P then the question 'Is S P?' has no sense.

White. Gray, your faith in ratiocination is pathetic. I can just hear you deducing away 'Is it *logically* or merely *physically* impossible to find out whether God exists? It's logically impossible, therefore it's a senseless question.' But don't you see that the new formula only reputs the question—puts it in the form 'Is it logically impossible to find out whether God exists?' A demonstrative argument only reputs a question, as appears when we reverse the antilogism on which it is based. Thus we may argue, 'The question whether God exists isn't senseless, therefore talk about finding out whether he exists can't be'. Or we may argue, 'The question whether God exists isn't senseless, the talk about finding out whether he exists is senseless, therefore talk about whether God exists can be sense while talk about finding out whether he exists is not.' Remember the question, 'Is this my duty?' the answer, 'Yes, to do it is to fulfil your filial blood-bond', and the renewed question, 'But is it always one's duty to fulfil the filial blood-bond?' Remember, 'Is the step from signs of germs to germs justifiable?' and the answer, 'Yes, by analogy', and the renewed question, 'But is this sort of extension of analogy justifiable?' There are no right words in philosophy, only lucky ones. There are reformulations such as 'What it is *logically* impossible to verify is meaningless'. But no reformulations are at last correct for then they vanish into logic. It is only that some are more seductive than others. And there is no sharp line between logic and philosophy. Logic is rhetoric, proof persuasion, and philosophy logic played with especially elastic equations.

Gray. Ah, all that's a little beyond me. Perhaps you would for the moment confine yourself to the point at issue. I would say that if and when it has no sense to talk of now finding out whether there are germs in a man's blood, bread in the larder or pain in Smith's mind then the questions, 'Are there germs in his blood?' 'Is there bread in the larder?' 'Is Smith in pain?' are also senseless. I wish to maintain in general that when there's no sense in talking of now finding out whether S is P then there is no sense in still asking whether S is P. Brown differs from me apparently. May I ask whether you agree with him or with me and Black?

White. Let us return to what you said. You said 'What Black and I hold is that if it is *logically* impossible to find out whether S is P then it is senseless to ask whether S is P'.

Brown. And I want to say that to say that decides what has all along been at issue. For what has been at issue has been this, 'Given that all that can be done to find out whether Smith is in pain has been done and that it is all in favour of his being in pain can't we still wonder whether he is really in pain, isn't it still meaningful to ask whether he is really in pain?' This has been the point at issue, and if you now say that if all that can be done to decide a question has been done, then it is no longer meaningful to ask the question, then you decide, in general terms, the issue which we have been considering in a specific form.

Gray. The issue has been, 'Given that all that can *actually* be done to find out whether Smith is in pain has been done and that it is all in favour of his being in pain can't we still wonder whether he is really in pain, isn't it still meaningful to ask

whether he is really in pain?' Now this issue is not begged by
saying what Black and I wish to say, namely, that given that all
that can *conceivably*, can *logically* be done, to find out whether S is
P has been done and points to S being P, then the question 'Is S
P?' would be meaningless. But it is not meaningless to ask
whether a man might not now and for ever give all signs of
being in pain now and yet not be. Hence it must make sense to
talk of finding out that what all the indirect evidence about a
man's state of mind suggests is after all quite wrong. And of
course this does make sense. The idea we have in mind is that of
knowing what is going on in the mind of another in the direct
way one knows what is going on in one's own mind.

White. So it seemed. And yet this knowing of other minds is
not merely rare but mysterious. It isn't quite clear to me what it
would amount to. To see into Diana's mind, would that be to
feel one had reached a place where it was always before breakfast in early spring, the brightness and the cold, the fields still
pale from winter, delicate, exquisite, unoppressive grace? And
how would the subtle and benevolent but relentless mockery
which appears in George's face and talk appear in his mind?
Would his images all be stamped with the features of a creature
that smiles but with its face in shadows cast by things now long
ago?

But this is all nonsense. The fact is one of three embarrassing
things has to be said if anything is said. (This will bring out
again how the best thing in philosophy is not to say anything, or
if you must say something, say it wildly—you're bound to go
wrong if you're careful.) To return, if anything is said one of
three embarrassing things must be said because three points are
involved.

Usually with the questions we ask one another we feel no
hesitation about their being substantial questions. I mean when
I ask my bedmaker whether she has lit the fire I feel no embarrassment but sometimes I cover up the philosophical questions I
leave on my desk because I am afraid of her thinking me silly.
And again when we ask everyday questions we feel no hesitation
in saying that there are ways of finding out their answers.
Philosophy begins when a question is raised and it seems a
sensible question, and there's a lot we can do towards answering

it, only it doesn't seem quite enough to be called finding out the answer, and yet there's nothing we would call putting the finishing touch to finding out the answer. It seems queer to say that it is still a sensible question whether a certain thing is so, when it makes no sense to say that it is still not known whether it is so because it makes no sense to talk of really finding out whether it is so or not. In face of this situation we feel we have either (1) to say that though it makes no sense to talk of finding out the answer to the question the question is a real question, or (2) to say that really it does make sense to talk about finding out the answer to the question although it requires some care to explain what the finding out would be, or (3) to say that the question isn't a real question though it seemed so real and sensible at first.

Now I can feel some inclination to say that while 'Could we ever know of the existence of invisible, intangible germs otherwise than by their effects' is senseless, nevertheless the question '*Are* there invisible germs here?' makes sense even when all their effects have been observed. Surely even under these circumstances one could still wonder what the germs were like.

But, as I've said, What sort of wondering is this? Remembering how such a question as 'Is it a dog or a wolf?' changes in character according to whether it is asked in a dim light or a good light and changes *gradually* in character the better the light and the more the means to answering it have been tried, I am inclined to say that when we have an interrogative form of words surviving when all the means to answering it have been tried then those words don't put a real question. As we have seen, if observations favouring one answer to a question, for example, 'Is it a dog or a wolf?', balance those favouring the other then it is usual, conventional and proper to say that a question remains. But the question which remains is very different from what it was in a dim light when lots of tests had not yet been done, and different in a way very relevant to the attitude or feeling of a person who uses the form of words, 'Is it a dog or a wolf?' For curiosity has become inappropriate. And it has therefore become *unpoetic* to call his question a question just as it may become intolerable to say 'That is Joan' when she has become an inmate of a mental hospital and her whole time occupied with absurd obsessions—intolerable, however correct.

And when all conceivable tests for whether there are leprechauns or germs in things have been done and all turned out *pro* then to ask whether there are leprechauns or germs there is to ask something which it is unpoetic to call a question. We have been into all this already.

Gray. May we now return to my point. What I said was 'It is of course absurd to talk of finding, apart from their effects, germs defined as invisible, intangible, etc., and so when all the effects to be expected are present it is absurd to ask "Are there invisible germs here?" where the germs are *defined* as invisible, intangible, etc.' But it by no means follows that it is absurd to talk of finding, apart from their effects, germs in fact invisible,[1] that is, germs which are always *in fact* detected by their effects. Now bread and the mental states of others are not defined as detectable only by their effects, although like measle germs they are in fact always detected that way. Consequently, White has not shown that the step from the effects of bread to bread and from the effects of pain to pain are not really steps but are immediate inferences or redescriptions. For bread and the mental states of others are like germs hitherto in fact invisible, like germs defined as invisible.

White. There is of course a difference between talk about invisible germs and talk about measle germs however much in fact invisible the measle germs have been. For if you say 'I've discovered a way of seeing the measle germ', I say, 'No! how, what?' and you say, 'Well, at sunset you sacrifice a goat, at dawn light a fire of laurel leaves and at noon draw off a little of the patient's blood. Then if he has measles you will see first, blood as it usually appears to the naked eye, then blood as it appears under a moderate microscope, then blood as it appears under an enormously powerful microscope, and, finally, you will see amongst the things you saw as small even under the enormously powerful microscope small organisms moving swiftly like bees about the blossom.' And I say, 'You don't say

[1] We have been into this a little already. See p. 25.
Someone may ask, 'Is it absurd for a human being to ask "But are these humanly invisible germs present?"' Compare Ayer on the knowledge of other minds in *The Foundations of Empirical Knowledge*.

so.' In contrast to this, if you say, 'I've found a way to see invisible germs' then I say, 'You mean you've found they are not quite invisible'.

This point has sometimes been brought out by saying this sort of thing: 'Though we cannot in fact see measle germs, the mountains on the other side of the moon, the stars beyond the fixed stars, the elephants in heaven, this is only a physical accident, so however much we've failed to find them it's still meaningful to ask whether they don't exist, it still means more to say that there are stars we can't see than it does to say that there'll be an eclipse of the sun on July 18th just as if there were those extra stars.' People say, 'Even though we've tried all ways to see fairies and still have never seen them so that we haven't any idea left as to what now to try, this doesn't make it meaningless to say, "But may be we will see them tomorrow', and thus leaves meaningful the question, 'Do fairies exist, unseen by mortal eyes?" This isn't meaningless like talk of things defined as invisible or talk of disembodied spirits (here remember Thomas Aquinas on the need for the resurrection of the body). Talk of fairies isn't meaningless talk like talk of disembodied spirits because we can describe what a fairy is like and thus what it would be to find one—

> "Wee folk, good folk,
>   Trooping all together;
>   Green jacket, red cap,
>   And white owl's feather." '

'And,' people would say, 'it's the same with the measle germ.

> "Its eyebrows of a vivid green
>   Have never, never yet been seen
>   But scientists who ought to know
>   Assure us that it must be so." '[1]

There is none of this I wish to deny, there is none of it I can deny. No one differs from anyone about what a sentence means and how far two sentences mean the same provided they both know the language and both describe the meanings of the sentences aseptically. No one differs from anyone about what sort

---

[1] Belloc, quoted by Broad in *Scientific Thought*.

of animal they've found provided they know the animal and describe it in aseptic words. 'Is it a lion?' may be a question, in view of its having stripes like a tiger, but 'Has it stripes?' 'Has it a mane?'—about this no dispute arises. Philosophy arises only because people ask questions to which they know the answers. It's one of those competitions which decide themselves, not one in which the editor's decision is final. Only of course no words are absolutely aseptic—a question may arise, 'Do these constitute stripes?'—only then no one can deny that the stripes are very faint and blurred and, on the other hand, no one can deny that the creature's colour is far from a uniform bronze. But to return. As I have said, I can see that 'Are there invisible germs?' is different from 'Are there measle germs?' in that there isn't anything one could call finding (apart from their effects) invisible germs, while though perhaps there is nothing one could call finding that there are no measle germs, and though one who says 'There are measle germs' doesn't at all mean that if you look with a microscope you'll find some, because he knows you won't, nevertheless there is something which, if quite unexpectedly it did come about, would lead people to say that at last they had seen the measle germ. And this inclines me to say that compared with 'Are there absolutely invisible germs here?' the question, 'Are there rather invisible germs here?' is a meaningful question. But I am not inclined to make much difference between them. After all I can imagine an absolutely invisible thing—he wears a smile no one ever sees. I can imagine God seeing the invisible germs.[1] Of course this as we have seen with the invisible leprechaun is an imagining which leaves my question, 'Are there invisible germs', very different from this question before all signs of them have been observed and very different from the question, 'Are there germs?' before we've looked. But then so it is with the imagining of ourselves finding measle germs when this imagining is the sort which remains when the microscope and all other hopes have been tried. True, the picture of fairies or germs remains undimmed however long we look for them without success. But if now, whatever ritual is

---

[1] Here compare Ayer, who in this way comes back to saying that all the questions he said were meaningless are meaningful. 'Not all' some patient defender protests. But it might as well be all.

suggested, we not only don't expect it to succeed but expect it to fail, then how like are we, though we say, 'I believe in fairies' or 'There *are* fairies somewhere', to one who says, 'There are fairies but they are all by nature invisible' or one who says 'There are no fairies'. Suppose A says to B 'This doesn't fall because it's held by a magnet'. B says 'I see no magnet'. A says 'It's further on'. B goes further on and says 'Still no magnet'. A says 'Further still'. B says 'Still no magnet'. After a while, though there's no saying just when, A's statement functions very like 'There is a magnet but at the point of infinity', which is very like 'There is no magnet though this behaves as if there were', which is very like 'There is an invisible magnet'.[1] 'There is a happy land' but 'far, far away'. Of course the line between having tried lots of hopes without success and having tried everything without success isn't a sharp one and so the line between a question where there is still a finding the answer and one where there is not is not a sharp one. And you may say that in such cases as 'There is a magnet beyond', 'There is a germ within', 'There are fairies somewhere' we *never* reach a point where *every* test about which there is *any* hope has been done, so that the question never becomes a joke.[2] We need not quarrel over whether we say 'They become utterly jokes at infinity', or say 'They never become utterly jokes though they come nearer and nearer to that'.

And if you like to say that the questions, 'Are there fairies?' 'Are there germs?' are meaningful, real questions because they never become untestable with *any* hope, then by all means do so. Or if you like to say that they are real questions or at least meaningful questions because even when they have become hopeless they retain an undimmed picture such that if by some means, however astonishing, we were to find facts to fit it we would answer the questions in the affirmative, then again by all means do so. But I don't call a question a question unless an affirmative answer expresses a real belief and I don't call a

---

[1] Compare (1) 'I believe in miracles but they are very few and one can never be sure there isn't some explanation', with (2) 'Miracles don't happen though often one cannot find the explanation of an occurrence', and (3) 'Put your trust in God and keep your powder dry'.

[2] Thus in spite of the extensive efforts of the Society for Psychical Research the question 'Do we survive death?' has not yet become a joke.

belief a real belief unless it's a bet,[1] and I don't call a bet a bet
unless it's a real belief and the backer differs from the layer in
what he expects. When in other days a man backed his own
horse against another or the clock that was a real bet, but to
back a horse because one must back something isn't to back him.
A man may back a horse like this and say, with a great show of
confidence, 'You see, he'll win'. But he's talking to make the
party go—his confidence is a pretence. He's quite different
from the elderly gentleman forsaking his usual reticence to
shout, 'Mahmoud in a cake walk', as the field for the Two
Thousand came by the Bushes with Mahmoud fast regaining
the length he lost at the gate.

Perhaps those who say 'There are fairies, there are germs,
though you may bet your life you'll never see them', would be
more pleased to see them if they did see them than those who say
that there are none. Or may be they would be less surprised to
see a fairy or a germ, however unexpectedly, than those who say
there are none. Perhaps it is these things which find expression
in 'You can't be sure there are no fairies'.

We have now gone over what the words about fairies and
germs do to people who hear them and what they register in
those who utter them and how these things are different in
different circumstances. After all this detail and refinement,
sketchy as it may have been, to ask to be allowed to present the
thing in one big black line, 'meaningful—not meaningful'
seems just crude. The question, 'Are they meaningful?' has
become a bore. We have seen the race and can do without the
shouting. Write it in red or write it in black, tell it with smiles or
tell it with tears that won't alter what's up the slide.

And now as to your point that bread isn't defined as invisible
or as unknowable except through its effects, so that to ask 'Is
there bread here?' is like asking whether there are germs here
where the germs are not defined as invisible.

First, as we have just seen, there isn't all that difference
between asking, 'Are there absolutely invisible leprechauns,
currents, germs here?' and asking, 'Are there rather invisible
leprechauns, currents, germs here?' However, as we recalled,
we can imagine a crash of thunder and then seeing a fairy or a

[1] Compare Mr. Moulder in *Orley Farm*, ch. lxvii.

germ. Is the bread case like this? There is no step or ritual in which I have any confidence for revealing noumenal bread. But more, I cannot say what would need to follow a crash of thunder, in order to lead me to say 'There now I've seen the noumenal bread'. Would it do to see spread out as on a diagram the several sides and internal structure of things? This would be a gift indeed—no more mistakes at Madame Tussaud's, no more Easter eggs without a filling. But still it hardly fills the bill. After all it's only another visual sensation. True, it's extraordinarily capable of preventing mistakes about subsequent sensations but that only means that it presents simultaneously and conveniently what we otherwise learn from subsequent sensations. It can't count as finding that what our sensations suggest is so is so.[1] There is nothing which would count.

And now the confidence of the agnostic about material things begins to be suspect. He's so sure. He says we can't find out that they exist. He's sure we never shall find out, he doesn't see how we could, and that not merely in the way he can't see how we could ever fly with our arms. We don't ever fly with our arms and we never shall, but we do in dreams, that is there is something we would call this if it did happen. That is, the agnostic about flying with arms must watch the newspapers in case there's a headline—Man Flies with His Arms. But the agnostic about the existence of a bread which is other than, because it causes, our sensations, he need not watch the papers. For no astonishing pattern of phenomena, no newspaper scoop, however astounding, can wreck his claim or cure his pessimism. As a doubt about whether there is bread in the larder becomes less and less practical it becomes more and more philosophical and more and more impregnable. And when it becomes quite philosophical it becomes quite impregnable and gains a more than physical necessity. At the same moment it becomes a senseless lament. The sceptic, like the rest of us, wants to be on a selection that can't lose.[2] He forgets that in heaven one's never

---

[1] There is an excellent account of this matter in Mr. G. A. Paul's fellowship dissertation, *Perception*, in the Library of Trinity College, Cambridge.

[2] The sceptic refuses to back anything, saying that everything may lose except Logic which doesn't. In saying this he appears to back something but he doesn't. For his own statement can't lose and doesn't run. This is in accordance with itself. It doesn't disprove itself. It describes its own nature.

down on the day only because there is no betting there or if you like there is but only first favourites win.

Gray. Well, drop the bread. The supersensual bread is, when one comes to think of it, like the invisible, the intangible germs and fairies. When one comes to think of it it makes no sense to talk of finding it apart from its effects, when amongst its effects are included all its effects on our sensations. And so when all these are present it makes no sense to ask whether it is present. But this after all is not what we are concerned with. What concerns us is the question, 'Is there anything which if it did occur we should call knowing, really knowing that Smith sees the Union Jack in red, white and blue"—is there anything we would call knowing this apart from its effects on Smith's behaviour?

White. The answer to that is 'Certainly there is'. Suppose that sometimes Jones gets a mental image in a blue frame with the word 'Smith' underneath, and when he does knows that that mental image is what Smith is seeing.

Gray. But how does Jones know that the image is an image of what Smith is seeing?

White. It isn't my business to say how he knows. The point is that it's perfectly possible to understand the statement that Smith knows whenever he sees an image of X with underneath it the device 'Smith', that X is what Smith is seeing, and that this would be knowing what is going on in Smith's mind apart from its effects on his behaviour. We might, that is, know what is in Smith's mind from our own inner sensations instead of from our observation of Smith's body, that is from our outer sensations. And then we should be knowing what is going on in Smith's mind and body in the way we know what is going on in our own mind and body.

Gray. No, no. We know what is going on on in our own mind by introspection and we know what is going on in our own body by inner feelings, and we can imagine, as you say, that we should come to know by inner feelings what is going on or going to go on in the bodies of others, e.g. that so and so is going to have a cold. But this wouldn't be really knowing what is going on in the minds of others—and that for two reasons. First, such knowledge would be indirect. For if you come to think of how Jones knows

that his image is an image of what Smith is seeing then you see
that his knowledge is a case of inference from effect to cause.
For it is by experience that Jones knows that such and such an
image signifies that Smith is seeing such and such a thing. His
image would tell him nothing if he hadn't, whenever he got an
image of X with 'Smith' written under it, then found that
Smith was seeing an X. But a knowledge which relies on past
experience and is indirect like this may always be wrong, isn't
really knowing.

White. Well, but still he knows, in a special way, what is
going on in Smith's mind. It is not without arguing from effects
to cause but it is without arguing from effects on Smith's body
to the state of Smith's mind. The question you asked was 'Can
one man tell what is going on in the mind of another apart from
its effects on the behaviour of the other?' And the answer to that
is 'Yes, in telepathy people do'.

Gray. Excuse me, No. I allow that you have shown that one
can imagine, even if one can't find, cases where what I will call
'the instantial basis' for what one person knows of the mind of
another is not an outer sensation of the bodily behaviour of the
other but an inner sensation of his own. And I own I had in fact
overlooked this when I put our question in the form 'Is there
anything we would call knowing that Smith sees the Union
Jack in red, white and blue apart from our knowledge of its
effects on his behaviour?' But you will remember I said that
there is a second objection to saying that the case you imagined
answers that question in the affirmative. This second objection
brings out how Jones's knowledge of Smith's mental condition
is still based in part though not so completely as usual upon
knowledge of Smith's behaviour. As I've said Jones's knowledge doesn't consist in having an image with the name 'Smith'
underneath it or in a special blue frame. It does not consist in
having an image which is in fact an image of what Smith sees.
'Jones knows', we might say, 'from the image what is going on
in Smith's mind.' But this is our usual carelessness. What
Strictly Smith knows from the image of X with 'Smith' written
underneath is that Smith will say he sees X and that there will
be nothing wrong with Smith's eyes, etc., and he knows this not
merely from the image but because in the past he has found the

image in his own mind always associated with certain behaviour on the part of Smith.

White. He might just know without any such experience of past associations.

Gray. Wouldn't his knowledge then be nothing but a blind intuition, a blind faith, a blind superstition? Of course if he had had such images for people other than Smith then he might reasonably trust the Smith images without further experience. But then once more his knowledge would be based on the association of his inner sensation or image with behaviour. He knows what he knows of Smith from what he knows of how Smith or others have behaved. And the further point remains that what he knows of Smith is after all only how he will behave, and not his mental state.

White. Well, if this knowing from pain that Smith's in pain, knowing from seeing an image of crossed swords that Smith is seeing crossed swords would not be knowing directly what is going on in Smith's mind, what would be? Nothing would be. When I ask 'Shall I be in pain tomorrow?' or someone says to me, 'You'll be in pain tomorrow', or I overhear someone say of me, 'He'll be in pain tomorrow', this means more to me than failing in tests for colour-blindness. Then that's because I shall have another way of finding out whether I am colour-blind. I might have, as we have just seen, another way besides observation of behaviour for finding out whether someone else is colour-blind. But this other way consists still in having feelings and sensations of my own and from these expecting other sensations of my own. And to talk of any other kind of knowing of anything lacks a sense, and in particular talk of any other kind of knowing of what is going on in someone else's mind lacks a sense. One who talks of knowing neither by observation of behaviour nor by telepathy of what is going on in the mind of another just doesn't know what he is talking about.

Black. No, I can't agree with that. You assume that no account can be given of any kind of knowing except knowing which consists in having sensation and basing on it prediction of further sensation. In your view no knowledge differs in kind from knowledge of what will win the 2.30. Apart from the fact that I wouldn't call this predictive and therefore problematic business knowledge at all, I must insist that you have given no reason for saying that all talk of knowledge, apart from this betting on future sensation on the basis of present sensation, is without sense. It leads, you should notice, to the conclusion that when on the basis of sensation from Smith's symptoms on Tuesday at 2, together with telepathic sensation at the same time, we have made bets on future sensations from Smith and these bets have all turned out well, then it is absurd to ask, 'Do we know that Smith was in pain on Tuesday at 2', except in so far as it is still possible to make still further bets on what Smith will do. Something like this conclusion we have already rejected. For we have insisted that the conclusion that Smith will be colour-blind means more than any story, however long, about what he'll do, that is, that however much information we have about the stimuli applied to him and the reactions he has made it still makes sense to ask, 'Is he colour-blind?' We may add now that 'Smith will be colour-blind' means more than any story, however long, about what sensations we shall get from Smith, *whether sensations of his behaviour or telepathic sensations from him.*

White. I quite agree that no telepathic knowledge on our part of what is in Smith's mind will do as direct knowledge of what is in his mind, for such knowledge is always still too little or finally too much. But I am returning to the conclusion that the reason why we never gain knowledge of what is going on in the minds of others is the same as the reason why we never find a perfect pulley on which W doesn't balance $\frac{1}{2}$.W, or reach the Islands of Perfection. It will follow, I know, that somehow there is something wrong in saying that in expecting Bobby to feel sick we do more than expect him to fall silent, turn green, bring up his breakfast, feel a bit sick ourselves if we are there, and so on. But now after all what more do we expect?

Black. Before coming back to that let's get quite clear about telepathy's not being what is wanted by the real metaphysician when he asks for real knowledge of the mind of another. What did you mean when you said 'It is always not enough or finally too much'?

White. What I meant was this: Besides the fact that any telepathy consists in predicting sensation from sensation and is thus (*a*) indirect and (*b*) still confined to the knower's sensations, there is the point that only if the telepathic sensations are *extremely* like those they are used to predict is there any inclination to speak of the facts of telepathy as direct seeing into the mind of another. At the same time if they are extremely like a new disinclination to say this arises in another way. I must explain. Suppose first that Jones's telepathic sensation of Smith's colour-blindness consisted in looking into a colour-blindness detector applied to Smith—he screws it on to Smith's head and looks into an aperture—and from the sensation he gets he is able to read off whether Smith is colour-blind or not. The simplest thing is to suppose that in the machine Jones sees the words 'Colour-blind' or 'Not colour-blind' according to whether Smith is colour-blind or not. Now, no one would be much inclined to call this knowing directly that Smith is colour-blind, especially if any-one else could with the detector do as well as Jones. Indeed, it would hardly be called telepathy, though of course it would be knowing what is going on in Smith's mind, 'not by the *usual* channels of sense'—if 'usual channels' means sensations of, or resulting from, Smith's bodily behaviour. If instead of applying the mental state detector to Smith's head and reading the word 'colour-blind' one held the machine between one's knees and gazing into it saw as in a mirror the world coloured or not coloured and knew in this way whether Smith were colour-blind, people would be more inclined to talk of telepathy—it would be like crystal-gazing for the past, the future or the distant; it would be more nearly seeing for ourselves Smith's colour-blindness. The situation would not differ in kind from the first thing we imagined—reading 'Colour-blind' in a machine applied to Smith's head. If from reading the word 'Pain' in a mental state detector applied to Smith's head we knew Smith to be in pain no one would call this telepathy, still less would they call it knowing directly Smith's pain and still less would they call it feeling Smith's pain. If by putting the mental state detector on one could feel pain, sharp when Smith's was sharp, stabbing when Smith's was stabbing, then I should feel inclined to talk of feeling Smith's pain when one put on the mental state detector. And if when one put on special spectacles one saw things a bit differently, blurred if Smith suffered from astigmatism, and colourless if he were colour-blind, one might then speak of seeing with the help of the spectacles what Smith sees. And if now one could do this without a machine at all so that just at will one could see and feel things as Smith saw and felt them then that would be telepathy, great telepathy. And suppose that Jones just all the time, at once and involuntarily, saw things as Smith saw them, then Jones would be spoken of as Smith's mental twin, and if Jones saw a thing grey like Smith and a third man saw it red then one might say that the third man perhaps is wrong until others came along and confirmed him. Then it would be said that Smith and Jones were suffering from a joint illusion. And it might be said that only Smith and Jones really know what is in Smith's mind. Again it might be said if Jones always thought the same thoughts and felt the same feelings as Smith that here was a case of the same person being in two bodies at once.

Suppose, lastly, that after an operation on Smith's eyes or after a clap of thunder Smith cries 'The colours fade', and at that moment not merely some small scene in a glass but all the world goes grey, not merely to Jones and not merely to you but to everyone. This would come nearest to our knowing, our all knowing as opposed to merely Jones's knowing, what was going on in Smith's mind. This would be everyone's having the highest class telepathy for Smith.

At the moment we reach this which we feel we might call everyone's knowing what occurred in Smith's mind, in Smith's private world, at that very moment Smith's private world becomes the public world, his psychical processes physical events. A complete insight by everyone into Smith's private world makes Smith's sensation, Smith's illusion, Smith's hallucination, not an hallucination but a real physical event, however mysterious. Thus at the moment we reach what we seek it vanishes into something we never sought. You can't have direct knowledge of a feeling, a sensation, without having that feeling or sensation. We can't all see a dagger-like patch without its being no longer an hallucination but a dagger. Jones can't have direct knowledge of Smith's feeling of depression without feeling that feeling himself there and then. But if when and as Smith or any other man felt depressed we all felt depressed then there would be no point in Jones or any one else saying 'Smith feels depressed'. It would do as well to say 'A depression this morning', 'An atmosphere of excitement last night', 'It's raining'. When we are confident of others feeling with us as we look at a house whose long blank windows face empty lawns stretching to the still trees which surround it, we say 'It's sinister', instead of 'To me it always feels sinister'. If when Smith sees a dagger in the air we all expect not only dagger-behaviour from Smith but also dagger-sensations for ourselves, then when Smith says 'A dagger in the air' we expect not merely Smith's hallucination of a dagger but—a dagger. No wonder we can't all have direct knowledge of Smith's hallucination of a dagger—for as our knowledge of it becomes direct so does its nature change from a mental aberration to a physical reality. No wonder we can't have *direct* knowledge of the *mental* condition of others.

Black. You are trying again to persuade us that the words 'real or direct knowledge of the mental condition of others' has no more sense than 'real, direct knowledge of the existence of invisible germs or supersensual bread'. But the position is different in this case of the souls of others. To talk of direct knowledge of germs is to talk of seeing germs because this is the appropriate way of knowing directly of the existence of germs as opposed to inferring it from a rash on the face. Consequently, to talk of direct knowledge of invisible germs is absurd. But seeing is not the appropriate way of knowing mental states. Direct knowledge of mental states is knowledge by introspection. Now you obtained your result, 'No wonder we can never know directly of the mental condition of others' by thinking that the meaning of 'direct knowledge' here was to be found by altering and improving for the purpose our telepathic and thus sensory knowledge of mental states. The result was that when the sensory knowledge had become suitable, good enough, for our saying that we could all know directly Smith's hallucination of a dagger, what we had got turned out to be knowledge of a physical thing. The truth is that what we have in mind when we talk of knowing the mind of another is not having the same sensations as another but having the same sort of knowledge of the states of another as each of us has of his own. We might call it introspective knowledge if introspection weren't by definition knowledge of one's own states. What we have in mind is an extension of an introspective faculty.

Just as when we ask of things so light we cannot feel their weight, 'Are their weights really such as these good scales indicate?' we mean 'What would we feel if our power of feeling weight were greater and we lifted these?' so when we ask of bodies whose pain we cannot feel, 'Is this behaviour really due to pain?' what we mean is 'What would we feel if our power of feeling pain were not confined to our own bodies?' This is what we mean when we talk about the pain of others and really knowing it. As with the weight of feathers we can't in fact use this method of knowing what causes the visual phenomena we observe. But just as it would be absurd on this account to say that weight is a visual phenomenon and a matter of a body's behaviour on scales, so is it absurd to say that pain is a visual phenomenon and a matter of a body's behaviour on a psychogalvanometer. If it is asked how we know the weight of feathers which are too light for us to feel their weight we get into many of the difficulties we have got into about pain in others. There is the inclination to say that when we speak of the weight of things whose weight we cannot feel what we mean is something about how refined scales will react to them, that when we say that A weighs the same as B we mean they will balance on scales and that therefore 'we can never really know whether feathers have weight' is a senseless lament. But of course the fact is that 'A is heavy', 'A weighs the same as B' *mean* the same when we are talkng of feathers as when we are talking of cakes and we don't then mean merely something about scales. No doubt we have to rely upon indirect means such as scales in order to ascertain the weight of feathers. We cannot in fact learn directly which of two feathers is the heavier. But if it is suggested that since we can't conceive of what it would be to know directly the weight of feathers therefore when we talk of their weight all we mean is something about what would ordinarily be called the effects of weight, then the answer is that we certainly *don't* mean merely that, and that therefore we must be able to conceive of knowing directly the weight of feathers and that in fact we *can* conceive of feeling their weight because we can conceive of our weight-detecting and weight-discriminating faculty so improved that we can detect the weight of feathers *in the way we detect the weight of cakes*. To say that dogs hear sounds we can't hear doesn't mean merely that dogs respond to whistles which when blown seem to make no noise, it means that the dogs hear what we would hear if our auditory acuity were greater.

White. And if anyone asks 'Do we really know that the whistle makes a sound?' Gray will reply, 'Yes, we know by analogy with cases where our senses do not fail us so soon', for example, cases in which a whistle is blown, we hear it, and a dog looks back.

And if anyone asks 'Do we really know the weight of feathers?' then Gray will reply, 'We know by analogy with cakes'. This is a real argument by analogy because we know here what it would be like to find that what analogy suggests is so is not so, because we know what it would be to actually feel the weight of feathers as opposed to merely inferring it from the movement of scales.

Black. And when someone asks 'Is this feather heavier than that?' what he *means* is 'Would this feather feel heavier than that if one were able to feel the weight of feathers?'

And when someone asks 'Is Smith colour-blind?' 'Does Smith feel more pain than Robinson?' what he means is 'What would we find Smith's mental states to be if our capacity for detecting mental states were extended. Talk of consciousness in the bodies of others where we can't feel it gets its meaning and justification from cases where we can, just like talk of sound and weight where we can't feel them get their meaning and justification from cases where we can.'

White. Like that is it? Exactly like that?

In that case it will be worth while your explaining to me specially carefully what an improved faculty for detecting weight would be.

Black. You know what superior auditory acuity is?

White. Yes, I think so. But I'd like you to tell me what it comes to. It isn't just that I can hear sounds when others hear nothing. I might do this because there was something wrong with my ears and not because they were specially good.

Black. Of course. It is when a man hears sounds which are really there of which others hear nothing that we say 'He has very good hearing'.

White. No doubt. Only what constitutes sounds being really there.

Black. Well, suppose a highwayman says 'I hear the sound of coaches' when the other highwaymen can hear nothing, and sure enough he's always right. Or suppose someone says 'I can hear the sound of moths chumbling the clothes in that chest', and sure enough they are.

White. And the other highwaymen know the one who said 'I hear the sound of coaches' was right because soon they too hear a coach and soon see it. That is, they find other tests soon confirm his statement that he hears the sound of coaches. And we should say that a man's faculty for discriminating weight is improved by taking opium, if after taking it he could tell the difference between weights which before felt just alike to him though now the scales and all other tests confirm his statement that they differed in weight.

Black. Yes, of course.

White. But the consequence is that the question, 'These scales tip towards the black feather but does this prove that the black feather is heavier—it feels to me to have no weight at all?' is a foolish question even if you insist that 'The black feather is heavier' means not merely that the scales tip towards it but that a person with superior powers of weight discrimination would feel it heavier. For if (1) 'a person with superior power of weight-discrimination' means one who feels differences of weight when *ever* and as the best scales show them, then the question becomes of the form 'A prefers this wine to that but which would an expert prefer?' where an expert is one who *always* agrees with A. And if (2) 'a person with superior powers of weight discrimination' means one who *has hitherto* always felt differences in weight when and as the best scales show them then the question becomes of the form 'A prefers this wine to that but which would an expert prefer?' where an expert is one who has hitherto agreed with A. The answer here is 'Heaven knows—probably he would'.

Brown. If the expert differed from the scales then we wouldn't know whether the black feather weighed heavier than the white as the scales indicate or whether there was something about a black feather which slightly upset the actions of even the best scales. Which hypothesis we should favour would depend upon surrounding circumstances. For example, if the movement on the scales were slighter than any hitherto associated with discrimination by the expert then we should say, 'It looks as if even Mr. Scales has failed at last'. On the other hand, if the movement on the scales were larger than in some other cases where Mr. Scales had nevertheless succeeded in detecting a difference in weight then we should say, 'Very extraordinary. Is Mr. Scales not quite well or is there something wrong with the scales?' and if when we added a hundred feathers just like the black one to the black one, and a hundred feathers just like the white one to the white one, the scales did not tip any more, although each feather singly tipped the scales against a single white feather, then we should be very astonished, and one of the things we might say is that it is impossible to weigh single feathers on the scales. But the point is not which we would say and what would make us say the one and what the other, but that since a conflict between the expert Mr. Scales and the scales would lead to doubt as to whether the black feather was heavier than the white, therefore its being heavier is not to be identified either with the expert's report or the scales' report.

White. Exactly. That is, Black was wrong to say that when even after finding all physical tests such as scales to be in favour of one one feather being heavier than another we nevertheless ask, 'Now, is it heavier or is it that all the usual effects of weight are here clustered in the usual way but no weight?' then what we mean is 'What would a person with superior power of weight discrimination feel if he felt these feathers?' And yet if this isn't what we mean what is? If such an expert couldn't find out what the real weight is who could? Surely you are not going to say that the fact that one thing is heavier than another is something over and above what happens to scales they are put on, what happens to bridges they are rolled on, how long they take to burn, and especially what they feel like when lifted? Or are you going to say it is some quality which we never directly know which causes in people certain sensations and which causes in scales certain movements.

Black. Well, I don't know. I can't identify the weight of things with the way scales behave when the things are put on them; weight isn't something you see happening—see with your eyes. And I can't identify it with what we would feel because lots of things have weight which we wouldn't feel at all. Nor can I identify it with what an expert would feel, because if an expert felt one thing heavier than another and yet everything else pointed to their being equal in weight then we shouldn't know what to say, whether to say the expert was right or the scales.

White. Just like you wouldn't know what to say if everyone felt a room very hot and all thermometers and physical phenomena within it pointed to its being rather chilly. And yet surely the heat of a room is a matter of how we feel in it, or a matter of that together with the facts that thermometers rise in it, butter melts in it, milk goes sour in it, water readily boils in it. If it is something over and above all this what is it and what would it be like to find that it is present?

Black. And yet since none of these things are essential to one thing's being heavier than another, and we may be perfectly informed about these things without knowing whether a thing has changed in weight or is equal in weight to another, surely it follows that they must be merely the signs and not the essence, much less the whole essence, of weight. What I mean is this: suppose Mr. Scales, the expert, feels that the black feather is heavier today than it was yesterday does it follow that it is? Not at all. May be it's just the same weight as it was in spite of Mr. Scales. Mr. Scales may have a black feather illusion like the size-weight illusion, and indeed if all other tests are against Mr. Scales we shall say that the black feather has not changed in weight though Mr. Scales, the expert, feels it has.

White. And yet, embarrassing thought, surely it would be *possible* that Mr. Scales was right and all the other reporters including the best of scales wrong.

Black. Exactly. And from this it follows that each of the other reports is not essential to weight, since weight may have changed without their changing or have disappeared without their changing. From all this it is clear that the phenomena which you have mentioned and which admittedly provide our only evidence as to the weight of bodies, do not provide a list of necessary and sufficient conditions of its presence, do not constitute weight—they are only signs of its presence, they are not of its essence. And this is confirmed by the fact that we might know all about the phenomena and be entirely uncertain as to what the weight was. This would happen if the phenomena gave conflicting indications.

White. But to say that weight is not a matter of what the scales do or of what we feel but of something we never directly know—isn't that very odd? I beg of you to allow yourself to feel the feelings that must lie somewhere in you, feelings that this sort of talk is, to use a phrase of Professor Moore's, 'the purest mythology'. And may I draw your attention to a result which is even more strikingly paradoxical than the statement that a thing might feel heavy, tip down the scales, etc., and still not be heavy. This last statement is not itself a denial of anything we ordinarily assert. It denies no one of our ordinary statements of fact for it is not a statement of fact at all. It doesn't conflict with a recognized law of logic or rule of language like 'A man may be the child of another man's parents and yet not be his brother'.[1] In itself then, queer as it sounds, it is not paradoxical in the way of conflicting with statements we ordinarily accept. But combine it with the premiss 'And we never know of weight except through these phenomena, the feelings we have, the tipping of the scales, etc.', and we obtain the result that we never know the weight of anything. For even Gray will hardly suggest here that we know of weight from scales and feelings by an argument by analogy and induction. There's been no golden age when besides putting things on scales or lifting them with our hands or feet we have directly observed, correlated with these phenomena, the real weights of objects. And owing to the generality of the ignorance claimed it is not possible to reply here that we have on occasion experienced something *like* weight. When the lament is the limited one that we don't know the weight of things which are so light we can't feel their weight then the reply is made that we know their weight by analogy with things whose weight we can feel. But in the general case

[1] The axiom of reducibility is not a law in a logic. It is law connecting logics. The relations between logical constructions and what they are constructed out of are always presented with an empirical air. This is because the relations between them are not within a logic. A logic gives the necessary relations between statements about things in a given category or order of logical construction, not the relations between statements about things in different categories.

this sort of answer is much more out of the question. And yet without it we are forced to the paradox, 'We never have the faintest ground for saying that one thing is heavier than another'. We are forced to this paradox unless we accept more mythology —a new mode of knowing. Ah! these new modes of knowing, these new modes of being, how swiftly, how easily they soothe our conflicting inclinations. How much more easily than the re-examination of the impeccable steps which have led to the impossible conclusion.

But I prefer that re-examination. Let us repeat, 'Sometimes we know of two things that one is heavier than the other and we know it by feeling them and weighing them'. I want to list at once the blunders that lead to the denial of this. First, from the fact that a phenomenon connected with one thing's being heavier than another is not a necessary condition of its being heavier, it is often taken to follow that it is not necessarily connected with its being heavier[1] and that it could not together with some selection of such phenomena suffice for and constitute its being heavier. Having cloven hoofs, having horns, having four stomachs are none of them necessary conditions of a thing's being a cow. But they are necessarily connected with a thing's being a cow, and if a particular animal has some selection of them then its being a cow is not something over and above its having that selection of characters.

Second, it is argued that the scales fall *because* of the weight of what's on them, and even that it's the weight that *gives* us the sensation we get when we lift the weighty object, and that the weight is therefore something in the object which is *responsible* for and *explains* the cluster of symptoms it exhibits, and that therefore as the *cause* and *explanation* it is not identical with its effects.

Thirdly, it is argued that we argue and argue problematically and for ever problematically from the phenomena to the weight and that the conclusion of *problematic* argument cannot be identical with the data, the *evidence*, by which it is supported.

Fourthly, but in close connection with this, it is said, 'However "conclusive" the phenomena exhibited, surely I may

---

[1] Mr. Clive Bell in his excellent and intellectually snobbish book *Civilization*, while explaining in a kindly way to an ignorant and stupid public the logic of his inquiry, makes this blunder as well as the cruder one of supposing that if there are non-S which are P then P is no part of the essence of S. See *Civilization*, p. 24.

wonder whether a thing which by all tests appears heavier than another really is, surely I can imagine the opposite?'

Fifthly, it is argued that since I can be certain about the phenomena and then if I find them conflicting remain uncertain as to the weight, therefore to know the weight is not to know the phenomena and therefore the weight is other than the phenomena.

The answers to these arguments are all of the same form. The answers are: 'Causes? Yes. Explanations? Yes. Problematic inferences? Yes. Wonder whether the opposite? Yes. Imagine, understand the opposite? Yes. Remain uncertain, remain in ignorance? Yes.' But there are causes and causes, explanations and explanations. It's the energy in the coal that makes it burn so well, the electricity in the wire that makes it give off sparks. And there is problematic inference and problematic inference, problematic inference that doesn't vanish towards immediate inference and problematic inference that does. It's a problematic inference from the symptoms of measles to measles. There is ignorance as to whether an animal in a dim light is a tiger or a lion and ignorance as to whether a striped lion is a lion—however strong the light. There is wondering and wondering. 'Ridden by a lady', says the dealer as we gaze at the extremely good looking and surprisingly inexpensive animal that his man is riding at so very collected a canter. 'Ridden by a lady', we murmur, half-reassured but remembering just in time the elegant but determined female we noticed leaving the yard as we entered it.

The monstrousness of the conclusion that weight is an unknown something which may or may not be behind the phenomena we fondly but unjustifiably take to prove its presence and its properties, leads one to look carefully at the steps which led to it. These steps cannot be said to involve logical slips or even ambiguities except in a stretched sense. The expression 'ridden by a lady' is not ambiguous. And we cannot say that there is a use of 'know' in which one may know that certain things are so and not know whether a certain thing is so although that thing's being so just is a matter of those other things being so. We cannot say this. There is not a well-marked usage of 'know' in which one may know P and not know Q although

Q is nothing but P. We can only say that such a use would be welcome, that we could introduce it with advantage. It would be useful in dealing with the puzzle 'Is demonstrative inference circular?' and it would be useful in the case in which a thing's being a cow would seem certainly to be a matter of its having horns, hoofs, etc., while yet one may know very well all about its having or not having the right horns and hoofs and yet to reply to 'Is it a cow?' with 'Well, I hardly know'. To see how readily there could be a use of words in which a puzzle would not arise enables us to see through it. We grasp how it arises not from the ambiguity, not from the vagueness, but from the *elasticity*[1] of language. 'Ridden by a lady', says the dealer truly, and his words are not ambiguous. But our picture of a certain non-typical lady gave us a better grasp of what he was saying, prevented our proceeding as if the word 'lady' had a narrower, sharper usage than it has.

Black. Well, I can see that it was wrong to say that the question, 'The black feather tips the scales but is it really the heavier?' means 'How would the black feather feel if our weight-detecting capacity were improved?' and at the same time I see that this is what the question *amounts to* when all other tests have been applied. What I mean is this: If 'S is P' means 'S is p_1 and p_2 ... and p_n' then 'Is S P?' asked in a context in which it is already known that S is p_1 and p_2 ... and p_{n-1} *amounts to* 'Is S p_n?' I see too how easily one might come to say 'Even if our weight-detecting capacity were increased we wouldn't know the weight of feathers because we would still be guessing from our sensations at something that is other than they and a source of those sensations', and how from this one might come to saying 'We not only do not know whether things whose weight we can't feel really have any weight but we never shall know and never can know'. I grasp how these words could be

---

[1] Wittgenstein has said of certain words that they have thousands of meanings when they have not. Sometimes his purpose has been to distinguish certain words with what I will call multiple grammars from others, but at times he has been referring to the *elasticity* of words when he would have done better to say, as he may have done, '*Every* word has thousands of meanings'. Some people, almost including myself, have tried to make this truer by talking of vagueness (*Mind*, October 1938, p. 489). But this won't do either. Some words are not at all vague. Elasticity is infinite vagueness or infinite ambiguity. If you say that a word has as many meanings as individuals to which it could be applied then ambiguity becomes elasticity.

interpreted as a genuine lament for our ignorance, for the absence of weight experts, and how the words give the lament a false importance by describing our ignorance as ignorance of weight and a false everlasting hopelessness since our abilities *may* improve at any time. I grasp how the words could be given an interpretation which would make the everlastingness of their hopelessness appropriate but would make it like the hopelessness that lines so truly parallel though infinite should ever meet.[1]

White. And doesn't the pattern of talk here remind you of the pattern of talk about knowing whether Smith's pain is greater than Jones's? You said to begin with that the cases are very like. The patterns of talk are indeed almost congruent. They run: *A.* I can't tell whether Smith's pain is greater than Jones's, whether the weight of the black feather is greater than that of the white. *B* Can't tell? But look at the sweat on his brow, look at the scales. *A.* Yes, but these things don't enable me to *know*, only to guess. *C.* Not merely guess but know by an argument by analogy. *A.* A very poor argument because only in comparatively few cases of sweat and scale-tipping do I find associated pain and weight. *B.* To describe the justifications for saying that Smith is in the greater pain, that the black feather is heavier, as arguments by analogy is muddling. The conclusion that Smith is in pain is just a redescription of his symptoms and a reminder of how in one's own case these symptoms are associated with pain. The conclusion that the feather is heavier is merely a redescription of what happens to scales it is put on and a reminder of how in other cases these symptoms are associated with a feeling of weight. *A and C.* But this is to make weight and pain in bodies whose weight and pain we can't feel nothing but visual phenomena, things to be detected by eyes and ears. And yet what we talk about, what we mean, when we talk of weight and pain in these cases is not different from what we mean when we talk about weight and pain in other cases. And in these other cases it is very clear that we are not talking merely, if at all, about what is to be detected by eyes and ears. We are talking about something which in these cases we can feel in a different way. And what we must mean when we ask in those cases where we can't feel weight and pain whether it is there and what is its

[1] With apologies to Marvell.

nature, is what *would* we feel in those cases if we could in those cases detect weight and pain as we do in the other cases. We must be asking what we would find if our faculties for detecting weight and pain were improved.

D. 'Is Smith in more pain than Jones?' 'Is the black feather heavier than the white?' can't mean 'What would we feel if we could feel their pain and weight?' because if we could feel pain on looking at Smith and pain on looking at Jones and more pain on looking at Smith we would still hesitate to say that Smith felt more pain if every other sign suggested that Jones was in more pain than Smith, and if we could feel more weight in lifting the black feather than in lifting the white we would still hesitate to say that the black was heavier if every other sign suggested the opposite.

A and C. It is true that 'Is Smith in more pain than Jones?' 'Is this feather heavier than that?' doesn't mean 'What would we feel if we had higher powers for detecting differences in consciousness and weight than we have'. All we meant was that in cases where all other signs favoured one answer there would, contrary to *B*'s suggestion, remain a question open, a question which in the peculiar circumstances would *amount* to 'What would we feel if our faculties were improved?'

B. This wouldn't really be a question. Because our faculties wouldn't be improved unless the answers they gave correlated with the other signs as to the nature and presence of consciousness and weight. The question would therefore be like, 'I like this wine but is it really good?' where this means 'Would an expert like it?' and an expert is a man with the same tastes as I.

A and C. But, as *D* said, it is perfectly conceivable that our faculties should be improved and then conflict with other signs. And if they were improved then when in cases in which all other evidence suggested that Smith was in greater pain than Jones, that the black feather was heavier than the white, we asked 'Which is really in the greater pain?' 'Which is really the heavier?' we should be asking 'What should we feel if we were to apply our telepathic and weight-discriminating faculties to this case?'

B. Certainly, and we should expect to get certain sensations on applying our faculties but we might be wrong, and not get them. But the question is not what would we mean if our faculties were different but what do we mean with our faculties as they are.

A and C. What we mean is that even in cases where the indirect evidence is of the best we don't know what our faculties for detecting pain and weight would reveal if only they were better than they are.

B. You might as well say that we don't know whether Charles I was beheaded because even in cases where the indirect evidence is of the best we don't know what our memory would reveal if it were more powerful.

A. Exactly so. That *is* what I say about the past.

B. But 'memory more powerful than it is' means 'memory correlated with indirect evidence more extensively than it is'. So you might as well say 'I like this wine and so do other judges but I don't know whether it is good because I don't know what the people who are not judges would think of it if they were much more expert than they are?'

D. This certainly isn't what's meant when we say we can't tell whether a wine is really good, can't really know the past, can't really know the future, can't really know the weight of bodies nor their states of consciousness. We are not just saying we don't know what feelings we would get from our faculties if they were greater, i.e. had correlated more with other clues as to consciousness, weight and the past. This comes out if we grasp that even if our faculties were improved they wouldn't give us the knowledge we lack but only other clues to set beside the old clues, only further indirect evidence. We don't know the absolute amounts of weights nor the nature of weight in itself. We know only that objects possess a certain quality in virtue of which they produce certain appearances to us.

B. Do we know that? Don't we know only that the objects produce certain appearances? Do we know that there are any objects? You say we know only the present appearances of the past? Surely this is all we know of anything. And surely each man knows only the appearances which appear to him, his own sensations.

Black. I have said that I have seen through this puzzling talk about weight and I have seen how surprisingly congruent is the

pattern of talk about consciousness and pain. But I must insist
upon a difference. Indeed I must insist upon a uniqueness in the
puzzle of consciousness. It comes from its involving the use of
'I', 'you' and 'he'.

I have said that even if we had an improved power of detecting the mental states of others this wouldn't be real knowledge
of their mental states. This is like what is said about the weight
of bodies whose weight we can't feel. But the reason for what is
said about the weight of bodies whose weight we can't feel is
different from the reason for saying that no telepathy gives
knowledge of other minds. If our faculties were improved that
would give the same knowledge of the weight as we have of the
weight of cakes. Consequently, if it is to be said that we *couldn't*
know the weight of feathers, it has to be said that we wouldn't
know it even if we knew it like we know the weight of cakes.
That is, it has to be said that we don't really know the weight of
cakes, and that is said on the mistaken grounds which lead to
saying that weight is something other than our sensations.

But it is not said that we don't really know the consciousness
and pain of those bodies in which we do feel these. On the contrary this knowledge and the knowledge of self-evident truths
are the paradigms of knowledge. One's own pain is not other
and beyond our sensations—it is one of them. And if we had this
sort of knowledge of the pain of others we should say we knew
their pain.

No, unlike the weight case, the result that we wouldn't be
knowing the mental states of others even if our faculties were
improved in the way described is reached by saying that the
knowing so obtained would not be the same sort of knowing as
we have of our own states, not real, infallible, introspective
knowing. When Gray said that we can conceive of finding our
conclusions from the behaviour of people as to their inward
states true or false, this was the kind of finding he referred to,
this is what would still leave meaningful the question 'Is Smith
in pain?', 'Is Smith seeing the Union Jack in red, white and
blue?' whatever our telepathic powers might become.

White. Let us look into this 'knowing one's own state of mind',
'knowing in like manner the states of mind of others', 'expecting
a sensation for oneself', 'expecting a sensation for another'.

Other Minds V

White. We came to realize last time that even when a question is one in which we can draw, paint and describe very satisfactorily what we would have to smell, taste, touch, hear or see as the consequence of doing something in order to know that the answer to it is in the affirmative or the negative, still the question may be quite unreal. It is quite unreal when we haven't an idea of what to do in order to see the necessary sight, hear the sound or smell the smell which gives the answer yes. If a man asserts that there are or may be fairies in the flowers or swing bands in heaven, a dispute with him is idle, however detailed and vivid his portrayal of elves emerging from foxgloves or Count Basie on a sea of glass. For there is no occasion on which he expects to see something like his picture while we don't.

We came, too, to realize that spirits are not even in the position of fairies. It isn't merely that we haven't the faintest idea of what steps to take in order to see them; we haven't the faintest idea what it would be like to see them anyway; trying to imagine seeing them always turns into trying to see ghosts or spirits of the air, of the water, of the trees. But dryads were of one shape and not another, just as much as gnomes or for that matter unicorns. We haven't an idea of what it would be like to see men's souls apart from their bodies however etherealized.

Black. Of course not. As I said, souls are by nature *invisible*. That doesn't prove that they are by nature unfindable by *any* means.

White. You overrun me. I was going to add that we last time came to realize that we not only have no idea what it would be like to *see* souls or spirits but that we have no idea what it would be like to *find* souls or spirits. As you say they are by nature invisible. Not only that, they are like invisible germs, by nature unfindable. We haven't an idea what it would be like to find out, when all signs point to the presence of invisible germs, that what

123

all the signs point to is so. It wouldn't be touching anything—or it would, and then the question, 'Are there invisible germs here?' would be a straightforward empirical issue—it wouldn't be hearing anything, it wouldn't be smelling anything. It wouldn't be anything. It is the same with souls. They are by nature invisible of course, but, further, no other means of knowing them apart from their effects has been conceived. Nor can be conceived. For it is not merely that we have attached no meaning to 'knows what is going on in the minds of others' like we have attached no meaning to 'Pirots carulize elatically',[1] it is that (i) there are certain meanings which all of us are inclined to attach to it, while (ii) all of us are inclined to do what some of us unhesitatingly do, namely reject every suggested meaning, like we reject every suggested meaning for 'an outsider was favourite', because it is an expression such that there are cir-cumstances the absence of which would disincline us to apply one part of the expression, while their presence would disincline us to apply another part of it.[2]

Black. But you assume that all real finding out, all real ascer-taining, all direct knowledge is either seeing or touching or smelling or hearing.

White. No. I know that I have a cold not only by seeing my eyes running—that indeed might be onions—but by the prickling I have in my throat—a feeling which isn't seeing or touching or hearing anything.

Black. Of course. I meant you assume that all experience, all direct knowledge is sensory. But your knowledge of your own mind isn't sensory. You know that there is a red patch before you, a buzzing in your ears, by your senses; but you don't see that you are seeing or know by hearing that you are hearing. You have a direct knowledge of your own mental states which is

---

[1] H. D. Oakeley, *Mind*, October 1940, p. 431.

[2] The whole difficulty arises like difficulty in a neurotic; the forces are con-flicting but nearly equal. The philosopher remains in a state of confused tension unless he makes the effort necessary to bring them all out by speaking of them and to make them fight it out by speaking of them together. It isn't that people can't resolve philosophical difficulties but that they won't. In philosophy it is not a matter of making sure that one has got hold of the right theory but of making sure that one has got hold of them all. Like psychoanalysis it is not a matter of selecting from all our inclinations some which are right, but of bringing them all to light by men-tioning them and in this process creating some which are right for this individual in these circumstances.

not sensory. It is often, though not always, knowledge of a sensory state, but that is not the point. The point is that you know directly that what the outward signs (sweat and tears) of your mental condition suggest is so, is so, and that his knowing is not the seeing, hearing, smelling or tasting of anything. And when Gray insists that it is possible to conceive of finding out whether what all the outward signs of a man's mental state suggest, is in fact the case or not, he is referring to the possibility of finding this out by some direct but non-sensory mode of finding out.

White. What would this be? We saw it would not be telepathy described as guessing from an image with the device 'Smith' under it what Smith will say he sees. This is still passing from one sensation of one's own to the expectation of other sensations of one's own on the basis of past experience. This becomes plainer the more the sensation of one's own from which one guesses Smith's sensation is unlike Smith's sensation.

Brown. Might not finding out that Smith's in pain be to see the sweat on his brow, the swelling in his cheek, to ask 'Is Smith in pain?' and then suddenly without any reason to feel an aching pain in one's tooth?

White. When you feel the aching pain, this is to be like Smith's pain and you are to know that it is like his?

Brown. Yes.

White. But this just is telepathy except that you have made the provision that it shall be done by having the same sensation as the person one telepathizes. No doubt if this provision is satisfied we are more inclined to speak of feeling what the agent feels, of sensing his pain. Suppose that when Alfred Smith sees a dagger before his mind's eye Bessie Smith does too, that when Alfred sees a long one then Bessie does too, that when he is scared by it, then she is too, that when he says he doesn't feel as she says he does then it always turns out in the end that really he was feeling like she said. This is the sort of case which I should be especially inclined to call real inside knowledge of the mind of another. Nevertheless, I am disinclined to allow it this title when I notice that it doesn't differ in principle from guessing from what one reads in a mind-detector at what Alfred will say and thus does not differ in principle from guessing from what one reads today in a crystal or the *Star* what will win the 2.30

tomorrow, and also that it doesn't differ in principle from seeing a dagger, and thus doesn't differ in principle from knowing from a man's dilated pupils that he will stagger if he walks, i.e. that it doesn't differ in principle from knowledge of future behaviour from present behaviour. I have two ways of seeing how this wonderful knowing of another's mind doesn't differ in principle from seeing a dagger. First, I think of a case, like we have just thought of, where I see a dagger and rightly anticipate, in virtue of experience which would justify me if I recalled it, (1) that Smith will say he sees a dagger, (2) that *no one* else will. This is what I've just felt inclined to call having inside knowledge of Smith's mind. It is also called sharing in his hallucination or having a like hallucination and knowing it. Next I think of a case in which I see a dagger and rightly and excusably anticipate that Smith and a *few* other people will do so too. The hallucination has now spread. Then I think of a case where I see a dagger and rightly and excusably anticipate that Smith and a few other people will do so too, *and also* rightly and excusably anticipate where treasure, a body etc., will be found. In such a case those who can't see the dagger that Smith and I and the elect can see are now inclined to say that we can see something, something real, which they can't see. Now this last case differs only in degree from that in which I see a dagger and rightly and excusably anticipate that *everyone* else will do so too, *and also* rightly and excusably anticipate that animals and cameras and magnets will do so too, and also that everything will hereafter behave suitably to there having been a dagger here now. But in this case what I do is to see a real physical dagger. Therefore the sort of thing which I at first felt inclined to call seeing into Smith's mind differs only in degree from seeing a real physical dagger. Now I feel disinclined to say that seeing into Smith's mind differs only in degree from seeing a physical thing, and so I prefer now to describe the first case by saying that I didn't see into his mind but had an hallucination like his from which I was able to predict that he had one. An astounding and valuable performance, but not different in principle from knowing in the ordinary way from what I see of his face what he is going to say, and not different in principle from knowing in the ordinary way from what I see of the church tower what other people will say the time is, and not different in principle from knowing in an extraordinary way from what I see in a crystal what will win the 2.30. This last would again be a striking and valuable performance. Here, again, we might at first feel inclined to say of a man with this gift that he can look into the future. And here again, we feel disinclined to say this when we notice that the gift doesn't differ in principle from being able to predict from the angle of an animal's shoulder that he won't get down the hill to Tattenham Corner. For it is all predicting from one sensation of one's own other sensations of one's own. Even if we allow that this guessing at future sensations from present sensations is knowing, there remains the problem of how we get from knowledge of these to knowledge of other things and, in particular, to knowledge of other minds; of how to pierce, in this matter, the veil of appearance, of how to escape, in this matter, from the egocentric predicament.

Gray. But whether you call this *looking into* the mind of another or no isn't the point. The point is 'Wouldn't this be *knowing* what is going on in the mind of another?' and it would be. What is more it would be knowing it in a very special way, not from his face and behaviour but in the sort of way one knows one's own mind. For with this gift I should know that Smith was in love by the way I felt and this is the way I know I am in love,[1] that is, this is the way I know what is going on in my own mind.

White. Undoubtedly what has been described would be something which it would be conventional to describe as 'knowing how someone else feels'. But I must insist that whether cases which would ordinarily be described as 'knowing how someone else feels' occur is not the point. We have known all along that they do. Ordinarily we say that we knew when he smiled that he was pleased, knew when he stopped smiling that he had fallen in love. My point is that many who complain against these cases that they aren't really knowledge of what is going on in the mind of another but only of knowledge from present behaviour of future behaviour, will still complain that telepathy or extended introspection of the sort we have described is not really knowledge of another mind. When such extended introspection is described they may, at first, staggered by the novelty and value of the

---

[1] Wittgenstein's invaluable example.

imagined gift, waver. But when they look into its cash value they will see that it doesn't differ in principle from what they have already rejected, that it buys still only the same sort of goods.

Gray. But it *is* different from what they have rejected.

White. It's different, it would be a private way of knowing what others have to learn by public means. But the market-place would not be made private by my having a private way to it. I know I have a cold in a way, by a means, by which you cannot know this. I know it by the feel I have in my head. I know I have malaria or something wrong with my tooth, or that my arm is moving, in ways which you can use to know whether *you* have malaria or something wrong with *your* tooth, or that *your* arm is moving, but which you cannot use to know whether *I* have malaria or something wrong with my tooth. Indeed, it seems now as if one has the same sort of private knowledge of one's bodily condition as one has of one's mental condition. Does my knowledge that I am in love differ in principle from my know-ledge that I have a cold? In the one case, from a prickling in the throat and a headache which others don't share, I anticipate seeing my eyes and nose streaming if I look in a mirror (sensa-tions which others will share) and hearing my voice thick (sen-sation which others will share), and further feelings in my head and back (sensations which others will not share) When I know I am in love, then, from a picture in my head and a heartache which others don't share, I anticipate seeing myself hurrying with flowers (sensations which others will share) and my voice saying this or that (sensations which others will share), and further feelings in my heart (sensations which others will not share). I know by introspection that I am in love. I know by introspection that I have understood the English sentence you have just uttered but not the French one. I know in the same way that I have a cold, and in the same way that my arm has moved. Therefore I know by introspection that I have a cold and I know by introspection that my arm has moved. Usually it is not in this sort of way that I know that the arm of the clock on the tower has moved. Usually it is on the basis of a sensation which others share that I know that. But I might easily—clair-voyants do—come to know this sort of thing from a sensation which others don't share and thus know by introspection that the arm of the clock on the tower has moved. Likewise, usually I don't know from a sensation which others don't share, a private, unechoed, sensation, what is happening in the body of another. But of course I easily might. I easily might come to be a famous doctor who knew that people had malaria by getting them on the telephone, murmuring a formula and then knowing from the peculiar sensation he got whether they had malaria—this peculiar sensation being one which others didn't share, unlike the sensations to be had by looking at the patients' faces or feeling their pulses. So I easily might come to know by introspection the bodily states of others. Likewise, usually I don't know from a sensation which others don't share what is the mental condition of another. I know from what I see of his face or hear of his voice, and these are sensations which others share. But I easily might become a famous—a famous *telepathist*, who knew that people were in love or were thinking of the Sahara by getting them on the telephone and then knowing from the peculiar sensation he got whether they were in love or not, whether they were thinking of the Sahara or the Karoo. So I easily might come to know by introspection, i.e. as you say in the special way I have of knowing my own mental states, the mental states of others. Only this knowing wouldn't differ in principle from knowing by a private sensation whether the clock points to ten to three or what will win the 2.30. And this again doesn't differ in principle but only in the fact that the basic sensation is private, from knowing in the ordinary way, by looking, that the clock points to ten to three or by reading in the *Star* what will win the 2.30. That is, if I came to have this extraordinary gift it would be a matter of my having sensations which others don't share and on the basis of these anticipating further sensations which others will share.

Black. This is where we were before. I said then that this couldn't be called seeing into the mind of another and I say it still. It is just predicting from one sensation of one's own another sensation of one's own.

White. It begins to look as if there can be no real knowledge of the mind of another which isn't direct, and this not on the ground that all indirect knowledge is problematic and therefore not real knowledge, but on the ground that all indirect knowledge will be rightly and excusably anticipating future sensations of one's own on the basis of a present sensation of one's own, and thus, like telepathy, not different in principle from expecting from the sweat on Smith's brow that he will say that he is in pain.

Brown. But, look here, surely introspection *is* direct knowledge? The way I know my own mental condition is different from the way I know from a stable whisper what horse will win a certain race on the following day, or from the present position of the heavenly bodies when the next eclipse is due. For my knowledge of the last two things is indirect while my knowledge of my mental condition is direct.

White. I know from how I feel now that I have a cold. This knowing is indirect, for it is because my past experience has been what it has that I know from my present feeling that I have a cold. This is the way I know a horse is going to buck, not only from the way he sets his ears, but also from the feeling I have of his humping his back. This is the way I know how many rooms there are in my house, not only from the note I have in my diary but also from the picture I have in my head. And this is the way I know my own mental condition. I know from how I feel now that I am in love. This is dependent on experience. I know from how I feel when you ask me, 'Do you know Wordsworth's "Ode to Duty" and Shelley's "Ode to a Skylark"?' that I know the former and not the latter. I know from the way I feel when I look at a man that I trust him though this trust is not put to the test.

There are six importantly different cases of indirect knowledge. (1) Where from a shared sensation or group of sensations I predict a group of shared sensations, e.g. where from a speck I predict a vulture, from a smell a carcase or where I predict from a vulture a carcase. (2) Where from an unshared sensation I predict a group of shared sensations, e.g. where from a memory image, a clairvoyant image, or a precognitive image I predict the number of rooms in my house, the presence of gold in the cellar, or the winner of the big race. (3) Where from a shared sensation I predict shared sensations and anticipate streaming eyes and anticipate a feeling of stuffiness in the head, or when from a beating heart I predict calling with flowers and anticipate a feeling of this or that. (4) Where from an unshared sensation I predict shared sensations and anticipate unshared sensations, e.g. when from a pricking in the throat and a headache I predict streaming eyes and anticipate a feeling of stuffiness in the head, or when from a heartache I predict calling with flowers and anticipate a feeling of this or that. (5) Where from a group of shared sensations I predict shared sensations and anticipate or predict[1] unshared sensations not for myself but for another, e.g. when from a film on a man's eyes I anticipate for him or predict his colour-blindness. (6) Where from an unshared sensation I predict shared senastions and anticipate or predict unshared sensations not for myself but for another, e.g. where from a telepathic sensation I predict a man's colour-blindness.

These cases of indirect knowledge are importantly different from one another. The question whether knowledge that a man is in pain differs from knowledge that he shows all signs of pain, and how it differs and whether if it does we ever have any justification for claiming the former over and above the latter is the question whether anticipating an unshared sensation for another is anything different from predicting the shared sensations of the signs of that unshared sensation, and how it differs and whether the former has any justification other than what there is for the latter. This is the question whether cases (5) and (6) are reducible, respectively, to cases (1) and (2). This, however, is not my point at the moment. My point is that there is no more reason for insisting that (6) is not reducible to (2) than there is for insisting that (5) is not reducible to (1). In other words: Anyone who complains that knowledge of the future from the barometer or the present position of the stars isn't really knowledge of the future will also complain that knowledge of the future from an unshared precognitive image isn't really knowledge of the future. For in both cases one may say, 'All the knower really knows is something about the present; so for all the knower really knows what he claims to know, since it is about a different time, the future, can without contradiction be false'. Anyone who complains that knowledge of the past from a history book isn't really knowledge of the past should also

---

[1] In this disjunction, this hesitation, lies the secret of the puzzles about the minds of others. See pp. 50-55.

complain that knowledge of the past from an unshared memory image is not really knowledge of the past. For (i) both are problematic, i.e. for all the knower really knows what he claims to know can without contradiction be false. (ii) There is no more reason for saying of the first case that all the knower really knows is something about his *future* sensations and therefore something different from what he claims to know, which is about the past, than there is to say this of the latter. In the same way anyone who complains that knowledge of the mental condition of another from his expression and behaviour isn't real knowledge should also complain that knowledge of the mental condition of another like one has of one's own, that is from an unshared sensation, is not really knowledge of the mental condition of another. Both are problematic, and some people will on this account refuse to call them real knowledge of anything. But this is still not the point. The point is that there is no more reason for abusing the former by saying that it is at best knowledge only of the knower's future sensations, or at very best of the behaviour of a body, than there is to say this of the latter— i.e. if ordinary knowledge from a man's expression isn't real knowledge of the mind of another, because it is only knowledge of how he will behave or of the knower's own sensations, then, on those very same counts, knowledge of the mind of another by extended introspection, by private feeling like one uses for knowledge of oneself, is still not real knowledge of the mind of another.

Brown. I think I see now what is wrong between us. I agree that what you have described as extended introspection would not be real knowledge of the mind of another. But then what you describe is not an extension of real introspection, which is a direct and infallible form of knowledge, but an extension of a so-called introspection which is fallible and indirect. In other words, when Gray or someone said, 'one might find out what is the mental condition of another because one might know it in the way one knows one's own, by a sort of introspection', you took this to amount to 'in the sort of way one knows one's in love'. Now there is no difference in principle between the way one knows one's in love and the way one knows one has a cold and, as you say, one only comes to be able to tell when one has a cold or a touch of malaria after considerable experience. One doesn't really *observe* that one has a cold; one has a sensation and in virtue of past experience predicts others to come. Likewise one doesn't strictly observe that one is in love. We are indeed inclined to speak loosely of knowing by introspection that one loves, hates or despises someone, but it is no more strictly true that one can observe that one is in love than it is strictly true that one can observe that there is a clock on the tower or that it points to ten to three, although in ordinary speech we loosely speak of doing so.

Gray. I don't understand you. Surely to be angry, to believe what Smith says and to doubt what Jones says, to understand one sentence and to fail to understand another, to remember an incident, to fall in love, all these are mental states and things the presence of which I can detect in myself by introspection though you cannot.

Brown. Of course you are better able to tell than others whether you are in love or can remember the coronation of George V. Or at least you have ways of knowing whether you are in love which others haven't, though they have these ways of knowing whether *they* are in love. We have just seen that this private source of information about yourself isn't confined to knowledge of what is in your mind. You have a private way of knowing whether you are digesting your breakfast. You have indeed a private way of knowing what took place in the vaults of the bank where you were on watch last night, because you can remember what took place and no one else can, since the man who was hiding there died of heart failure when the alarms went.[1] But these sorts of knowing are dependent on past experience. Of course you might and babies may have confidence in memory images without any experience to back it, just as you might have confidence in certain images as representing the future although you had never had precognitive images before. But your confidence in the rosy images of the future—rosy to distinguish them from images of the past—doesn't become justified until you have found out by experience their value. You

[1] It might be thought that this case differs in principle from the others since someone else might have been there. But someone might develop the gift of being able to feel whether you were digesting your breakfast.

have experience which justifies your confidence in memory images and sensations of palms and water.[1] But experience though it justifies confidence doesn't prevent mistakes, and knowledge that here are palms and water, that here the accident occurred and that one is in love, is all liable to error. It is dependent on past experience, it is indirect, it is fallible. However characteristic the prickling in one's nose still one may turn out not to have caught cold at all—it was only the hay dust. However strong the feeling that this has all happened before, it may turn out that one is not remembering, but suffering from paramnesia, a feeling of *déjà vu*. However clearly one sees a figure in the dusk, still may be there's no one there. It is well recognized that though we speak of knowing what will happen in the future we never really know the future, that we at best have only a reasonable confidence that it will turn out to be this rather than that. Our knowledge of the future is indirect, based on our knowledge of the present and supported by past experience, though often we have forgotten this. It is fallible because no statement about one time is incompatible with a statement about another and therefore the contradictory of any statement about the future is compatible with any present and any past.

It is less well recognized that though we speak of knowing what has happened in the past we never really know the past, that our knowledge in memory of the past is indirect, being based upon our knowledge of the present and supported by past experience and, therefore, fallible.

It is still less well recognized that most of our so-called knowledge of the present is not really knowledge. We do not really know the physical states of things. This knowledge is based on what we immediately see and hear and is supported by past experience—it is indirect and fallible. We do not know the mental states of others. Even if we had the telepathy which we have just been imagining this would still be indirect and fallible. But, finally, it is least well recognized that many statements about our own minds we don't really know—or if you like that there

---

[1] This falsifies the situation in a way which comes out when one says that memory-sensations and perception-sensations are not distinguished from others by being of a special colour or having 'memory' or 'perception' written under them, but by the confidence they give. The confidence itself comes by experience to be its own excuse. See *The Rocking Horse Winner* (last page especially), by D. H. Lawrence.

are many statements about one's own mind that one doesn't really know. Indeed, the only things one really knows appear to be the contents, the immediate contents of one's own mind at the moment of knowing. A man may say that he knows he has a pain in his foot. But all he really knows is the immediate contents of his own mind as he speaks, the feeling as of pain in his foot. He doesn't know that he has a pain in his foot. All he really knows is what he knows by introspection, and all he knows really by introspection is what he really knows—namely, the feeling as of pain in his foot. He doesn't really know anything about his foot, he can't tell by the feel that he has a pain in his foot because he can't tell by the feel that he has a foot. Of course he can tell by introspection that he feels as if he had a pain in his foot, and this is sometimes misleadingly expressed by saying that he can tell by introspection that he feels a pain in his foot. But it is necessary to realize that this last is true only if one either does not mean real introspection, direct and infallible, or does not mean by 'pain in the foot' more than a certain kind of sensation which as luck will have it has been constantly found connected with a thorn or tin-tack in the foot.

Now what I wish to suggest is that though in fact we never do have that sort of knowledge of the mind of another which each of us has of the immediate contents of his own mind, we could have it.

White. And what I now want to assert is that this is impossible, that it is an absurd idea. And that therefore real knowledge of the mind of another is impossible.

Black. That's what I've been saying all along.

White. Yes, and I want to say that what you have been saying is true—only necessarily true.

Gray. But I thought that you had been disagreeing with Black.

White. Ah! but now I've come to see that what he says is true, I have indeed come to see how *very* true it is.

Gray. To say that it is necessarily true that we don't know what is going on in the minds of others is to say that it is impossible that we should know what is going on in their minds. Black didn't say that this is impossible but that it never happens, and up till now you haven't said that it is impossible but that such talk lacked any sense.

White. Yes, but that was quite inadequate. The phrase 'know what is going on in the mind of another' isn't just a phrase without a use like 'Pirots carulize elatically'. It isn't merely that when someone talks of knowing, really knowing, what is going on in the mind of another we have no idea of what he means. On the contrary, we have an idea of what he means, but on examination find that it is out of the question—not merely something that is in fact out of the question, like providing everyone with gold teeth or a pair of elephants, but something that is unimaginable because it hides a contradiction.

Black. As for me, I did in fact say not merely that we never *do* but that we can't know what is going on in the minds of others. True, I didn't then realize what sort of 'can't' this was—whether like the 'can't' in 'I can't make out what the people on the next floor do in the evenings', or like the 'can't' in 'I can't get a triangular flag with four corners'. But I realize now that it is the latter it is like. When first one says, 'We can never really know whether a thing is going to happen till it does', or 'We can never really know what lies in the future', it feels as if this were because the door to the future is one to which we happen to have no key. But on trying to think of what it would be to really know today what will happen tomorrow, it soon appears that it is more like the impossibility of seeing perfectly clear streams. For to really know of the occurrence of an event seems to involve observing it as opposed to observing something other than it from which one infers its occurrence. But if today I observe the occurrence of an event such as the birth of a baby then that event is not something that's going to happen tomorrow.[1] So the 'can't' in 'We can't really know the future' turns out to have been a logical 'can't'.

If you like, it isn't that my 'can't' in 'We can't really know what is going on in the minds of others' was really a logical 'can't' all the time though I didn't realize it but that it was a 'can't' of a sort all its own, a metaphysical 'can't', or 'can't'

[1] Not that this proof is worth much. It is nearly as easy to say, 'If today I really know of the occurrence of an event, that event is not something that's going to happen tomorrow', as to say, 'If today I observe the occurrence of an event then it is not something that's going to happen tomorrow'. And it is as easy to say, 'No, why shouldn't it be possible to observe the events of the future just as one can in memory observe the events of the past', as it is to say, 'No, why shouldn't one really know of the occurrence of events in the future just as one can in memory know of the occurrence of events in the past'.

which is between, or a mixture of, a factual 'can't' and a logical 'can't',[1] and that it has now become purified into something quite logical. Thus at first I didn't very well realize that in saying that we can't know what is going on in the minds of others I was saying anything very different from 'In order to know what is going on in the minds of others we have to rely upon inference from what we observe of their behaviour'. It was only when something was submitted which refuted the second statement though I could not accept it as refuting the first, that the first really came to mean for me something quite different from the second.

Gray. But surely either what you meant was the factual statement which is false, or what you meant was something which is necessarily true. I still don't understand why you say that your 'can't' was neither factual nor logical, nor what you mean by its *becoming* logical.

Black. Take the case of someone who says 'A leopard can't change his spots', and then when we describe the leopard who at the zoo (in the colder climate) lost his spots, says 'I really meant wild leopards'. Does it matter whether we say '*All the time* he *really* meant "*Wild* leopards can't change their spots"' but he expressed himself carelessly or maybe even he wasn't quite clear himself as to what he did mean', or instead say, '*First* he asserted that leopards can't change their spots but *then* he gave up that when we reminded him of the leopard Burchell brought to the zoo, and *now* he says that *wild* leopards can't change their spots'. We may choose to describe him in the second way because, after all, what he did say, was 'Leopards can't change their spots', although it would have been quite easy to say 'Wild leopards can't change their spots', and also when we reminded him of Burchell's leopard he paused for a moment in slight embarrassment and then saved himself by saying 'I meant real, wild leopards'. On the other hand, we may choose to describe him by saying that what he *really* meant *all along* was 'wild leopards'. We shall be the more inclined to do this the more immediately and easily he ignores Burchell's leopard, and the more the previous discussion had been all

[1] Those who know what Wittgenstein has been saying will understand why at this point I again remind people that I owe a debt to him and of how large it is.

about *wild* animals we'd found and how wild zebras lose their stripes as they get older. Or we may choose to describe him by saying, like psychoanalysts, that he meant both—only how could he mean both?—or say that he meant neither—only then what did he mean? nothing at all? But it doesn't matter what we say once we know all about him. Suppose now that someone instead of saying 'I meant wild leopards', says 'I meant real leopards', and that it then turns out that taking into account what he means by 'a real leopard' the statement 'Real leopards can't change their spots' is necessarily true. Then, again, it doesn't matter whether we say '*All along* he *really* meant what he calls real leopards', *or* say '*At first* he was making a statement of fact about how animals of a sort we all know never change their colour in a way they very conceivably might, though they seldom or never do, *but when* we reminded him of an exception to his statement then he changed his position and also the sort of thing he was saying, so that he came to be saying something necessarily true'. It doesn't matter which we say provided we are clear about what happened in him. At first he brought out his original statement with an air and feeling of worldly wisdom like one who says 'Never trust a man with red hair', or 'Once a thief always a thief', and he expected from us the sort of respect which is due to people who learn these things, and appropriately he was a bit taken aback when we mentioned Burchell's leopard. All this inclines us to say 'Originally he meant to make a statement of fact'. At the same time he wasn't so astonished and impressed by our producing this case of a leopard who lost his spots as we had expected he would be and he still went on talking, as if this did not refute what he had wished originally to say. For, reminded of the faded leopard at the zoo, he replied, after a moment's pause, 'The animal you describe wouldn't really be a leopard would it? More of a puma with a peculiar past'.

It is the same with me. When first I said 'We can't ever know what is going on in the minds of others', I brought this out as if it were a 'can't' like 'Whippets can't catch hares' and not like 'Parallel lines can't meet', and I wasn't clear that telepathy, even if it occurred, would provide no exception to my statement. But when telepathy was concretely described *then* I became clear that it would provide no exception. And with that I became clear that nothing would, that is, that my statement was un-exceptionable, that is, that it was necessarily true. Now you know all about me in this, so there is no need to bother about whether we say that first I made a statement of fact which turned out to be false, and then in the same words a necessary statement, without very explicitly acknowledging that I'd over-looked the facts which made the statement of fact false, or say instead that though I used a form of words which might express a statement of fact, I really meant all the time to express by them something necessarily true.

And I am not peculiar in this. This is the sort of game which again and again people play with the sentence, 'We can't know what is going on in the minds of others', like they do with 'We can't know what is going on in the future', or 'A good horse can't have a bad tail'. And roughly speaking it's because of this[1] that I said that the 'can't' in 'We can't know what is going on in the minds of others' *starts* half-factual and only *becomes* purely logical.

White. Well never mind about what we did do. . . .

Black. Ah! but it's important. Because in examining this matter of what was originally being said we examine philo-sophically philosophical progress.

White. Well anyway we both realize now that the truth 'We can't know what is going on in the minds of others', is more than we first thought it. I realize that it isn't merely the statement that a certain expression, 'know what is going on in the mind of another', is meaningless, and you realize that it is no mere matter of fact, like it used to be a mere matter of fact before X-rays that we couldn't know what was going on in the belly of another. We both realize now that the philosopher's discovery that no one can really know what is going on in the mind of another expresses not something that may be otherwise to-morrow but an eternal necessity that lies in the nature of things.

Brown. I have agreed that telepathy and, what comes to the same thing, the sort of extension of our powers of knowing of our own mental states which you, White, described, do not prove

---

[1] It is not only because other people play this sort of game with it, It is because some people play this sort of game while others to the end make the statement factual, while others from the first make it logical.

that real knowledge of the mind of another is anything but an impossibility, an absurdity. The out-of-the-way possibilities we have imagined do not provide a meaning for talk about real knowledge of the mind of another; they are not what is wanted; with however plausible an air we place them on the counter, one who seeks real knowledge of the minds of others rejects them as not what he wants. But it doesn't follow that there is nothing he wants or that what he wants is impossible. It does not follow that it is impossible to have real knowledge of the mind of another in *any* way. In particular, it doesn't follow that it is impossible to know the mind of another by that real introspective observation, direct and infallible, by which one knows the sensations, images and feelings which one is having at the moment.

White. I believe that it is impossible that a man should know the mind of another in the sort of way he knows his own sensations of the moment, but it takes time to see why. And I believe that when we look into (1) why it is that ordinary and telepathic knowing of the mind of another aren't really knowing of what the knower claims to know, and why perception isn't real knowledge of what the knower claims to know, and why most introspection and all knowledge of future sensations isn't really knowledge of what the knower claims to know; and (2) why only in knowledge of his sensations of the moment does the knower really know what he claims to know; and (3) why such knowledge of the mind of another is impossible, then we shall see that *no* knowledge of the mind of another could, like knowledge of the immediate contents of one's own mind, lack those very features which in all other knowledge make it not really knowledge of what the knower claims to know. For we shall then see the connection between the nature of knowing and the nature of what is known, and how this connection is not accidental but necessary, so that (i) 'We never really know the minds of others, never really know anything beyond their behaviour', is not only true but necessarily true; (ii) 'We never really know anything beyond our own sensations' is not only true but necessarily true; (iii) 'We never really know anything beyond our own sensation of the moment' is not ony true but necessarily true; (iv) 'We never really know anything' is not only true but necessarily true.

Other Minds VI

Black. Let's 'look down that lonely road' which leads past abandoned illusions to the security of Solipsism. Let's see what's wrong with the common or garden claims to knowledge, and by refusing in those cases to speak of knowledge set our minds on higher things, gain a glimpse of perfect knowledge, though perhaps without hope of reaching it. We shall have to reject much, indeed most, of what the common herd unthinkingly accept as real knowledge, most of what we ourselves in unthinking moments have taken to be real knowledge. To begin with, we shall have to recognize that we never really know what is still in the future, much less what would happen if this or that were to come about, or what would have happened if things had been otherwise. For when a man says 'I know he'd have won if Richards had ridden him' we know that the most he really knows is that the horse turned round as the tapes went up and thereby lost some three or four lengths, that he nevertheless was beaten by no more than half a length, and that horses seldom or never turn round at the gate when Gordon Richards is riding. Does such knowledge absolutely guarantee what would have happened in this case? Certainly not. No one knows what would have happened. Maybe *this* horse would have turned round in spite of Gordon's subtlest persuasions. Maybe this horse would not have exerted himself if he had not been left behind at the start. Maybe if he hadn't got left he'd have got bumped or jumped the path across the course, or anything of too many things. Nor is it otherwise with cars. With horses it's obvious that there are a thousand accidents and follies that may 'upset your calculations', with horses it's notorious that 'you never can tell', that 'one never knows'. What's not so obvious is that this is fatal to all knowledge. It is, however, tolerably easy to see that with cars, too, one never really knows. True, if the Bentleys are beaten by very little, and then a small but definite defect is detected in the superchargers used by the team then we feel very sure they would have won with better superchargers. For our experience assures us that another 0.05 of a mile per hour could have been got out of them, and knowing by how little they lost it is then a matter of mathematics to decide whether they would have won or lost. But is it? Or, if you like, do we know that they would have lapped 0.05 of a mile per hour faster? Even if we know that, fitted with faultless superchargers, they would have gone faster, this doesn't guarantee that their average speed for the race would have been better—on the contrary, some other part of the mechanism might have failed to stand the slightly greater strain of the slightly increased pace. And, worse still, do we *know* that faultless superchargers would have increased speed? We do not. We should be surprised to see a horse get away badly with Richards riding, but of course it might happen. We should be astonished if a car did no better with a superior supercharger. But of course it might not. The very change which in other cars, even in other cars of the same make, has resulted in a better performance might, in this car, have no effect, or only make it worse. Speaking of a horse, someone may say, 'Then for some unknown reason it refused to move', or 'Then for some unknown reason it rushed down that side turn by the White Farm. As if it hadn't been along that road a hundred times and never turned it's head'. And often the tone of voice in which the speaker says 'for some unknown reason' makes it plain that only his scientific upbringing prevents him saying 'Then for no reason at all it . . .' It is worth noticing that instead of saying 'Then for no reason . . .' or 'Then for no discoverable reason . . .' or 'Then for some unknown reason . . .' the story-teller may say 'Then he *took it into his head*, e.g. to rush down that side turning'.[1] It's the same with cars. A man may say, 'My car has a mind of her own. Sometimes she'll go, sometimes she won't'. Or a man may say, exasperated by the non-uniformity of nature into speaking animistically, but obliged by the prestige of science to speak jokingly, 'My car goes when she chooses'. Notice not only the 'chooses', but the

---

[1] The two may be used together, 'For some unknown reason he took it into his head'. But nevertheless there is an association between the absence of a cause (magic), the undiscoverable cause, and the psychological cause.

'she' or 'he'. If one morning you see this man struggling with his car and say pleasantly, 'Won't go this morning? What's wrong?' he will look up with scarlet face and say, 'There's nothing wrong. The damn thing just won't go'. You will shake your head at the naughty boy. So would I. We are sure that a calm and skilful mechanic would find something wrong. We are more sure of that than we are that the man who knows a lot about horses, or better, *understands* them, will find what's wrong when one of them refuses to go. He will get the horse to go, but he will quite likely not know why it stopped. But of course the mechanic may not be able to locate the trouble, that is, may not find any difference between this car and a normal car, which explains why this one won't go, and which if altered does the trick. True, when the mechanic can't find the cause of the trouble, we are sure that if the car is taken back to the makers then they will find the cause. But of course we are not *quite* sure. Maybe they'll say they can't find anything wrong, and pull the car to pieces, and perhaps make it again, or perhaps not. And if they do maybe it will go and maybe it won't. The owner of the car, who is an animistic man and believes in magic, says 'I told you there was nothing wrong'. Even if we have had a modern education, and know that what he says can't really be so,[1] we are no better off than he for predicting the future. Even if we know that when one car which seems just like another behaves differently, then there is always some explanation, if only we could find it, still we are no better off than he. For our confidence in the connection between knowledge of a car's present condition and knowledge of its future condition is greater than his only in so far as we have reduced our confidence in our knowledge of its present condition. The fact is, even with the simplest machines we get surprises. In face of these we may save the accuracy of science at the cost of its completeness, or both at the cost of confidence in the accuracy and completeness of our observations. Sometimes we watch more carefully, sometimes we say, 'one of these other things must be at work here', only at last we do say, 'the ultimate laws for these phenomena are statistical, i.e. they have free will'. But

[1] Nowadays it's not done to say there was no explanation. See G. A. Paul, *Mind*, July 1938, pp. 373, 374.

whichever we do the surprises teach the same lesson—'one never knows'.

And it isn't only that because of our carelessness or ignorance, or because of the overwhelming complexity of the world, we never *do* really know what would have happened if things had been otherwise, it is that we never *could* know this from information about the present and the past, or for that matter, about the present, the past and the future. And it's equally plain that we not only never do know what's going to happen in the future, but that we never could know this from information about what is now the case and about what has been the case.

Gray. But surely if we were to know (1) that a car is exactly in the condition of one which went perfectly when the starter was pressed, and (2) that if two machines or, in general, two things, are exactly alike and in exactly the same surroundings, they always react exactly alike to the same stimulus, then we would know that that car would go perfectly when the starter was pressed. Even if we haven't any such general premiss as the uniformity of nature, but only a more specific premiss that if two *cars* are exactly alike, then they always behave alike, still we should, armed with the information that this car is in the same condition and surroundings as the one which went so well yesterday, be in a position to deduce that this car will go well today.

Black. But what is to be meant by '*Always* in our experience when two machines are exactly alike, if one goes right the other goes right?' Does this mean merely that this always has been so? Then, as Aristotle said, no conclusion follows as to what will happen in the future in the case of the car before us. Or does it mean not merely that this always has been so, but also that it always will be so? And then, though now the premisses entail the conclusion, the argument now involves, as Mill said, a *petitio principii*. Though the premisses *appear* not to include a statement about the future, really they do.

Gray. It's only a negative or a hypothetical statement about the future.

Black. Nevertheless, the whole difficulty of our knowledge of the future now flows into the question 'How do we know that if two machines are exactly alike they behave alike?' In the same way, if you say that you know that the wheels of a bicycle will go round if the pedal is turned because you know there is a connection between the two, then the whole difficulty of the questions 'How do you know the future? How do you know the wheels will turn?' flows into the question 'How do you know there is this connection? Do you infer it from regular association, or do you come to see it at least in favourable cases? Indeed, what is knowing of the presence of a *causal* connection as opposed to knowing of the presence of a *steel* connection? Do you see it there, or do you guess it's there, like you guess there's a connection between two wheels if they turn together? In a factory you see a wonderful machine which performs a sequence of operations with machine-like regularity—first an endless band brings a jar to an opening, a valve opens, the jar is filled with Pumpkin's Pickles, an arm seals it, bang! and the show begins again. It doesn't take you long to know what's going to happen next. Even if the sequence of operations were ever so much longer and more complicated, still by watching long enough you might well come to know what was going to happen next. You might come to know this without taking a peep behind the scenes, without ever examining the machine. But of course if you could examine the machine, so much the better. Then you really would know. Then you would come on the flaw in the mechanism which makes the machine miss every hundredth jar. Our talk about causation is dominated by an unconscious phantasy[1] of this sort: Caught by a giant, you are shut in a cell. Past the windows fly birds, red, green, blue, golden, and of many other colours. If you come to be able to tell what coloured bird is coming next, you will live, but every time you make a mistake you lose a drop of blood. Soon you begin to notice a regularity in the way birds appear together, or in succession. You may rely on statistics about this for your predictions. But if on looking carefully you can sometimes see wires connecting one bird with another, though usually you are not quite sure of this because it's rather misty outside, you will use what you see of the wires to supplement your statistics, to help you to guess what bird is coming next, and to guide you as to what hypotheses about the

---

[1] I here put the psychoanalytic expression 'an unconscious phantasy dictating our conscious life' instead of Wittgenstein's 'We have the idea that . . .', 'We have the picture of . . .'. At the risk of being tiresome I must repeat that all this article comes from Wittgenstein. He has resolved the conflict.

way the birds follow one another are best worth testing by careful watching. These hypotheses you will verify, not merely by careful watching of the birds. You will vainly wipe the window pane and peer through the mist for the wires.

But causal connections aren't wires in a mist. You say that you know there's a connection between the turning of the pedal of a bicycle and the turning of the back wheel, and that this is how you know what is going to happen at the other end of the bicycle as soon as you turn the pedal. It's true, of course, and plain enough, that you know that to turn this pedal will turn the back wheel, because you know they are connected—*by a chain*. But the question we are concerned with is 'How do you know that to turn the pedal of a bicycle—a machine in which a pedal is connected by a chain or a cam-shaft with the back wheel— how do you know that to turn the pedal of such a machine will result in the back wheel revolving?' It's no good answering that you know by knowing that there's a connection between the one sort of happening and the other. For here the connection is not something like a wire which can be observed in addition to, and judged to be responsible for, the fact that when one thing happens then another does, like the wires which were responsible for the fact that when one bird appeared another did too. The fact that there's some connection between drunkenness and disorder just is the fact that very often when a man is disorderly in the public streets he's drunk. If the connection is close, very close, then it just is the fact that *whenever* a man is disorderly he's drunk. But if the 'whenever' does *not* include the future, then we can infer nothing about the future from the connection (Aristotle). And if it *does*, then the major premiss couldn't be known without already knowing the conclusion (Mill).

Brown. Couldn't the connection be a *necessary* one which experience of association enables us to *see*, like experience with marbles enables the child to come to see that $2+2$ must always make 4?

Black. This amounts to turning the general premiss into a principle and claiming that from what is happening now one can deduce by an immediate inference without any further premisses what is going to happen.

Brown. And surely one may. From the fact that this wheel is engaged in that one, and that this one is turning I know that in a moment that one will turn. I allow that I wrongly gave the impression that knowledge of the necessary connection was knowledge of an additional premiss. And of course it is no more an additional premiss than is '*What is foreseen must happen*' an additional premiss when I argue 'I shall fall, for God foresees that I shall fall and what is foreseen must happen'.

I ought to have said plainly that there appear to be cases in which the occurrence of one sort of thing *by itself* necessitates, or *by itself* justifies an inference to the early occurrence of another. But now if there are such cases, then you are wrong in saying that it is impossible that we should from the present know the future. And I want now to say plainly that there are such cases. Our friends let us down, our horses go lame, but 'one cogged wheel can't fail to turn another', and, as Mace says, though not in so many words, 'If two ivory billiard balls approach one another, then we know what will happen when they meet'.[1]

White. Now the whole difficulty flows into the question 'How do you know they are ivory?' You don't understand the significance of your own admissions. If you admit that if the connection is necessary, it is a principle and not a premiss, and therefore provides no further information about nature, can't you see what sort of 'knowing from' this is, and what sort of 'premiss-about-the-present' this is? When to 'I am putting a lever under this log', taken as descriptive of something we really know of the present, we add 'Long levers lift logs', taken as descriptive of something we really know about the past, then we have secure premisses but they give only a problematic inference to the future.

We can make the inference demonstrative by making the major premiss more powerful, but it is not powerful enough until it includes our conclusion and shares its insecurity.

We can avoid this by making our major premiss the necessary proposition, 'Long enough levers lift logs'. But this security in the step from premiss to conclusion is gained only by making the minor premiss include our conclusion and share its insecurity.

Mace saw this, but unfortunately did not smile. Rightly he

said 'There are necessary connections between the present and the future'. But no chuckle escaped him.

Black. But *are* there necessary connections between one time and another? I don't see that Mace and Stout[1] prove it with their examples.

White. This is a tedious business you are introducing. It doesn't matter whether there are or there aren't. If there aren't then the connections between premises about the present and conclusions about the future are problematic. If there are then the premises aren't really about the present and are problematic. So that whichever is the case, conclusions about the future are problematic.

Black. I must confess I don't follow you. It does seem to me that if there were a necessary connection between a fact or facts about the present and a conclusion about the future, then I might know the latter from the former. What I want to insist upon is that Mace hasn't shown that there are necessary connections between the present and the future. He says truly that when two billiard balls meet then they must rebound. But do we know that they will meet? It is is self-contradictory to say that a brick has passed through a window without breaking it, but it is not self-contradictory to say that a brick is now hurtling towards this window but the window will not be broken.

Brown. If yesterday I fed a certain cake to a large herd of cows and today they are all well, then the cake *can't* have been poisoned, and if there is arsenic in this that I am giving them now they *must* be dead by morning.

Black. Perhaps they'll disappear.

Brown. Not if they are real cows. In fairyland a hurtling brick may turn to dust just before it reaches the window, but then that proves it's a fairy brick and not an ordinary physical brick.

Black. But even if the brick were an ordinary brick, mightn't a hand come down from the clouds and clutch it in mid air? Mightn't an invisible gypsy administer, in the nick of time, an antidote to the arsenic?

Brown. Yes, but then that would be magic or the hand of God. What I know about the future when I see a brick hurtling towards a window is, if you insist on pedantic accuracy, not that

[1] *Aristotelian Society, Suppl. Vol. XIV.*

the window will be broken but that it will be broken unless some hand from the clouds clutches it or it turns to dust before it reaches the window or in front of the window there's wire netting or something.

White. Or something!

> 'So tell your papa where the yak can be got,
> And if he is awfully rich,
> He will buy you the creature or else he will not,
> I can not be positive which.'[1]

Brown. Well, I can put it another way. If I know not merely that I am dealing with an ordinary brick, not a fairy brick, but also that I am not in fairyland, then when I see a brick hurtling towards a window I know the glass is going to break.

White. And isn't fairyland where the glass doesn't break, where what's fragile sometimes survives?

Black. You mean that the connection isn't necessary between what I know about the present and what I am to learn from it of the future until what I am to know of the present includes what I am to infer about the future?

White. Exactly. You don't know that one cogged wheel will turn another unless you know that they are both of steel, the best steel, i.e. steel that will not break—any other sense of 'best' won't do; 'comes from a reliable firm', 'of a particular appearance', 'already tested'—none of this will do. For there's no more contradiction in supposing that steel with the best pedigree, most impressive 'form', and most perfect conformation should fail us than there is in supposing that a horse with these things should do so. It is nowadays logically impossible for both a standard-bred trotter and his parents to fail to trot a mile in 2 minutes 30 seconds. But this wasn't always so. This bit of logic was made quite recently in America. For 'a standard-bred trotter' was defined as a horse 'with a record of 2.30 or less or whose parents have a record of 2.30 or less'.

Black. Even if you know that the steel is the best steel, you don't know from the present what will happen in the future, because it may cease to be the best steel by tomorrow, in half an hour's time, in a second's time. When you know it is the best

[1] Hilaire Belloc.

steel, all you know is that if *now* the pedal were turned the wheel would turn—nothing follows about the future.

If when she hears that he has been drowned she isn't at all upset we are apt to say 'She can't have loved him'. And we might say 'You had better not come to see her tomorrow. I am going to tell her of his death, and if, as you say, she is very much in love with him she's bound to be upset'. But of course 'she's bound to be' means 'it's extremely probable that she will be', or at least that is all it ought to mean. This is quite plain when we consider, 'You had better not come to see her when you return at the end of the year because I am going to tell her then what has happened and if, as you say, she's very much in love with him, she is *quite likely* to be considerably upset, although of course twelve months is twelve months'. Here we say 'quite likely' instead of 'is bound to', 'can't but', etc. Here, where between what is now the case—that she loves him—and what is predicted—her distress—is a *long* interval, we are not at all inclined to speak of a necessary connection. Even if we are told that during that time nothing will happen to change her feelings, such as the appearnace of other suitors, we feel that the mere lapse of time may well make a difference. For, as the vocalists insist, 'Time on my hands with you in my arms' is one thing, but the former without the latter quite another.

We may say, 'There is no explanation why Fidelity still loves him while Amaryllis already confuses him with Alfred—it's just that with Amaryllis love is very evanescent'. It is clear that the fact that Fidelity was distressed to hear the news of his death while Amaryllis was not does not necessitate that Amaryllis did not *ten years* ago love him. Now is there some number of minutes n such that if we say of a person that she loves another now then if within n minutes she hears of his death and is not distressed, it follows that we were wrong in thinking she loved him though this does not follow for $n+1$ minutes? There is no such number of minutes. And therefore the fact that Amaryllis loves him now does not *necessitate* that she will be distressed if a *minute, a moment*, hence she hears he's been drowned. Even supposing it true that *if* a moment hence she *still* loves him then she must be distressed at the news it nevertheless does not follow from the fact that she *now* loves him that she will be distressed. For from the fact that she *now* loves him it does not follow that she will ten years, two years, or a moment hence still love him.

White. Supposing a child[1] says he knows what twice three are but when we ask him he says 'Seven', and when we say 'That's wrong' he says 'I know it is but I know now what it is' but when we ask him he says 'Eight', and next says 'Eighteen', and then says 'I know when you don't ask me'. We don't think much of his knowing. And if he says he knows the twice times table but always makes a mistake before the end and then he says he always knows at the time he says he does and when he starts but forgets it before the end, then we give a queer sort of grin. This is so in spite of the fact that if we ask him a *week* later and he fails we don't say 'He *can't* have known it when he said he did', we say, 'He may have known it and forgotten it by now', or we may say, 'He can't have known it *very well*'. (She can't have loved him very much. It can't have been very poisonous.)

Exactly how many minutes after the child has claimed knowledge of the twice times table he must be able to get through it correctly if his claim to know it is to stand one cannot say. But it doesn't follow that there is no number of minutes such that he must be able to deliver the goods for that number of minutes if his claim is to stand. One cannot say exactly how many hairs a man must have to make good his claim that he isn't bald, but undoubtedly two are not enough. Suppose a man with only two hairs on his head says he's not bald. 'Not bald', we say, 'what d'you mean?' He says, 'Well, you wouldn't call me bald if I had twenty thousand hairs, and if I had twenty thousand less one you wouldn't call me bald for the loss of that one hair, nor if I had twenty thousand less two, nor, etc.; and I have two hairs'. Notice two things: (1) We are half inclined to allow he's right, and that a man isn't really bald unless he has no hairs on his head, that is, we are half inclined to say that being bald necessitates having no hair, while not being bald does not necessitate having more than two hairs. This inclination to accept such a notation is almost unconscious. We repress it because it would result in such very eccentric behaviour. We say 'No, no', but we smile a half-condoning smile. Although he's wrong we feel he is not as wrong as one who says of a round

[1] Another Wittgenstein example.

penny that it's square.[1] We feel he's reminding us of something
and when he suggests that we should speak not of baldness but
of baldishness, we feel that he is suggesting a notation which
brings out what is concealed by our ordinary notation which
puts us in difficulties when asked whether a betwixt-and-between man is bald. And the man who says 'A man isn't really
bald unless he has no hairs on his head' is recommending the
same sort of change in notation, though he prefers to avoid talking of everyone as baldish and to speak of them as so far and not so
far from being bald—while they still have a hair on their heads.

When you, Black, say 'There's no necessity while there's an
interval', aren't you doing the same sort of thing? The truth and
value of your statement consists in the reasons you offer for
it. You point out that we do offer the mere lapse of time as an
excuse for a past statement ascribing a property to a thing
which property it now fails to manifest.

And you point out that we have an aversion to saying of n
minutes that they provide a sufficient excuse while denying this
of $n-1$ minutes. But you then claim that we must do this or say
with you that the excuse is valid however few the minutes. But
you are wrong. We can do what we do do, namely count some
periods as sufficient excuse, hesitate over others, and count
other shorter periods as insufficient excuse. It is as absurd to
say that we are wrong in doing this as it is to say that we are
wrong in calling a bald man bald because he is continuously
related to the unbald, or wrong in calling a sofa a sofa because it
is continuously related to an armchair.

Black. It is *immensely* improbable that the best steel should
lose its strength by the time I have finished speaking, but the
suggestion doesn't differ in kind from the suggestion that it
should lose its strength in ten years' time.

White. But does differ in kind from the suggestion that it
should inexplicably turn pink with blue stripes, utterly improbable as the latter suggestion is. The best steel has never
turned pink with blue stripes, so it has regularly avoided this
sort of thing just as much as it has regularly avoided losing its

[1] And we are right. Or are we? For though, if ever there is a difference in kind
between one thing and another, there is between a thing that is round and a thing
that is square, nevertheless this embarrassing technique beginning 'Is this still
square?' might lead one to say 'There is no difference in kind even here'.

strength and turning to dust. According to you, there should be as much necessity about the not turning pink as there is about not turning to dust. But, in fact, its reputation is bound up with the latter in a way it's not with the former and that in the sense that we shall say 'It cannot *have* been the best steel' if the moment we try it it fails us. The fact of the matter is that just as there are not only cases where we argue from *This is* S to *This is* P merely because of a uniformity of association of S with P, but also cases where we do this from a necessary connection between S and P, so there are not only cases where we argue from *This is* S to *This will be* P merely because of an association in sequence of S with P, but also cases where we do this because of a necessary connection in sequence of S with P.

I prove this as follows: When someone says 'The Kalmuks give their cows poison every night but they do well on it' we say 'A queer poison', with a queer look on our faces. This look is quite unlike the look on our faces when we say, on first seeing a diplodocus, 'What an extraordinary animal'. But it *is* like the look on our faces when someone says, 'I found a leopard without spots and a giraffe with a neck like a cow'.

Black. Do you or do you not want to say that there are necessary connections between the facts of one time and the facts of another, and thus between what is at present the case and what will be the case?

And do you or do you not want to say that we have knowledge of the future in virtue of these connections?

White. With great patience we draw a pretty detailed picture of the animal you and I met in the wood last night. You recognize the picture but at once you tear it up and ask, 'Was what we saw a man or a horse?' In the same way, for the detailed description of the relations between individual statements about the present and individual statements about the future you want to substitute a formula. This sort of wish is the root of philosophical difficulty. In the management of horses, even in the limited field of proper tension on the reins, there is no formula such that any ignorant and insensitive fool can be trusted to unwind from it, as occasion arises, suitable treatment for the infinite variety of situations he will meet. Likewise with sentences, even in this limited matter of necessity.

However, if you insist upon a mnemonic formula, I prefer to say that there are as necessary relations between facts separated by an interval as there are between many facts not so separated, though this necessity is, in the way we have seen, by no means independent of the interval. The longer the interval the more its adverse effect upon the necessity, but this adverse effect diminishes towards zero as the interval diminishes.

If now it is asked 'Are there really any necessary connections between any one fact and another whether they be facts of the same time or no? And can one from one know another?' then I want to laugh. We have looked at a great many cases of connection and in some there is no inclination to speak of a necessary connection, although the things connected have been associated thousands of times without exception, while in other cases there is, without any more association, an inclination to speak of a very necessary connection. And between these extremes are intermediate cases where there appears to be an approach to, or if you like degree of, necessity.[1] When we look into (1) what it is which alters as the degree of necessity alters, and look into (2) what it is which makes the difference between a logical and a natural curiosity, we are able to describe the situation in a way which makes the question 'Are there *necessary* connections between *one* matter of fact and *another*?' vanish.

Take the matter of natural and logical curiosities. When a man says to us, 'In the wood at noon today I met a centaur—a creature with the body of a horse and the torso of a man', then we are very much surprised, and say, 'What an extraordinary animal!' but we don't feel that there is in his story that sort of queerness and absurdity, that incorrectness and self-contradictoriness, which we feel there is in that of the man who says, 'In the wood at noon today I met a horse, only it had the torso of a man'. And yet, this is the point, *they tell the same story*. We react to the second man's story with a pattern of words, namely, 'What an extraordinary horse', very like the 'What an extraordinary animal' with which we reacted to the first man's story. But we bring out 'What an extraordinary horse' with that queer look we have mentioned, the logical look. The look is connected with the fact that the word 'horse' not 'animal'

---

[1] See Dr. Ewing, *Aristotelian Society, Suppl. Vol. XIV*, p. 68

appears in our second response, and because of the way the word 'horse' is used in the second man's story. Although the two men tell the same story, they do so in different words. And the second man uses the word 'horse' in a way we feel he ought not, although we are well aware that neither he in making nor we in accepting his statement are expressing any misapprehension about what the animal he saw was like, such as might exist it he had seen it in a fog. His misapplication of the word 'horse' does not arise from ignorance of the thing to which it is applied. He is making a logical mistake.

This prepares us for what we notice when we examine the differences in a necessity series. As we imagine animals less and less like horses we find it becoming more and more absurd to call them horses. And this increasing absurdity, though it is represented as a matter of increasing improbability—the probability of their being horses or true horses—is not of that nature. On the contrary, the cases imagined are ones in which the nature of the animals is very well known indeed, in the light of noon, nothing is in doubt about them, and no betting is done on the nature of their insides or what they most like to eat. What then, is our feeling of doubt as to whether they are horses, whether they can be horses? What is plain is that more and more of us more and more hesitate when asked 'Are they horses?'

We notice that the same thing is true when we doubt whether a man whose head we can very well see is bald or not. The doubt is correlated with the degree of hesitation one has in whether to call him bald, but this correlation does not arise in the way it does when we can't see his head very well. In the latter case, besides the hesitation as to what to call him, there is a lack of confidence as to what to expect when he takes off his hat. In the case in which we can see his head very well there is no lack of confidence about how much hair there is on his head (Tautology). That is, unless his being bald is not a matter of how much hair there is on his head, there is nothing about us in favour of saying that we are doubting whether he is bald except our hesitation as to whether to call him bald. This comes out in the fact that when we can see his head well we sometimes would ask, not 'Do you believe he's bald?' nor even 'Is he bald?' but 'Would you call him bald?' I submit that in the circumstances described the only thing that is against saying that the questions are identical is what makes one say that the second is a plainer, less confusing way of asking the first.

Black. There is a very much more serious reason. 'Is he bald?' is objective in a way in which 'Would you call him bald?' is not. In this particular case it is most unlikely that, having said you would call him bald, you would afterwards say, influenced by argument perhaps, that now you would not call him bald. But if you did you would say that you were wrong when you said he was bald, although you would not say you were wrong in replying that you would call him bald, since at that time that is what you would have called him. And I must point out that though here there is very little difference between 'Is he bald?' and 'Would you call him bald?' there are other logical questions where there is the greatest difference.

White. You mean in those cases, as in arithmetic, where a man to begin with says one thing and later corrects himself, or at first does not know what to say and then gives the answer. But now the point I want to make can be put this way: In the case in which we can see a man's head well, the question 'Does he now *seem* to you to be bald?' means 'Do you now feel inclined to call him bald?' as opposed to the case where, when we are unable properly to see a man's head, 'Does he *seem* bald to you?' means 'Does his appearance at this distance lead you to expect he has hardly any hair?' The consequence is that just as 'Is he bald?' means, when you can't see his head, 'Would infinite investigation, including inquiry of others, leave you inclined to call him bald?' so does 'Is he bald?', when you can see his head, mean 'Would infinite reflection and inquiry of others leave you inclined to call him bald?' Here (as usual) objectivity is nothing short of infinite corrigibility, infinite liability to correction from experiment. But here the experiments are *all* on ourselves with our own language.[1]

Having grasped the peculiar nature of these 'baldness' *doubts*

[1] We all talk of infinite corrigibility in terms of something (a point) beyond the series, behind 'a Veil past which we can not see, a Door to which we find no key'. We all have the fatal phantasy of the prisoners in the cave which Plato brought up from the unconscious. But this phantasy, this way of talking, leads to our failure to grasp how objectivity is a matter of the infinity of the subjective. Remember the phantasy of the real unfelt and invisible weight of feathers and then of everything else.

and *questions*, we can grasp the peculiar nature of the growing *absurdity* of refusing to call bald a man who is fast losing his hair, or of insisting upon calling an animal which is getting less and less like a horse, a horse

It is soon obvious that these betwixt-and-between questions and doubts are matters of words, and then that the correlated semi-absurdities and semi-necessities are matters of words. It is then obvious that the utter absurdities and utter necessities at the ends of the series are matters of words. One says that it is utterly absurd to call a certain animal a horse when one feels that, however long one reflects, one will feel disinclined to do so, and is confident that other people will be with one over this. To say that it is absurd is to vent this feeling, though it is not to say that one feels it.

We would now say that Black was right in saying that there is no difference in kind introduced by lengthening the time interval. But now we should add that this is not because there is in no case no necessity, however short the interval, but because there is in some cases some necessity, however long the interval.

I want to try to explain in another way what I mean about the degrees and nature of necessity. The sights and sounds we see and hear appear in patterns in space and time, patterns which repeat themselves. Seeing some part of one of these patterns, one anticipates and wishes to lead one's friends to anticipate the remainder, and then one calls out a word. If to one's disappointment the remainder of the pattern fails to appear one often says one was wrong when one shouted the word. But sometimes one does not. Sometimes when one refuses to retract everyone else would also refuse, for example when to one's astonishment one finds a black swan, or a cat that likes water, or even a cow on skates. Sometimes one refuses to retract when everyone else would retract. There are again two cases: first, where everyone permanently refuses to 'agree with' one; second, where everyone in the end agrees with one. In the first case, one is wrong with a wrongness which would vanish with a new language, not because what one had said would become true, but because then one couldn't make the statement one had made (Tautology). In the second case one is right in one's counting, and the opposition is proved wrong. In the first case, one remains eccentric. In the second case, one becomes the fashion. This second sort of thing may happen when an animal is discovered rather like a zebra. On reflection (not investigation) someone says 'No, it's not a zebra', but you say 'Not a zebra! Not with those stripes?' 'Not lovely! Not with those eyes?' This is demonstrative proof. Or is it? It isn't if it fails. But it succeeds. And therefore it is. And its *infinite* success is the necessary connection between having such lovely stripes and being a zebra. The same sort of thing constitutes the necessary connection between being a zebra and preferring grass to meat. Or is this last not a necessary connection? Wouldn't you call an animal a zebra even if it preferred meat to grass provided it had those ears and those lovely stripes? With arsenic, however lovely it looked, if it didn't kill the cattle I wouldn't call it arsenic. By 'arsenic' I mean a poison of a certain sort, and by a poison I mean what kills cattle, and when I say this *does* kill cattle I register my confidence that it *will* if given to them at once before it's had time to go bad or anything. So if I know this is arsenic, then I know it will kill these cattle in a few minutes if Smith now, i.e. this very moment, gives it to them, and if I know I *was* right when I said it was arsenic and know that Smith is at this very moment giving it to these cattle, then I know these cattle *will* die or get ill. So from two matters of fact '*about the present*' (if Brown likes), namely that this is arsenic, and that Smith is now giving it to these cattle, I know '*another*' (if Brown likes) matter of fact, and it is one about the future, that these cattle will die. In the same way if I know these wheels are engaged in one another and are of the best steel, and that the first is turning, then I know that the second will turn. And I know that the black knight's armour will turn that light sword.

Black. Unless indeed the sword is the good blade Excalibur.

White. Or the cattle come from the herds that graze the Elysian plains and are immortal.

Other Minds VII

Black. '*Are* immortal'!

White. Yes, *are* immortal. A flash reveals that the road we are on leads to Solipsism. Elijah mounts the flaming car and at that instant, in that moment, gains immortality; and we begin to see how in all the present is hidden the future, from the bird always renewed to the flower that fades so fast.

'Is now immortal', 'is deadly', 'has a soporific power', 'is a poppy', 'is a silver rose upon an azure field'—each of these is a claim about what the nature of something is at the moment the speaker speaks, yet each makes a claim about the future. Even if the exclamation 'A rose on azure' is used as no more than a description of a pattern we can see and makes no claim as to whether what we see is a flower we can pluck or a sign in heaven we can never reach, still it makes a claim about the future. For whatever you may see above there's no rainbow there if no one sees it too.

Of course there's a difference between a pattern and a poison. 'It's poison' obviously makes a claim about the future in spite of its present tense, 'Poppies' less obviously, 'A halo' or 'A rainbow' (purely visual) still less obviously. For a rainbow carries its character in its face and the more a thing does that the less does anyone who tells us that it's here make any claim about the future.

Gray. But surely the more a man's face tells us of his character the more it tells us of the future.

White. But a rainbow's face doesn't tell you of its character, it *is* its character. A man's face may tell you about his character and tell you wrong. A rainbow's face never does, never can. But this isn't because Iris is so ingenuous. However ingenuous she were she might at any time be tempted to be disingenuous. No, a rainbow's face can not mislead as to its character for this

159

best of reasons—a rainbow has no character at all or if you like
its character is its face.

Black. Surely what you are *now* saying is that 'There is a rainbow (purely visual) in the sky' does *not* make any claim about
the future. What did you mean when you said that it does? Of
course if we take a rainbow as a token of a covenant, so that a
coloured bow is not a rainbow unless there is sunshine to follow,
then 'There's a rainbow' does involve the future. But then its
character isn't its face. If 'There's a rainbow' is taken as you
have reminded us it may be taken, namely, as a statement that
there's a many-coloured bow-pattern in the sky, then surely it
becomes a statement purely about the present and not involving
the future.

White. Relatively it is a statement about the present. I mean
that in the ordinary way we should say that 'There's a rainbow'
is a statement about the present, and we should also say that it
is categorical and in these ways oppose it to such statements as
'There will be a rainbow in about five minutes' time' and 'You
will see a rainbow in five minutes' time' and 'If you look out of
the window in five minutes' time you will see a rainbow'. Even
when we have considered such statements as 'That's poison',
'That's the best steel', 'Jones is very strong', and decided to say
that these are really about the future and are really hypothetical,
we may still insist that 'There's a rainbow' is really about the
present and categorical, especially, very especially, when we
have explained that we are thinking of a use in which 'There's a
rainbow', unlike 'That's arsenic' or 'That's cheese' involves no
claims about the reactions of rats, cameras, dictaphones, or
even about what we shall smell or taste, that is, is about an
utterly ineffective and purely visual object.[1]

In spite of all this it is quite possible to think of statements
which *still less* involve anything about the future, and then one
begins to say of even the purely visual use of 'A rainbow!' that
really it involves a claim about the future. And this inclination
is increased when one sets out those features of its use which
make it different from those other, even more cautious statements, about which one feels, 'Now these really are statements

[1] Compare: 'is poisonous' is a dispositional property but 'round' and 'sweet' and
'red' are not and can be detected in *one* glance.

about the present, categorical, and such that one may know them to be true'.

We have taken a use of 'There's a rainbow' which involves no claim about what cameras or other instruments will show. You now ask, 'Isn't this a statement about the present?' Now even when only purely visual rainbows are in question one may very well say, 'There must be a rainbow', or 'There must be a rainbow somewhere', even when no one sees a rainbow. It is at once clear that this statement makes a prediction. For if some-one looks and sees no rainbow he will say, 'No, you are wrong. You look. There's no rainbow.' It is clear that this objectivity makes the statement involve a prediction. For it now involves that anyone who looks will see a rainbow. Of course this must not be taken to mean that if Jack looks and fails to see one then there isn't one there. If one thing is heavier than another then that involves that if we try them on a pair of scales the one will tip the other but if this doesn't happen when they are put on my scales it doesn't follow that the one isn't heavier than another. There may be something wrong with my scales. There may be something wrong with Jack. 'It's a cow' involves that it chews the cud but, of course, if it doesn't, then provided it gives milk, is born of cows and bears cows, it's a cow which doesn't chew the cud. Probably there's something wrong with its internal struc-ture. But possibly not—you never know—and even if there isn't it's still a cow. Here appears again how every fact is a matter of an infinite pattern of facts fading but never disappearing in the distances of Space and Time.[1]

Black. But surely the *present* existence of the rainbow isn't *constituted* by its being seen or seeable in the future.

White. Is the actual and present poisonousness of arsenic something different from the hypothetical fact about the future that if an animal takes it it will die? Is the immortality which Elijah has now gained anything more than the fact that he will not die? Is the weight of a cake or a feather a liquid hidden within it, like water in a sponge, which will cause it to depress scales in the future? Isn't it rather that the cake's being heavy, as opposed to the sponge's being heavy, just is a matter of its

[1] See R. B. Braithwaite, 'Propositions about Material Objects", *Proc. Aris. Soc.*, XXXVIII.

depressing scales and giving a feeling of tension in the muscles of
of those who lift it, i.e. feeling heavy to those who lift it? And
isn't the softness of a feather that sort of thing too? And its
whiteness.[1] Indeed the whole feather? And is our rainbow any
less a matter of what people will see if . . .?

It sounds queer to say that the giving of a gift involves the
future. If you give a man a gift of a thousand pounds at two
o'clock on Tuesday do you give it him then or not till later? For
'after all', and 'if you come to think of it,' as the philosophers
say, what you really give him is nothing but a piece of paper—a
cheque—and if it isn't honoured you didn't give him a thousand
pounds, only a worthless bit of paper. Every statement is a
cheque drawn on the bank of Time.

Black. But take the case of a man who while actually seeing a
rainbow exclaims, 'A rainbow'. Surely then his statement involves nothing about the future.

White. It involves nothing about the future only if it is used to
describe only what he can see, in other words his own sensation
at the moment. Otherwise his statement still involves claims
about what others will see if they look. In other words what
makes the statement objective also makes it predictive.

Black. Suppose that everyone who hears him is actually seeing
a rainbow as the speaker speaks and that sudden and inexplicable disappearances are the usual thing with rainbows so that
what they see or fail to see a moment later counts not at all
against their statement, 'A rainbow.'

White. Notice how in so far as for each man the statement is
less about the future it is less informative. That, however, is not
the point at the moment. The point is that for each hearer in so
far as the statement is objective for him that far it is predictive
for him. The statement is objective for each hearer while in
accepting it he is prepared for the echoes in others of his sensations of a rainbow; I mean that when he asks others, 'Do you
see a rainbow?' then he expects them to answer 'Yes'. The statement would be subjective for him if you took it as you would in
the following case: a doctor gives you a dose of a new drug and

---

[1] Whiteness and softness can be felt in a moment. But so can immortality. Maybe
behind the celestial horses Elijah *felt* immortal all the way to Heaven but so no
doubt did Mr. Walter Winans on Brighton front behind a pair of trotters.

then says, 'A purple circle, a rose on azure, a rainbow round a railway train bound for the Golden Gate', and to your astonishment he thereby describes very well the sequence of your images. His statements involve for you no predictions and therefore no predictions which for all you really know just conceivably might not be fulfilled. You know his statements to be right. But then they are just statements about what you are seeing, about your sensations at the moment he speaks. And it is precisely because they are just that that they involve no prediction and thus are known, not from the smell, not from the present, not *from* anything, but completely and thus absolutely directly, and it is just because they are known directly and without any 'knowing' what will happen *from* what is happening, that they are known without the possibility of error and thus really known.

Black. You mean that unless the hearer knows that others are seeing a rainbow then even if he is seeing one he doesn't know whether the statement, 'A rainbow', is correct unless he takes that statement as descriptive merely of his own sensation. But imagine that all the hearers are also speakers, that everyone sees a rainbow and that everyone shouts 'A rainbow' and hears everyone else shout it. Surely there is then no prediction and no possibility of error in their statements although the statements are still objective.

White. Given that the statement, 'A rainbow', is used in the way described and that it is uttered by everyone whom its use makes relevant and that each of these is seeing a rainbow then nothing in the future can make that statement false. But it is not true that each speaker is given all this. He just sees as it were a rainbow and hears as it were shouts. So that it remains true that the shout, 'A rainbow', involves for each hearer no prediction only in so far as it is descriptive for him merely of his own sensations of the moment. Does he count anything else or doesn't he? If he doesn't then the shout 'A rainbow' amounts for him to 'It will seem to you just as if there is a rainbow and just as if everybody is shouting 'A rainbow' '. If he does count something else, such as whether people are really shouting or really seeing what they say they see then 'A rainbow' means to him something real, outside his mind, and is not merely the description of the moment. But then what would this something else counting be? What, for example, is the difference between a man for whom it matters whether people really saw what they said they saw and one for whom this doesn't matter? The difference is this sort of thing. Suppose that most of those who shouted 'A rainbow' subsequently confess that they saw no such thing. When this happens one of those who saw a rainbow says, 'So there wasn't a rainbow after all. You were all lying. You were all pretending you could see a rainbow', and turning to his doctor friend he says, 'Jack, you said there was a rainbow, but it wasn't true, it wasn't real, it was only another illusion'. This is the man for whom something else counts. Another man says, 'No. All they said was true. For it meant to me just the colour and the shouting. That was there and can't be taken from me, and when like the rest I shouted "A rainbow" I was right, for that is all I meant, that there was a rainbow for me, that come what might it was a rainbow moment.' For this man nothing counts but his own vision of a rainbow and his own hearing of sympathetic shouts. The first man was one for whom not merely his own sensations but also something else counted. And we say this because he counted the confession he *subsequently* heard.

Take another case. Suppose 'A rainbow' means nothing to a man about what cameras or even other people see. It may still be more for him than a description of his own sensations of the moment. Suppose that he has been suffering from waking nightmares or that there are four or five waking nightmares from which people suffer. For each nightmare there is a dominant hallucination which appears in all its changing scenes, for one nightmare a rainbow, for another a dagger, and so on. Characteristic feelings accompany the varying patterns of scenes. Then when a man says 'A rainbow', he will say this because he sees a rainbow and takes this as the precursor of a well-known pattern of hallucinations. And he and his friends may come to use the sentence, 'A rainbow', in such a way that if the well-known pattern fails to follow they say, 'No, I was wrong, it was only a passing vision' as an alternative to 'So it wasn't real *rainbowenia*'. Under these circumstances the words 'A rainbow' have come to mean to each of them much more than a temporary sensation of a rainbow. True, the words no

longer mean to the person to whom they are addressed anything about what others may see and mean only something
about what he will see. In that way they are subjective. But
they are much more to him than a description of what seems to
him to be so at the moment and in that way they are objective.
Of course we can again reduce the claims about the future and
so reduce the risks. But again the risks don't vanish till the
claims have vanished too. Only if 'You have a cold' means
merely 'You feel now just as if you have a cold', do the feelings
you have in your nose and throat suffice to decide whether the
statement is correct or incorrect. They don't suffice to deter-
mine whether you really have a cold. And the logic of love is
the same—of real love, real hate, real understanding and real
doubt. A psychological reality is an illusion that lasts. In other
words: Statements based on introspection, statements about
one's own state of mind, when they are not descriptive merely of
one's immediate experiences, differ from statements based on
perception, statements about material things, only in the sort
of subsequent pattern that is relevant to them.[1]

Gray. But is *every* statement which goes beyond the sensations
of the moment predictive? And in particular must every statement about the mind of another, even about what *sensations*
that other person is having *at the time*, mean to a hearer something about the future? *Does* 'Smith is now in pain' mean to
Jones something about the future?

White. The actual present weight of a thing is really no more
than the fact that it will tip scales and cause certain sensations
and so on. Opium is an anodyne and its being so is no more than
the fact that it will stop pain. Arsenic is the opposite and its
being so is no more than the fact that it will start pain. The
luminosity of paint is its looking white in the dark, and the
greenness of a frock is its looking green by day and not merely
in the light by which the assistant is showing it to you. The
greenness of a thing and one's having a cold, in so far as they
are not merely matters of a thing's seeming to one at the
moment green or snuffly, involve what will happen or what
would happen if . . . And for you, in so far as Smith's pain is not
merely his seeming to you now to be in pain, to that extent Smith's

[1] Pp 125-127

pain for you involves what will happen or what would happen if . . .

We have seen this already. For in passing from a real, physical, material rainbow to a private, mental rainbow, we on the way considered the change from a non-physical and purely visual but still public rainbow into a purely private rainbow. In doing this we set out what changes a statement about what others see into a statement which is merely about what one oneself sees. For to take the statement, 'A rainbow', as one about a public, objective though not physical thing is to count against it the failure of others to see any such thing while to take it as describing a private rainbow is to count only one's own sensations at the moment. And the changes from the statement about a public rainbow, like all the others on this route to security, consisted in the reduction of claims about the future and led in this instance to the reduction of such claims to zero. The reverse of the change is the restoration of those claims.

Gray. I feel that there's trickery here and that you have slyly introduced Materialism and Behaviourism under the cloak of Idealism, Sensationism and Phenomenalism. I feel that you begged the question by slyly asking, 'Surely what makes for Jones the statement, "A rainbow", one about a public rainbow and not merely about his own sensations, is his counting against it any signs he may subsequently find of others not having seen what he saw?' The argument runs: And what do you mean by Smith's pain *for me*? And anyway, Smith's pain for him isn't merely a matter of the future. So how *can* it be for me?

White. Was what we said true? A circular proof is a valid proof. And it is not futile provided it is sly. True, a demonstrative proof decides nothing. The old difficulties about the conclusion will be there still And the better the proof the more they will reflect on the premisses. But demonstrative proof is not therefore futile. It musters for us those things which tend to make us accept the conclusion and forces us to bring out those things which tend to make us refuse the conclusion and therefore the premisses.

However, the immediate issue is not Behaviourism but Predictionism, the doctrine which Professor C. I. Lewis so well sets out in a passage including the words, 'Is it not the case that the simplest statement of objective particular fact implicitly asserts something about possible experience throughout all future time ....?'[1] The subtle and conflicting connections between what we have been saying and Behaviourism we must look into later. But the immediate issue is: Is it true that for Jones even such a statement as 'Smith is now in pain' really involves a claim about the future?

As I said, I am assuming that the mere fact that 'Smith is in pain' is categorical and about the present is not what makes you hesitate to allow that it is really about the future. After all we are no longer startled by the statement that 'Timbuctoo is now in flames' means to a man 200 miles away with a speedometer at 200 m.p.h. that if his speedometer keeps steady while his clock revolves once he will find warm ashes when he steps from his plane. We are not startled by the doctrine that what lies beyond the horizon is a special sort of future, one that comes only if we employ not only a clock but also a car or a camel.

Gray. Well, I don't know. Surely 'There is now a fire beyond the horizon' doesn't *mean* 'There will be ashes in an hour by train'.

Brown and Black. For heaven's sake don't let's drag in the puzzle about things beyond the horizon.

White. The puzzle about how we can ever know what lies beyond the horizon throws a flood of light upon the puzzle about what lies in the spiritual world behind the veil of matter. For example: Does 'There's a bonfire in Trafalgar Square' mean the same to a man on the spot as it does to one in the country? And yet they speak the same language. However, forget it if you like and remember only those many statements we have already noticed which appeared to be purely categorical and about the present and yet really involved claims about the future and consider whether we have not been right in saying that the very reasons which have made us say this of them are present to make us say this of statements about the sensations of another. Relatively to 'There will be poppies when summer comes' the statement 'Poppies' is about the present. But when we remember how 'Poppies' involves the claim that men who eat these flowers will sleep we say that 'Poppies' really involves

1 Quoted by N. Malcolm, *Mind*, January 1942, p. 20.

a prediction. If someone were to say 'Poppies' without meaning anything about their soporific powers then this reason for saying that 'Poppies' is a prediction would have gone. But others would remain. For if winds don't stir them nor mirrors reflect them they would be queer poppies. If someone were to say 'Poppies' and mean nothing about their physical effects or responses but only something about their appearance, their sensory qualities, then still more reasons for saying that he was making a prediction would have gone. But others would remain. For even if he meant to say only something about what could be seen, this would involve the claim that anyone brought to the spot would see as it were poppies. Even if we suppose that several people are on the spot and all exclaim 'Poppies', this still involves the claim that if others were brought they, too, would see as it were poppies. Of course the speakers may be gods and count no one but themselves, and then, when on seeing the poppies they cry 'Poppies', nothing but what is already so is involved in their statement. And on this account we may say if we like that at last we have a statement which really does not involve a prediction. We may notice that at the same moment we reach a statement which can't be wrong. We may notice, too, that this is because at the same moment their joint statement merely describes their joint sensation. But if we say that such a statement is not a prediction and cannot be wrong we must remember that just what made it true that while they counted others their statement was predictive, also makes it true that for any sub-group of them the statement is predictive until that subgroup decides not to count the others and thus the statement becomes descriptive merely of its sensations. And this holds when the subgroup has only one member. 'Poppies' is for him, in so far as it is not merely a description of his own sensations of the moment, a prediction. This is so whether his sensation is as of poppies or as of poppies with as it were voices crying 'Poppies'. For just as before it involved the claim that not merely did it seem to him that mirrors were reflecting poppies but that there were real mirrors really reflecting them so does it now involve the claim that not merely does it seem to him that people are seeing poppies but that there are real people really seeing them. Its involving the claim that mirrors and cameras could 'see' poppies was a complex matter made up of such things as the speaker's counting what he found when he stretched out his hand and felt no real mirror or looked and found no photograph. Likewise whether a man takes 'Poppies' to claim that other people will see poppies is a complex matter made up of such things as his counting what he finds when he stretches out his hand and feels no real people or asks, 'what do you see? and gets no answer or the answer 'Nothing'. Of course a speaker may neglect all this but just that transforms his statement into one merely about his own sensations. While it is about the sensations of others he counts all that. And while he does the statement involves a claim about the future. That is while it is a statement about what another sees it involves a claim about the future.

Therefore this as well as every other statement of fact, except one descriptive merely of one's own sensations of the moment, involves a claim about the future and therefore by our sixth discussion cannot be known.

If we now push on from Solipsism to Scepticism and see how with knowledge of the sensations of the moment we have no more reached perfect knowledge than we have made a perfect man when we have made it inconceivable that he should err, if now we see why this knowledge isn't knowledge, or, if you like, what sort of knowledge it is, then we shall see how it is as absurd to speak of knowing the feelings of another in the way one knows one's own as it is to speak of knowing the future in the way one knows the present, or the distant in the way one knows the near. If we knew the distant as we know the near it would be near. If we knew the future as we know the present it would be present. If you knew how things now seem to me in the way I know how they seem to me that would be their seeming so to you. If you knew my present sensations as you know your own they would be yours. This is not grasped only when one has not grasped what sort of knowledge one has of one's present sensations and confuses it with the knowledge one may or may not have of the sheep or teaspoons one has at the moment.

'He is in pain and knows it', and 'He is in pain but doesn't know it' are queer expressions. So is 'He fancies he's in pain'. And 'He is in pain but doesn't feel it' is a contradiction, unless a use is carefully provided.

'He is in pain but doesn't know it' is not only unlike 'He is in bed but doesn't know it' but also unlike 'He is in love but doesn't know it'. And 'He thinks he's in pain but he isn't' needs careful explanation as compared with 'He thinks he's in bed but he isn't' and even 'He thinks he's in love but he isn't'. And the consequence is that 'He's in pain and does know it' is very queer too. What would it be to be in pain and not to know it? Well of course 'I am in pain' isn't so sharply separated from 'I am in love' as this question suggests. Nevertheless we may imagine it more sharply separated so that a speaker uses 'I am in pain' or 'I have a pain in my foot', so that subsequent sensations, such as those of finding he has no foot or the sudden disappearance of the pain, are quite irrelevant. This is the use we are concerned with; for otherwise we have not got what the Solipsist would call a pure description of the sensation of the moment. The purer, the less predictive the description the queerer the question, 'What would it be like to feel pain and not know it?' or again, 'What would it be to think oneself in pain and be wrong?'

What is it to have a sensation and not know one is having it? Although this expression has not an established use it is easy to describe a use which will tempt everybody. We say: 'When I came into this room I heard a buzzing but I didn't then know I was hearing it. *Now* I do.' When we ask ourselves, 'And what's the difference?' we are apt to answer, '*Now* I am *saying* I am in pain'. I am not merely uttering the words, I also understand and accept them. I can understand the words 'I am in pain' when I am not in pain just as I can understand the words 'I am in bed' when I am not in bed. So if knowledge that I am in pain is infallible it is not infallible like necessarily true statements, which are infallible because one can't understand the words of them without their being true.

To know directly that one is in pain is to say that one is and to say it on the basis of being in pain. To know that one hears a buzzing is, on the basis of hearing a buzzing, to say that one hears a buzzing. This account of knowing and not knowing that one has a sensation fits very well with the few things we do say about this. People have said that animals feel pain but don't know it. Well, of course animals never say anything. And then a person may say to an analyst, 'I felt this ache in my chest yesterday when I mentioned ... but I didn't realize it'. And once the patient really says he has a certain feeling it is absurd to say that he has it but doesn't know he has it.

But if we use 'know that I have the sensation S' in this way we must realize that it is a queer kind of knowledge. Knowledge that jazz isn't music or that 1 plus 1 makes 2 is knowledge; but it's a queer kind of knowledge. To know that something is so, is with a proper basis to believe that it is so and be right. That is not be wrong. And to know, in the direct way we are thinking of, that one is in pain is to believe it on the basis of feeling pain. But what would it be for this belief on such a basis to be wrong? There is no answer. And thus no point in adding 'and the statement is right', no answer to 'What would it be for such a statement made under such circumstances to be right, not wrong?' We may say if we like that when a man says that S seems now to him to be P on the basis of its seeming now to him to be P then this isn't knowledge because there is no account of what it would be for him to be wrong and thus no account of what it is for him to be right—that as he can't be wrong he can't be right. Or we may say: As he can't be wrong he must be right and this is perfect knowledge. The last is a confusing way of speaking; for we use the expression, 'must be right', in quite other connections—namely where we find that a man has compelling though not demonstrative evidence that he is right. And while we talk in the same way of a man's knowledge that he is in pain we feel that this is the same sort of thing only more so. But in the cases in which the evidence is not demonstrative the whole point of adding 'he can't be wrong', 'he must be right', depends upon the non-demonstrativeness of the evidence, i.e. on the fact that he can be wrong. So if we say of a man who on the basis of feeling pain is saying he is in pain that he really knows he is in pain then we must remember that we are simply saying that he is in pain and that he is saying that he is. That is, we must realize how the nature of the possible rightness of the belief, of the statement made, and thus the nature of the knowledge, depends upon the nature of the possible wrongness and ignorance.

To put things another way: The peculiarity of statements of the sort, 'X is in pain', 'X sees as it were poppies', in short, of sensation-statements, does not lie in the fact that they can't be wrong. Even if it were a fact it wouldn't be peculiar to them for '1 plus 1 makes 2' can't be wrong. Besides they can be wrong. They can be wrong even when their subject makes them; for X may lie. True, if X having the sensation in question, says that he has it then he can't be wrong. Nor can anyone else who says the same, i.e. says that X has the sensation in question. This is not peculiar to sensation-statements. If a man who is in London says he is in London he can't be wrong. Nor can anyone else who says the same. And the peculiarity of sensation-statements does not lie in the fact that one who knows the basis of such a statement knows it's right. For if on the basis that Y is the child of a child of a child of his father's parents X states 'I have a second cousin Y' then he knows he is right. No, the peculiarity of sensation-statements lies in the fact that when they are correct and made by X then X knows they are correct. To put it shortly: the peculiarity of a statement of the form X *has S* (a sensation) lies not in the fact that given its basis it is correct nor in the fact that if X is given its basis he knows it is correct but in the fact that given its basis X knows it is correct.

To put the thing yet another way: As with every sort of statement, the peculiarity of a sensation-statement shows in the peculiarity of its basis. And this peculiarity is not safely expressed by saying that its basis is the fact it states. For this is true in a sense of a statement made on demonstrative grounds. The peculiarity of, e.g. 'I am in pain' lies in the fact that one can *not* say that its basis is knowledge of the fact it states while *yet* its basis guarantees that it is correct. One can say that the basis of a statement made on demonstrative grounds is knowledge of its basis or premiss, but here to have the basis is to *know* the premiss and so to have the basis is in a sense to know the conclusion. The charm of X's knowledge of his sensations lies in the fact that although having the basis guarantees that what is stated is so, and thus guarantees the knowledge, it yet is not identical with the knowledge. This happens because here the basis isn't knowledge at all—it is a sensation, or if you like the having of a sensation. But of course the basis guarantees the knowledge of what is expressed in the statement although the basis is not the knowledge, *only* because the knowledge is no more than the basis plus the statement. This is another way of saying that to know one is in pain is to say on the basis of pain that one is in pain.

In consequence of all this if someone says to me, 'At last I have found something I really know—not merely something I would know if I knew something else and not a mere tautology. At last I really know a real truth. For I know I feel a doubt-ache, I know I feel pain, I know there is a smell of poppies—at least to me there is'—then I reply, 'Quite so. But why do you say "at last" as if you had gained what you first tried to reach by imagining a man to have more and more basis for saying "Poppies" and then tried to reach by making him claim less and less with "Poppies". You say: When it looks to me as if a man is eating poppies and I claim that he will fall asleep I know I am right, or at least if I claim merely that here's a man eating poppies I know I am right, or at least if I claim merely that here's something which looks like a man eating poppies I know I am right, or at least if I claim merely that here's some-thing which looks to me like a man eating poppies I know I am right.'

In all the cases except the last the connection between the conditions stated and the consequence, 'I know I'm right', is dubious. This is why each is followed by 'At least . . .', and then a statement in which the connection is less dubious. In the last the connection is not at all dubious. And it is easy to see why. The reason is the usual one, it is that the consequent now adds nothing. And it is easy to say why it adds nothing. 'X knows that S is P' if (1) he says that S is P, (2) he has a basis for what he says, and (3) he is right, i.e. S is P. Now in all the if . . . then statements above the antecedent provides for conditions (1) and (2), and therefore the consequent adds something only while 'I am right' adds something, and this adds something only while 'I am not wrong' adds something. But 'I am not wrong' adds nothing when it has been said that I say 'S seems to me P' on the basis that S seems to me P. For what would it be to be wrong under these circumstances? If on the basis of a sensa-tion of pain I say I have a sensation of pain then what would it be for me to be wrong?

Brown. But surely a man may misdescribe his own sensations?

White. There is a sort of way in which a man may be wrong

about his sensations and this yields a sort of way in which he may be right. Indeed our confusion about the knowledge which a man has of his sensations of the moment is due not only to our losing hold of the connection between the possibility of being right and the possibility of being wrong, and not only to the fact that statements about his immediate experience are not sharply separated from other statements about his states of mind at the moment, which statements can be wrong, but also to the fact that even statements about his immediate experiences can have a sort of wrongness, and so a sort of rightness.

True, when 'I feel a pain in my foot' or 'I see a rainbow' have become merely reports of sensation they have become exclamations in all but the indicative shape of the sentence used. But an exclamation can be inappropriate, and so be wrong and if you like false. So if someone says 'Surely a man may misdescribe the sensation he is having?' the answer is 'Certainly—but notice, don't forget, that misdescribing has become no more than mis-naming, and not misnaming in the way in which I misname Jack when I call him Alfred, thinking him to be Alfred, but in the way in which knowing him to be Jack I call him Alfred, thinking his name is Alfred *or not caring a damn what his name is*.

Because in such a case I can be only verbally wrong it is tempting to say that I am making a verbal statement. And in so far as I am making a statement at all by calling him 'Alfred' or saying 'Ow!' I am making a verbal statement to the effect that this sound is appropriate But the fact is I am not saying of a sound which in fact is inappropriate (or when I am 'right' appropriate) that it is appropriate; I am using a word which in fact is inappropriate (or when I am 'right' appropriate) inap-propriately (or when I am 'right' appropriately). What fixes whether I speak appropriately or not is the same as what fixes whether the statement that the word I use is appropriate, is true or false. The facts which make the verbal statement false and unacceptable make the exclamation 'Alfred' or 'Ow!' or 'I am in pain' inappropriate and misleading to others though not to the speaker. Or if you like they make the exclamations 'Alfred!' and 'Ow!' inappropriate and the 'statement' 'I am in pain' 'false'. But if you speak like this it will be very necessary to remember that for the speaker 'I am in pain' cannot be wrong in two ways like 'Here is Alfred' said of a figure in the mist, which may be wrong because Alfred isn't the right name *or* because the figure isn't the man the speaker thinks it is.

If we wish to use 'wrong' so that a man is wrong if he says 'I see as it were a rabbit' when he ought to have said 'hare' or when he says 'Ow!' when he ought to have said 'Psha!' then if we want a case where he is making a statement which he can *know* to be right we must take the case in which he is not claiming to speak appropriately, i.e. doesn't count anything he subsequently discovers as to how people use the words he has used.

Gray. Have we such a case when people play the game of giving 'appropriate' names to passers-by, or when one says 'The Union Jack is really a sort of Stars and Stripes', or when Mr. Nash calls his picture which the crude might describe as book-cases in the clouds by the more penetrating name, 'The Mansions of the Dead'?

White. No—even these don't do. For such 'statements' may be winners. And by the same fact may be losers. For if people don't 'see it at all' even when one says You see here, from the centre, spreads the star, here, round the outside are the stripes', or Mr. Nash says 'You don't feel these cold and hopeless but untroubled spaces?' then the speaker loses. Of course Mr. Nash may reply, 'I never expected anyone else to feel the same as I', and then he can't be wrong because they don't. He may even not expect that he himself will want to give the same name tomorrow. Even so, if, after he has said 'The Mansions of the Dead' in front of his picture, we ask him, 'When you spoke you felt that that was the appropriate title, didn't you?' and he replies, 'No, not at all', then we shall protest saying, 'But you spoke as if you felt that title appropriate'. If we wish to avoid even this sort of wrongness then he must not when he speaks be taken to be claiming appropriateness for his air of finding an appropriate name nor even to be claiming appropriateness for his air of naming. Appropriateness and inappropriateness, whether of the words in the sentence or of the 'sentential' air, whether relative to the practice of others or the speaker's own practice, mustn't be claimed. Only then will it be true that the utterance's context in time can never be bad for it. The 'speaker's' feelings make him utter a certain sound—like an infant's first whimper. The infant can't be wrong. But then also he is not knowing anything. For to know implies being right and being right is not merely not being wrong. It involves making a claim and not being wrong. It we choose to say that an infant when it's whimpering knows it's in pain then we must remember that to say that it knows it's in pain is to say that it's in pain and whimpering.

Of course there is a difference between the new-born infant and the philosopher who, having searched for something to say which couldn't go wrong, fixes his attention on a patch of colour or on a feeling in his head and says 'Wuf—there I can't be wrong over that'. About the philosopher there lingers the air of using language, especially if he says 'This is wuf', though of course he might just as well say 'Wis is thuf'. We may say if we like just because of the pattern of sound and the serious air, that he is making a statement.

But it isn't a statement. What is now more than ever apparent is that if, and in so far as, a statement is a statement then and that far it's a prediction. Which is only to be expected. A banknote means nothing to a baby. But it does to me. I cling to it, anticipating champagne or seats at the cinema. It's the same with a cheque, a ticket and a statement. And *what* they mean to me is a matter of *what* they lead me to anticipate—much or little, this or that, Bethnal Green or Central Park.

Black. People sometimes say, 'I know it means nothing—but say it—it means a lot to me'. And florists advise us to say it with flowers. And flowers aren't promises.

White. Nor are they statements—unless they are roses in Spain, when again they are promises. As to other flowers. Though they aren't statements they wouldn't mean so much while meaning nothing if they weren't wrong in certain contexts and right in others. But no context can make the philosopher's statement wrong. So far from being a statement it's not even an exclamation, not even an exclamation in his own language.[1] It is only an 'exclamation' in his own 'language' *of the moment*. Or if you like it is an *absolute* exclamation. The name

---

[1] People who have heard Wittgenstein will know how much this about such a sentence saying nothing comes from him.

is a good one because it suggests that it is that sort of utterance which remains when we have removed more and more and finally all those features of exclamations which permit us to say that they are still a sort of statement. These features had to go because they are the very ones which compel us to allow that a speaker who makes one can be wrong in a sort of way and so doesn't altogether know that he is right. It is better not to call them statements, for then, intoxicated with the fact that made under the prescribed circumstances they can't be wrong, we are apt to forget that though we have gained on the roundabouts what we've lost on the swings we have also lost on the swings what we've gained on the roundabouts.

If we insist on calling such extremely out of the way utterances statements and descriptions we needn't be surprised to find that they logically can't be wrong, and we must remember that just this is what we mean by saying that they are logically bound to be right. If we call a 'walk over' a race we needn't be surprised that there are races on which one can't lose. But it will then be well to remember that this is all we mean when we say there are races on which one is bound to win. I prefer to say that a 'walk over' is not a race or that there are races on which one can neither win nor lose.

It is inappropriate to be surprised by the fact that there are pairs of numbers such that when the first is added to the second the sum is no greater than the first, once we have said that 0 is a number.

It is the same with statements of the form *If S then P*, such as 'All men are mortal' or 'With a movable pulley W will balance $\frac{1}{2}$W' or 'No statement can be really known to be true'—they become more really knowable, more necessarily true, the fewer future facts can make them fail and they become quite knowable and quite necessarily true only when no future fact can make them fail. This is so when what makes the speaker call a thing S makes him call it P, that is, they may be reached by increasing what is given in S or reducing what is claimed in P until these are equal. And then the statement is a tautology. At the moment a statement becomes a necessary one, i.e. such that wrong or right it can't be wrong in the way that a contingent statement is, that moment it can't be right in the way that a contingent statement is. Of course if we call it wrong when the speaker's use of 'S' and 'P' is eccentric then we can call it right when it isn't. There is here again an inclination to identify a statement in which words are used as others would or as they wouldn't use them with the verbal statement that others would so use those words. The cause for this is again a grammatical muddle. What makes the verbal statement false makes the necessary statement eccentric, i.e. wrong in the way in which it can be wrong. Likewise for right.

Another point from the categorical series is reflected here. If we wish to avoid calling one who makes a necessary statement wrong just because he is eccentric, we may say that he is right in his own language or we may choose a speaker who is claiming to be right only in his own language. Such an utterance we may call a *private* tautology. If we wish to avoid his being wrong on account of eccentricity relative to his own language we shall have to say, 'He was right in the "language" he was speaking at the moment he was speaking', or we must choose a speaker who is 'claiming to be right' only in the 'language' he is speaking at the moment he is speaking, i.e. disregarding not only others but himself at other times. This is an *absolute* tautology. And about such a statement the speaker knows indeed that there can be no mistake. Here again is perfect knowledge, and here again the absolute exclamation. The route is different but the journey's end the same.

Conditional or categorical, critical or factual, necessary or contingent, public or private, about others or about oneself, about what is or about what seems, the same principle holds: No stakes, no winnings. Like the man with the rainbow-moment, we reach at last a place where Time and Chance can do no more. But alas too late. For the moment that security is reached that moment it is worthless.

Other Minds VIII

Gray. This result is quite absurd. You profess to have shown that, apart from mathematical truths, no man knows anything except his own sensation of the moment. But your whole proof has rested upon the fact that even in those cases where we should say that a man has the best of reasons for making a statement it is nevertheless *possible* that he is wrong. This fact does not lead to your conclusion except upon the assumption that if a man really knows that something is so then it is *impossible* that it isn't so. And as Mr. Norman Malcolm has explained in an article called 'Certainty and Empirical Statements',[1] this assumption though true in one sense is false in another. Consider the use of 'impossible' in which when someone points to Jones who has, unknown to me, undergone a severe operation and says, 'That's Jones', I reply, 'Impossible'. Here, for 'Impossible' I would readily substitute 'It can't be', 'It isn't'. In this sense of impossible it is true that if a man knows that something is so then it is not possible that it isn't; for it is absurd to say 'I know he is in but it's possible he isn't in', and it is absurd to say 'Henry knows he is in but it's possible he isn't in'. But it is not true that if a man knows that something is so then it is *logically* impossible that it is not. To say 'then it is logically impossible that it is not so' is to say 'then it is self-contradictory or absurd to say that it is not so'. Now it is not only not true but absurd to say that if a man knows an empirical proposition, *p*, then not-*p* is self-contradictory or absurd. For this implies that if a man knows an empirical proposition then it is not empirical.

Black. The first thing that disturbs me about what Mr. Malcolm says is that a philosopher who says 'If a man knows that something is so then it is logically impossible that it isn't' is speaking the truth. He wouldn't be if he meant what Malcolm says he means. It must therefore be perfectly proper to mean

[1] *Mind*, January 1942.

something different from what Malcolm says he means. And it is. If I remember that I had eggs for breakfast then it is logically impossible that I didn't have eggs for breakfast, although it is not true that if I remember that I had eggs for breakfast then the statement 'I had no eggs for breakfast' is self-contradictory. And if a man is drunk then it is logically impossible that he is sober. In general: Whenever we may say 'It is logically impossible that *p* and not-*q*' we may also say 'If *p* then it is logically impossible that not-*q*', without meaning that not-*q* is self-contradictory. It can't be true that you know you had eggs when you didn't. In logical language this can be put: It is logically impossible that both (i) X knows that S is P and (ii) S is not P. And this may be put: If X knows that S is P then it is logically impossible that S is not P. This is the principle which philosophers have used to prove that we never do and never can know an empirical fact, and whether they have used it well or ill the principle is correct.[1]

Gray. Malcolm might reply, 'I am obliged to you for providing a premiss from which it is even more plausible to suppose that philosophers have mistakenly stepped to their mistaken conclusion that if a man knows that something is so then it is logically impossible that it is not, in the sense that its denial is in itself logically impossible. I am the first to recognize the importance in philosophy of giving the right account of how a mistake was made, but I must now insist that I was right in saying that sceptical philosophers arrive at their absurd conclusions that we do and can know nothing, because of confusions about the use of 'possible'. I do not allow that the confusion I pointed out plays no part, but I am prepared to allow that the one you have pointed out plays much more part. Indeed this is what I now wish to insist upon. Philosophers have argued: If a man is to know that *p* then it must be logically impossible that not-*p*, i.e. not-*p* must be logically impossible, i.e. not-*p* must be self-contradictory. But when *p* is an empirical proposition this is never true—never, not however favourably placed we imagine the man to be. Therefore no man ever knows an empirical proposition.'

Black. This is still not a fair account of what sceptical philo-

[1] Malcolm at some places says this.

sophers have done. The confusion between 'If X knows that *p* then it is impossible that not-*p*' and 'If X knows that *p* then not-*p* is impossible' is easy to fall into, I allow. And it is partly from this cause that philosophers have said so confidently, 'Actually, whenever a man claims to know that *p* it is not impossible that not-*p*'. But what they really wanted to say was this: (i) If a man knows that something is so then it is impossible that it is not so. (ii) Actually, whenever it is claimed that man knows that something is so, for all he really knows it may not be so. Therefore, actually, no man ever knows what he claims to know.

Gray. But in his second premiss the Sceptic begs the whole issue, since if the claim is that Henry knows that S is P then to assert that for all Henry knows S may not be P is to assert that Henry doesn't know that S is P, since if among the things that Henry knows were included the proposition that S is P then it would not be the case that for all he really knows S may not be P.

Black. You haven't understood what the Sceptic means by 'really knows'. When a man says that S is P or that he knows that S is P, as for example that there is a rat in the room, he always bases his claim on other statements such as 'I can smell one can't you?' i.e. we all smell a ratty smell, 'I can see one can't you?' i.e. we all see a ratty sight. In support of his claim this is all he does offer, this is all he can offer. 'Now', says the Sceptic, 'what men know of this sort of thing as a basis for such a claim as "There's a rat in the room" or "I know there's a rat in the room", never suffices for that claim. Therefore their knowing what they do in the way of such statements as "I can smell a rat", "You can smell a rat", never constitutes their knowing that a rat is present. Of course there is a sense of "I smell a rat", "I see a rat" which entails the presence of a rat and in which to see a rat is to know that a rat is before one, just as there is a sense, and that the most usual, in which to remember an incident implies its occurrence and in which to remember an incident is a way of knowing that it took place. But this is not the sense in which "I smell one", "I see one", provides a basis for "I know there's a rat in the room".' If when the Sceptic asks, 'How do you know there's a rat in this room?' you reply, 'I can see one and it follows from this that there is one and that

I know there is', he will simply say, 'Let me put my question so as to exclude this irrelevant answer of yours. How do you know you see a rat? How do you know you smell a rat?' To avoid this questioning of your basis you must use 'I can smell one' so that you are giving the same answer as one who says 'From the smell'. (Compare 'from the feel in my bones I know I have a cold'—or malaria.) If a man says 'That's a Tetrarch colt' and you say 'How d'you know?' and he says 'I can see it is', then there is (i) a sense of 'I can see it is' from which 'That's a Tetrarch colt' follows, but, *ipso facto*, this is a sense in which 'I can see that's a Tetrarch colt' is open to every source of doubt to which 'That's a Tetrarch colt' is open. There is (ii) a sense of 'I can see it is' in which this means 'From the look of it' or 'From its colour and conformation'. In this sense it gives the basis of the claim 'That's a Tetrarch' without including that claim. But unluckily it at once becomes possible to say, 'For all you really know it's not a Tetrarch'. And from this it is very tempting to step to 'You don't really know it's a Tetrarch'. The temptation is less when the play on 'know' is removed. But it remains even when the matter is put more fairly in the form, 'For all your experience of colour and conformation amongst thoroughbreds and for all you can see and feel of the colour and conformation of this colt he may not be a Tetrarch so you don't really know he's a Tetrarch'. The temptation is less now that the play on 'know' is removed. But it is still strong. For if his past experience and present data don't guarantee the expert's claim and he has no other evidence then he is as surely betting on a pedigree when he says 'That's a Tetrarch' as he is betting on a performance when he says 'That's a winner'. All he really knows is that it's grey and that all the grey thoroughbreds he has seen and heard of have been Tetrarchs. But knowing this doesn't constitute knowing that it's a Tetrarch. Is what he referred to about himself when he said he knew that the colt before him was a Tetrarch something other than or more than his possessing the admittedly convincing evidence which he has? If so *what* is this something more? If not he must allow that he didn't know that the colt was a Tetrarch, that it was merely highly probable on the basis of what he did know.

In just the same way whenever a man claims to know that

there's a rat in the room his past experience and what he knows in the way of 'I can smell a rat', 'I can see a rat', never constitute his knowing what he claims to know, and there's nothing else about him, nothing over and above his experience and his smelling this and feeling that, which constitutes his knowing. It's that or nothing which is the reason for saying 'He knows', and that is not enough.

White. This argument is extremely compelling. There are two curious points. One is that the bloodstock expert will answer, 'I don't care what you say, I know that's a Tetrarch. What'll you take about it?' Is he misunderstanding the issue? Weren't we doing philosophy? Can it be appropriate to ask a price about a philosophical issue? The second point is another aspect of the first. When the Sceptic says 'We never *do* know' is his only reason that we never *could* know? Is what he says not only true but necessarily true?

Brown. Never mind the curious points. Is the argument sound or isn't it? I believe that one of its premisses is false. For it isn't true that when a man says 'There's a rat in the room' then there is nothing about him relevant to this claim except his past experience and what he now smells and sees and feels. For he not only knows what pattern his sensations have taken in the past and what patterns they are taking at the moment, he also knows a lot about what patterns they will take if this or that occurs. If a child who has been burnt sees a fire he knows what he will feel if he tries to hold the flames, and a dog which smells a rat knows what to expect when you lift the straw. From the pattern of its sensations in the past a creature is prepared for its present sensations to continue on this pattern and not on that. And to know how the pattern will continue is to know that a rat is before one.

White. There are sceptics whose scepticism arises from not accepting your last step, from denying that even an infinite knowledge of the actual and potential patterns of appearance gives knowledge of reality. These are those whose scepticism goes when and if they grasp what sort of difference of meaning there is between, on the one hand, statements about physical objects, causal relations, and minds, and, on the other hand, statements about their manifestations. These sceptics do not say that we do not know *any* empirical proposition, *any* matter of fact, but only that we know *only* those about how things will *seem* to us. It is with a wider scepticism that we are now concerned. This scepticism has a different source, namely the denial that from the present we can know *any*thing about the future. Sceptics of this sort say, 'You may say if you like that knowledge is possible at the point of infinity, and that when time and with it distance is no more then error will have become impossible. For then the objective will have vanished into the subjective, the subjective into the objective, and we shall know not through a glass darkly but face to face. But this way of describing our ignorance by talking of knowledge in an impossible situation doesn't affect our claim that no man knows anything. You are quite right when you say that when a man claims to know that there's a rat in the room then there's a great deal besides his past and present sensations which is relevant to his claim since there is a great deal about what sensations he will get if this or that occurs, which is relevant to his claim. Where you go wrong is in saying that he *knows* these things about his future sensations. These things about what he will see or hear if this or that occurs are not things which he claims to know directly. On the contrary if asked how he knows these things he will offer just the very same reasons he offered for "There's a rat in this room". And these reasons no more constitute knowledge of his claims about his future sensations than they constitute knowledge of the presence of a rat.

'So once more we say: When a man claims to know that there is a rat in the room or, if you like, that things will continue to seem just as they should if there were a rat in the room, nothing beside his past experience and present sensations counts. Maybe he takes sugar in his tea, maybe he's first-rate at snooker, but that's beside the point. Everything's beside the point except his smelling the smell he smells and his being such an expert ratter. That's why when he snuffles and wags his tail we say, "He knows there's one there, good old Trusty, he knows". But his smelling the smell he does and his having had the experience he has had don't *constitute* his knowing that there's a rat there or that things will continue to seem just as they should if there were. For his past experience and present sensations are compatible with any

future pattern and with their being no rat there while knowledge that a rat is there is not. Therefore all about him that
counts is not enough and he no more knows that the rat is a rat
than the bloodstock expert knows that the grey is a Tetrarch or
the doctor that the patient has chronic anaemia.'

Gray. And yet undoubtedly men and dogs often know that
there's a rat in the room. And we should often say, 'I knew
he was a Tetrarch the moment I set eyes on him', and we should
say, 'The doctor knew at once that there was no hope'.

Besides, these cases are different. If someone says of the bloodstock expert that he doesn't know that the colt is a Tetrarch I
understand very well what is meant. What is meant is that he
hasn't done all he might have to make sure. He has looked at
the colt but he hasn't written to Weatherbys, and so on. And
when someone asks me, 'But does the doctor really know?'
again I understand very well what is meant. It is not merely
the academic point that always anything *may* happen, it is the
point, 'Do the doctors know in such a case?', in other words,
'Is this doctor's prediction well supported, that is as well or
nearly as well as an astronomer's prediction?' But if someone
asks, 'Do you know that glass is fragile, that fire burns, that
cheese is soft?' i.e. 'Do you know when you see a glassy looking
thing that it is fragile or, if you like, that it is glass? Do you know
when you see as it were a fire that it will burn, i.e. that it is fire?
Do you know when you see a *cheesy* looking thing that it is
cheese?' then I don't know what he means unless he wishes to
contrast my case when I merely see cheese, with my case when
I see, touch and taste it all at once. But if that *is* what he is
doing then, though it seems to me that he is being eccentrically
strict, I can still understand him, I still know what he would
call knowing.

But if he says that even when I am seeing, touching and
tasting cheese still I don't know that there is cheese in my mouth,
then I don't know what he means. Then I am no longer surprised that he says not merely that we don't know but that we
never can know. For then we cannot conceive of what it would
be to know. It now isn't merely that the use of 'know' has been
been eccentrically narrowed, it has been narrowed to nothing.
Further, it has been made a *self-cancelling* expression like the

expression 'ride a motor cycle' as used by someone who is determined to use 'ride' only where what you ride is something living. Here the Sceptic has decided to use 'know that S is P' only when nothing not entailed by what he directly knows and therefore nothing in the future, can shake S is P, while like the rest of us he will not call S is P a 'statement of fact not about the speaker's sensations' unless it makes a claim about the future.

Black. Not at all. Allow me to explain. You say that if when you are looking at a cheese someone says to you, 'You don't know whether there is cheese before you', you understand. You understand even when he asks you while you are looking at the cheese in a well-lighted larder, not a dim séance room.

Gray. Certainly. He means I am not like one who is eating the cheese, in short that I am not tasting cheese.

Black. Exactly. You don't say that you can see a willow pattern when all you can see is a Chinaman on a bridge, because there's more to a willow pattern than that. To see a Chinaman on a bridge is not sufficient because you may look further and fail to find the necessary pagoda and birds. Of course, if you lift the cloth which covers half the plate and see at once the Chinaman, the bridge, the pagoda and the birds then at once this is enough to make it true that you are seeing a willow pattern. When you see all the parts of the pattern that you claim exists when you say, 'A willow pattern', then you see a willow pattern, but not before. Likewise if you see a dancer do a 'natural pivot turn' and then look away because someone drops a plate, you don't say you saw him do a 'running right-hand turn'—whether he in fact made that pivot turn the first part of a running right or went on in some other way. If, and only if, you did not turn your head but saw the whole of that pattern in time which constitutes the running right-hand turn do you say, 'I saw him do a running right-hand turn'. Now when a man claims to see a rat all he really sees is perhaps one side of its head or at best the whole of one side of it. And this is not to really see a rat, any more than seeing a Chinaman and a bridge is really seeing a willow pattern, or seeing a natural pivot is seeing a running right. Of course while Nature keeps orderly you may very reasonably guess that here's a willow pattern, especially, perhaps, if what you do see is blue and has a certain glaze; and if the dancer were very regular you might very reasonably guess that this natural pivot is the first part of a running right; and if you see the head of a rat or the whole of one of its sides then, because Nature is orderly about these things, you may very reasonably guess that here is a rat. But all this is guessing and not really seeing and knowing.

Gray. But here you make the *same* mistake as you made in saying that since it is perfectly natural and intelligible to say of someone who merely looks at an animal and says, 'It's a Tetrarch', that he doesn't really know it's a Tetrarch so it is perfectly natural and intelligible to say of someone who looks at and tastes a food and says, 'It's cheese', that he doesn't really know that it's cheese. It is true that it is perfectly natural and intelligible to say of someone who sees only part of a willow pattern that he doesn't see that willow pattern or know that it is before him. But this is just because there is something which you would call his really seeing a willow-pattern as opposed to only half seeing it. The running right-hand turn looks more like what you want because there is an inclination to say that it is impossible to see a running right-hand turn because by the time you are seeing its last phase its first has died away, while yet it is perfectly natural and intelligible to say of someone that he didn't really see a running right, only something from which he might reasonably guess at a running right. But if we speak more carefully we shall see that this, so far from supporting the intelligibility of the impossible, shows up its unintelligibility. For what made intelligible our statement 'You didn't really see a running right?' It was the statement 'you turned your head away', that is it was the understanding that if you had not turned your head away you would have seen the running right. The moment it is suggested that even if you hadn't turned your head and so had seen the suitable later phases, you still would not have seen a running right, then at once we ask, 'What d'you mean? Why not?' The moment it becomes impossible, that moment it becomes unintelligible—its name becomes not merely an unexplained expression but an unexplainable one. For suppose that it is merely unexplained and that the speaker, the Sceptic, can explain as follows: 'It wasn't done in a room with mirrors', or 'It was done so slowly that your memory of its earlier phases could not be relied upon by the time you were seeing its last phase'. At once we may mend matters. We fix the mirrors and raise the tempo to 6o bars to the minute.

The Sceptic may say, 'Even so you had to rely on your memory, it wasn't done in an instant'. If he says this his demand is plainly self-contradictory—his language inexplicable. For he he will not speak of a running right and nor will we unless upon a certain movement (a natural pivot) *succeeds* another (a running zigzag) and he will not speak of seeing or really seeing unless what is seen is instantaneous, that is not a matter of one thing succeeding upon another.

But the Sceptic may reply more subtly. He may say, 'I don't demand that the turn should be done in an instant, that is plainly self-contradictory. But even at 6o bars to the minute it takes too long.' Suppose that however fast the tempo a professional can be found who can do the turn at that tempo. Neglecting for a moment the unintelligibility of this supposition, imagine that every time we increase the speed the Sceptic says 'It's still not fast enough'. Then the situation is a curious one and of great importance for philosophy. For we cannot say that the Sceptic is making a self-contradictory request, that he is lamenting that parallel lines never meet. It has been said, e.g. by Wisdom, that that is the sort of lament he is making. But he isn't. He would be if he were asking to see in an instant a running right-hand turn done in an instant. But he allows that that is self-contradictory. Can we say that his expression, 'to really see a running right' though not self-contradictory,[1] has no meaning? But he explains its meaning by explaining with a perfectly intelligible phrase, namely 'too long', how what he wants differs from what actually happens. So we cannot quite say that it has no meaning. On the other hand, there is something about his explanation which I feel inclined to express by saying that it is 'never completed'. However, I don't wish to insist that that epithet either is properly applied here. What I mean by it here is that his explanation is not completed like it would be if, at last, when the tempo had reached 100 bars to the minute and we had

---

[1] I am aware that 'self-contradictory' "properly" applies to predicates and propositions, and to avoid grammatical confusion, it is safer to use of symbols the word 'self-cancelling'. But this is a new word and so has no life.

turned to him asking, 'Is that fast enough?' he had replied, 'Yes'. But as he never does this his explanation suggests that not until the complaint, 'took too long', becomes impossible will we reach what he calls 'really seeing an event'. And this complaint becomes impossible only when the event takes no time, i.e. is not an event. In other words he speaks *in accordance with* the principle which he allows is self-contradictory. Because of this I say that his account of really seeing an event is *surreptitiously* self-contradictory.

Black. I quite agree that such a Sceptic is not only altering, narrowing, our actual use of 'see an event' but introducing an inapplicable, impossible, self-contradictory use. And I see how by proceeding subtly he conceals this. And I confess that I haven't emphasized the fact that actually we speak of seeing a pattern and of knowing that a pattern is before us when we don't see quite the whole. The Sceptic if you like misrepresents and narrows our actual use of 'know'. But the use he recommends is 'the actual use, only more so', and it is a perfectly intelligible and explicable use.

Actually, I know, we say of a man who sees merely the head of a rat that he sees a rat, and knows that there's a rat in the room. But I must remind you that we are inclined to say of a man who sees the whole of a rat, or if you like the whole of one side of a rat, that he knows better still that there's a rat in the room. So one thing we may count against saying that a man knows that there's a rat in the room is the little he can see of it. And there's no sharp line between regarding the tail or even the head of a rat as insufficient for knowledge and regarding as insufficient everything short of seeing the whole or, if you like, the whole of one side of the rat, with mirrors arranged for its other sides while smelling and tasting and touching it and hearing its well-known voice. Consequently, while any of these possibilities remains unrealized there lingers in all of us an inclination to say and feel that we don't really know that a rat is a rat until and even when we are shaking it like a dog. We must say this if we wish to use 'know' *consistently*, that is, so that what in one degree we count against its application we count in all degrees. Such a use is eccentric but entirely understandable. It isn't merely that one wishes for a convenient and pretty notation, it is that one feels, and rightly, that a notation in which one speaks as if there is a difference in kind when there is only a difference in degree has something of a lie in it—like there is in speaking of those we love and those we hate when there is so much hate in so much love.

Brown. But after all when this has been realized—for example, how much we hate those we love—it is necessary to remember that the distinction we marked with our old notation was a distinction. Maybe Anna Karenina soon hated Vronsky but even on that last morning her feeling for him was very different from that of Irene for Soames Forsyte.

Gray. It isn't merely that the Sceptic by narrowing the use of 'know' is robbing us of our means of marking a distinction we need to mark, it is that he is narrowing the use of 'know' to nothing, narrowing it so that 'knowledge of matter of fact' becomes a self-contradictory expression because part of what we look for in order to speak of 'matter of fact other than his own sensations' is included in what precludes our speaking of 'knowledge'.

Black represents himself as saying merely that one who sees only the head of a rat or merely *sees* a rat, doesn't know that a rat is before him. But really he is going much further than that. For he says that even a dog who has a rat in his teeth doesn't know that he has a rat in his teeth. What I want to insist upon is that he is there contrasting the dog with no one, that he is giving a not merely eccentric but impossible use to 'know'. Even in our strictest moments we demand only that a man should have the best basis conceivable for his claim that a certain object is before him.

Black. You mean by 'has the best basis conceivable' 'senses as much favourable to his claim as he conceivably could at a given moment'? But isn't it true that we are inclined to count also the nature of his past experience?

Gray. I confess I had forgotten for the moment that we sometimes say that a man, a doctor perhaps, doesn't *know*, not because he hasn't thoroughly investigated the case before him but because there has not been that experience of regular connection between the wild phenomena with which he is dealing, which is so necessary to the prediction of the future, however extensive our knowledge of the present. Some of us are stricter than others about this but no doubt we all of us count it. And I must explain that what I really want to say is that even in our strictest moments we demand for knowledge of a claim involving future sensation only that a man should have the best conceivable basis in past and present sensation. What I want to insist upon is that if the Sceptic demands more than this then his statement is *necessarily* true, i.e. he is remarking on the absence of the self-contradictory.

Black. But even a man who is eating a rat has not the best basis he conceivably could have for 'There's a rat in the room'. There is still evidence obtainable which he hasn't obtained—for he hasn't yet ascertained whether it bursts into flames on the way down his throat.

Gray. It is true that at the time of saying, 'There's a rat here, I know there is', there is always obtainable evidence that has not been obtained, because it is always true that if the speaker waits he can gain more evidence for his statement. But this doesn't prove that he could have done better than he did at the time he spoke. What I mean is this: There is an important difference between the sense in which a man who might have been touching a rat as well as looking at it might have had evidence which he hasn't and that in which this is true because he doesn't yet know whether it will burst into flames on the way down his throat. The point is contained in the advertisement 'That's Shell, that was', in which the speaker is understood to see a car appear and pass while he speaks.

Black. I agree that we count in favour of saying that a man knows that there is a rat in the room his having the best basis he conceivably could have up till the time of speaking—that is his *having done* all he could. But I must insist that we *also* count against knowledge the possibility of his *still doing* better. For we say of even a man who is eating cheese or drinking brandy that he doesn't know that he is eating cheese or drinking brandy *as well* as he will when he has waited a little longer to see whether it turns to ashes in his mouth or bursts into flames in his throat.

Consequently there is an inclination in all of us to say that a man knows *best* when it is no longer true that he would know *any* better if he waited *any* longer, i.e. that he doesn't really know that there is a time pattern before him until he has seen, sensed, the whole pattern or (necessarily vacuous alternative) enough of it to *deduce* the rest.

Gray. I admit the inclination, I admit that I ought not to have represented us as not even in our strictest moments counting the possibility of still doing better. But I claim that if, like the Sceptic, we yield without limit to this inclination then we have left nothing but an impossible, unintelligible, use of 'know a matter of fact'.

Black. You can always understand 'would know better if he waited longer' can't you? Well then surely you can understand 'would know no better if he waited longer'? And this expression gives the nature of real knowledge.

Brown. I feel this is a very clear explanation.

Gray. Exactly. You feel that the Sceptic is contrasting the engineer, the dog and the beer drinker, not with any mortal being but with one who waits till the end of Time, or better, since the memory of so old a man might begin to fail, sees in one moment the panorama of all moments from all places and can already hear the whimper with which the world ends.[1]

Black. No, no. I don't want to talk of knowing the future as one knows the present: that is as absurd as talking of knowing the distant as one knows the near or of seeing in the dark as well as in the light. And to talk of knowing the whole future as one knows the present is, if possible, more absurd. What I said was this: We in fact speak of a man's knowing that, e.g., what he is drinking is beer, when we should also say that he would know better if he waited to see a little more of what is going to happen. I concluded that a man knows *best* when his knowledge has none of this defect which, when present in some degree, makes us say that he will know better when it is present in less degree; that is, I do not say a man has perfect knowledge when although his claim involves the future he can deduce this future from the present; nor do I say that he has perfect knowledge when all claims about the future have been subtracted from his claim so that it comes to nothing; but I do say that he would have perfect knowledge if he made his claim and then waited till it was not true that he would do better by waiting longer.

[1] With apologies to Mr. T. S. Eliot.

Gray. And what I say is that just as 'makes an objective claim purely about the present' hid a contradiction, just as 'deduce the future from a statement purely about the present' hides a contradiction, just as 'sees the future as he sees the present' hides a contradiction, so does 'waits till he really knows about the future or about an animal or a thing' hide a contradiction.

White. But isn't this exactly what Black is saying? You are saying that the opposite of that ignorance which Black says is inevitable, is impossible.

Gray. I want to do two things. First, I want to get it quite out in the open that Black is not stating a mere matter of fact when he says that we can never know anything about the future or about things and animals. I want this out in the open because with such statements as 'All knowledge is imperfect', 'We can never know anything about the future', 'We can never know that what seems to be a so and so is a so and so', 'We can never really see an event', 'We never see a perfect circle', 'We never really know what is happening beyond the horizon', 'We can never see in the dark like we can in the light', 'All love is imperfect', although it is possible to take them so that their contradictories are self-contradictory and senseless, it is also possible to take them as statements of fact, and people are often neither definitely doing the one nor definitely doing the other. Even if someone says, 'To really see a running right-hand turn done it would have to be done in no time', it is not clear that he is not saying merely that it would have to be done like a flash of lightning, which is over in no time. It is only when he rejects the best we can offer and insists with remarkable assurance that no novelty in nature will ever provide what he wants, that we begin to understand that what he speaks of is not merely a temporary accident but an eternal necessity. And at the same moment we understand why he is so confident that what he says never happens never will happen. For realizing that what he stated was for him an eternal truth and not a matter of fact was not other than the process of realizing that though there are things which if they were to happen would lead some men to say that they had seen such and such a thing done in no time, there is nothing which would induce him to do so.

Black. Just as I am now prepared to say plainly that 'We can never know the mind of another' expresses a necessary truth, so I am prepared to say plainly that 'We can never know any-thing—or anything beyond the sensation of the moment' expresses a necessary truth. It is not something that may be remedied at any time.

White. Let me understand this. You mean that when you say 'We can't know the future' you are not merely deploring the rarity or non-existence of precognition. You would say that reasonably and rightly predicting from pictures in a crystal or in one's head is not what you would call 'really knowing the future'. And when you say that we can never know the future the accent is not on 'we' is it? You mean that neither we nor the angels nor God in heaven can know the future.

Black. Well I don't know about that. Certainly I don't count precognition, that is only another form of the 'know-ledge' we already have. But I don't say that there might not be a being who, knowing in quite a different way, really knows what we can only guess.

White. Ah! Then you do not say that we can never know, you allow that some time we may know, even if you insist that we should have to change our methods and must in the process become divine. Now what would it be to know in this divine way you contemplate? You see, you sound to me like a man who says, 'There's no such thing as real love of a place'. Then we suggest this and suggest that, and he says, 'No, that's not real love of a place, we can't really love a *place*', and we say, 'I don't believe you know what you're asking for. What would you call real love of a place?' and he says, 'I mean something quite different, something different in quality', and we say, 'Do you mean love a place like we do a person', and he says, 'Yes, that's more like it, only that's not possible, is it, really? Because then the place would have to be a person', and we say, 'Well, what *do* you mean?' and he says, 'Oh, I mean something quite different, something that is real love and yet love of a place'. Oh, unknown species of love! Lost, not in Tauris and too long ago for us to well recall it, but somewhere in the labyrinths of logical space.

It is nowadays obvious to all that it is absurd to talk of know-ing a future fact like one knows a theorem, i.e. as a deduction from necessary truths. And you have said that to say that perfect knowledge is gained when we can deduce the future from the present or when we know it as we know the present is so much talk. And by now it is obvious why these things are so. It is because the ultimate species of knowledge are defined by the sorts of things known. You have indeed explained that the kind of knowledge you have in mind is the kind of knowledge we do have improved out of all knowledge. And when you say that we can't attain this improvement I am sure you don't mean that we can't for fear of becoming more than human. You mean that such knowledge is impossible to *us* because *it* is impossible.

Black. All right. But I insist that it is perfectly *intelligible* to say that neither we human creatures nor any other being can ever really know the future or that such and such a thing is before us, because we can never reach a state in which, making such a claim, we wouldn't know better whether we are right by waiting longer.

White. Let us first see what you do do with these expressions 'perfect knowledge', and 'waiting till there is no good in waiting longer'. Having ascertained the facts we can fix up the abusive and laudatory epithets later. I'm sure you are doing something with these expressions—indeed I confess I understand you, only I share with Gray the feeling that there's some *jiggery-pokery* here and that what you are doing is not what one tends to feel you are doing.

What would you call 'knowing the future as one who waits till he'd know no better by waiting longer'? Suppose I say 'This pain will last till 4 p.m. and then relief will come'. The longer I wait the better I know whether I was right; indeed until 4 p.m. it is always true that I shall know better if I wait longer. At 4 p.m., however, this is no longer so. Some people would say that by waiting this long I have gained real knowledge of the future. If you were one of these people you would be quite wrong in saying that we never can and never do gain knowledge of the future. But you are not one of them. For you, I take take it, would say that by 4 p.m. it's too late and that what I then come to know is that a statement about how I was going to feel, which I did make, has turned out correct, so that what I learn is something about the past and still the retreating veil before the future remains unpierced.

When and if you say this it becomes obvious that there is nothing we have conceived of which you would call 'real knowledge of the future', or 'being in a state in which one would know the future no better by waiting longer'. But more than this. After all we can't conceive of anything you would call 'a red Monday'. But with 'real knowledge' and 'real love' it is more than this. Real love and real knowledge are impossible but a red Monday is not. What is this more? You are not *averse* to applying the expression 'a red Monday', still less to applying the expression 'a red abracadabra'. But you are averse to applying the expression 'real knowledge'. And this aversion is not aesthetic. It arises from your education. For your education makes any attempt to apply the expression to anything, whether in actual or logical space, produce a conflict in you. Take the promising cases we imagined. Up to 4 p.m., though inclined to speak of knowledge of the *future*, you refuse to call it *real*, because improvement is possible. After 4 p.m., though inclined to speak of *real* knowledge, you refuse to call the knowledge knowledge of the *future*, and this is just because 4 p.m. is the last time referred to by the statement, 'This pain will last till 4 p.m.' It is this which makes knowledge, real knowledge, of the future, inconceivable to you as opposed to not in fact conceived of by you. And that which makes it inconceivable is that which makes it impossible.

Black. And is it the same with knowledge of things?

White. Well, is it? Suppose that one man before the start of a race points to one of the horses and says, 'That is the winner', while another man says nothing until in the final furlong one of the horses goes to the front. Another man says nothing till one of the horses has passed the post first. He is never wrong. True, he isn't what most people would hope for if you said, 'I know a man who always knows the winner'. But perhaps this is what you call 'waiting until one really knows that the thing before one is the sort of thing one says it is'. Or again, one man looking very carefully at a caterpillar and referring very carefully to his butterfly book says, 'That's a caterpillar of the Hawk moth'. Another waits till at the proper time the caterpillar has formed a proper chrysalis. Another man waits till the proper moth flies away. Perhaps this is another example

of what you would call 'waiting long enough to really know that
a statement about a thing or an animal is correct', or should we
say 'was correct'. Perhaps that's the trouble. Our cautious
friend at the races was always right. But his friends laughed at
him. And this was because of his air of doing the same as they
did, only without the defects of what they did, when really
'That's the winner' was losing more and more of its meaning as
the race went on, and he didn't speak till it had lost all its
meaning, or if you like, had become merely a description of
what they had seen and were seeing.

Black. No, my trouble is that he still has not waited long
enough.

White. You mean an objection may be lodged and sustained
against the winner, as the race cards call the horse first past the
post, and then he isn't really the winner.

Black. And even if that doesn't happen, the camera is the
only infallible way of judging a race. Besides, a man may fancy
he sees a race and then find it's all an illusion. Suppose that
abracadabras were animals which showed seriatim in their
foreheads the digits in the development of π. Then no man
would live long enough to know whether the animal before him
was a true abracadabra, i.e. to really know whether the animal
before him was an abracadabra. i.e. to *know* that the animal
before him was an abracadabra.

Now a rat is only an abracadabra with a more complicated
prognosis. So is a Hawk moth caterpillar and a winner, cheese
and beer and biscuits. True, there is a particularly striking
point in the prognosis of the caterpillar and the winner which
makes us inclined to say, 'Well, that settled, nothing further
matters'. But really there remain other predictions involved
which differ only in degree from this one, admitted on all hands
to be of the first importance.

White. I see. Your point is this: You yourself wouldn't particularly mind calling 'a statement about a thing' a statement
which made a *limited* prediction as to the future, and such a
statement could be known to be true in the way we have seen,
but what you are saying is that in fact those statements, such
as 'There's a rat in the room', 'Cheese in my mouth', 'Beer in
my throat', which we call 'statements about things and animals',

claim a temporal pattern *without end* and that you do very much object to saying that statements can be known to be correct when only a part of the pattern they imply is really known.

Black. Exactly.

White. Suppose a man says to you, 'Perfect love is impossible'. You say, 'What d'you mean?' He says, 'Love should stand the test of time, and other things being equal a love which has stood a longer test is better than one which has stood a shorter. Now, however long a love has lasted it is conceivable that it should last longer and thus be better. So, however long a love has lasted it is not perfect.' You say, 'Oh, I see'. You understand him now and understand too why he is so sure, just as you understand why a perfect map is impossible, because however large its scale it might be larger. When the pessimist says 'Perfect love is impossible' he speaks as if he is remarking on a shortcoming which he has noticed in all loves—a coming short of something he can dream of but never find. At the same time he conveys the impression that the shortcoming is inevitable. It is indeed inevitable, it is of the essence of love. Not merely of human love—for it isn't that the pessimist points to the greeds and hates that mar the loves of men so that as we mount with him his staircase to the stars we realize that when and if we reach the top storey our companions once too human will by then be too divine. It is that for him there is no top storey, so that in heaven, too, love is imperfect, and this is no accident but of the essence of love. If we mean by 'the winner' what's first past the post, it doesn't matter what objections are lodged and sustained; if we mean by 'love' what lasts a day, or three score years and ten, then perfect love is possible. But if we say 'These people have loved for a day so it doesn't matter what happens tomorrow' then the pessimist says 'That's not what I call love', and indeed he says this whenever we try to add 'so it doesn't matter what happens tomorrow' no matter how many days the love has lasted. And this procedure isn't arbitrary; may be it caricatures our actual usage but it comes naturally out of our actual usage. It is derived from our actual usage by *the consistency procedure*, that is, by counting as fatal in any degree what in a high degree we already count as fatal. True it exaggerates the way we count points in the pattern remote in time, i.e. it neglects the fact that we tend to count points in the pattern less the more remote they are in time. The patterns of things, whether rats, love or steel, not only become distorted by time and distance—our skeletons are different from ourselves —they also fade. But the fact remains that a usage of 'love' in which it is never correct to say, 'Well, it's ten, twenty, a hundred years since I said "This is love", so I was right no matter what happens tomorrow' is closely derived from our actual usage. Further, just as there is no time, say a day or a hundred years, after which events are suddenly irrelevant as to whether love *existed* before, so there is no time after which events are suddenly irrelevant as to its *quality* or perfection, and it is never true that failure of love wouldn't detract at all from that perfection and further love add to it. Now, if love isn't perfect while tomorrow can add to it and love isn't love when it can't, then indeed perfect love is impossible.

So it is with perfect knowledge of an abracadabra and a *metadrummer*, which is an animal which repeats in endless succession the digits 1, 2, 3, 4. Statements of the form, 'This is now, at t_1, a metadrummer and is saying 1', imply 'This will say 2 at t_2', 'This will say 3 at t_3', and so on without end, that is, there never comes a moment when what will be heard at the next moment is irrelevant to the original statement 'This is now, at t_1, a metadrummer'. Hence if we mean by perfect knowledge that a thing is a so and so, that that knowledge cannot be improved by waiting, and if we mean by this that there is something relevant to whether it's a so and so and still not really known because not known to the knower in the way he knows that the thing seems to be a so and so nor deducible from anything he so knows, then perfect knowledge that a thing is a metadrummer or an abracadabra is inconceivable. Put it another way. It is self contradictory that I should know perfectly now that my pen is an abracadabra. For I don't know this perfectly unless I wouldn't know it any better by waiting. Now I would know this better by waiting if there were something relevant to it which I would know better by waiting. I would know better by waiting how my pen will look ten minutes hence, since I don't know this like I know how it now looks nor can I deduce this from how it now looks. Therefore I don't know perfectly that my pen is an abracadabra unless how it will look ten minutes hence is irrelevant to whether it is an abracadabra, i.e. unless an abracadabra is not an abracadabra. Now if knowledge that a thing is an abracadabra isn't perfect while tomorrow can add to it and knowledge that a thing is an abracadabra isn't knowledge that it's an abracadabra when tomorrow can't add to it then indeed perfect knowledge of an abracadabra is impossible.

And in so far as rats, beer, cheese and every sort of animal and thing also involve endless patterns, so knowledge, real, perfect, knowledge of them is impossible, self-contradictory.

Indeed, nothing short of this would satisfy you. For you are claiming that it is not merely an accident that we have never gained real knowledge of these things but that inevitably we never shall, that such knowledge is inconceivable. You have claimed, and rightly, that this does not imply that, used as you recommend, expressions of the sort 'real knowledge of a meta-drummer', 'real knowledge of a rat' are senseless, that is, are expressions our education gives us no inclination to use or not to use. On the contrary it implies that these expressions have a meaning and that our education gives us an inclination not to use them for anything, by making their use involve a conflict of inclinations.

You want to insist too that with this strict use of 'know', with this strict use of 'wait' you are not doing something arbitrary but are saying something which is based upon and reveals our actual use of 'know' and of words for things.

And you are right. When a man holds a mug of beer in his hand we understand perfectly well what you mean if you say 'He will know still better that that beer is beer when he has it in his mouth and can feel it inside him, indeed, nowadays no one knows that beer is beer till he has done this, and strictly speaking of course this is always so, and still more strictly speaking it is still so when he has the beer inside him. We understand this strict sense of 'watches to see whether a thing, e.g. a winner, is what it seems, so long that there is no good in watching any longer', and we understand the words 'beer', 'a rat', 'an abracadabra', and we understand them in the combination, 'watches to see whether what seems to be an abracadabra is really one, and watches so long that there is no good in watching any longer'. Not only that. The expressions, even when strictly used, play a useful part, i.e. can be used in sentences with which we tell the truth, *necessary* truth. Suppose we say, 'One can never listen to a metadrummer to hear whether it is really one, so long that there is no good in listening any longer'. Now of course this sentence could be used to state a matter of fact, to contrast a metadrummer with an abracadabra in the respect that while we have never come on an animal which for ages showed the development of π and then became eccentric we have come on animals which for ages showed 1 2 3 4, 1 2 3 4 . . . and then became eccentric. But if the expressions are used *strictly* then the sentence is being used to state a *necessary* truth. It will be drawing attention to the fact that if we use words strictly then if we speak of a man's watching an animal to see whether it is really a metadrummer, so long that there's *no* good in waiting any longer then we shall be contradicting ourselves. And because such use of 'waiting till it's no good waiting longer', of 'real knowledge', of 'knowledge' and of 'metadrummer' or 'rat' are not arbitrary but derived from our actual use of these words we shall be bringing out by caricature something about our *actual* use of these words, about the connection between the essence of knowledge and the essence of metadrummers and rats.

Black. And what we are bringing out is just that which is neglected by Subjectivists, by Gray, when he says, 'When the Sceptic turns on the plain man and says, "But even when you have cheese in your mouth you don't know it is cheese", then he is suddenly correcting the plain man's application of "know" in just the case where he has been taught to say it'.

It is misleading to say that the Sceptic is saying 'Don't say "know" here' just where the plain man has been taught to say 'know'. To say this suggests that the Sceptic is like a man who having taught a child to say 'Union Jack' when both the cross of St. George, the cross of St. Andrew and the cross of St. Patrick are present, suddenly when all the crosses are there says 'No, that's not a Union Jack', or 'Perhaps that's not a Union Jack'. But the case of the Sceptic and the plain man is most importantly un-like this. True, we say to a baby 'Rats' or 'Fire' and point to the bushes blazing on either side of the path down which we are pushing his pram. He turns his head and finds the sight engaging. Next day we say 'Fire in five minutes', and he turns his head and is fed up with us when he sees no fire and he says we are liars, and we say, 'No, no. *In five minutes*', and begin counting 'One, two, three, four, five', and next day when we say 'Fire in five minutes' he counts 'One, two, three, four, five' before he takes the trouble to turn his head. The next day we say 'Fire, five miles away', he looks, sees nothing and then maybe tries counting but failing to see anything worth mentioning he begins to abuse us as before and we say 'No, no, five miles away not five minutes', and hurry him along counting 'One, two, three, four, five' and pointing to the mile stones as they flash past. Arrived at the spot we shall, if we are lucky, find the fire still burning but we may find only ashes and then we shall have to go through the business of showing the baby how fires die down to ashes and thus explaining that there was a fire here at the time we said 'A fire five miles away'.[1] If now one day when we and the baby find ashes and everything and he says 'There, I was right when I said "There is a fire five miles away" ' we turn on him and say 'You don't know', or 'You oughtn't to say "I was right" but "It looks as if I was right", you ought to say "Probably" ', then this is a typical philosophical *turning on* someone and it is true that we are refusing to let him say 'There was a fire' and 'I knew there was a fire' in a case which appears to him to be and may appear to us to be, and may in fact be, just like those cases in which before we have encouraged him to say these things. But while we have taught him that given his data that this is a flag bearing (1) the cross of St. George, (2) the cross of St. Andrew, (3) the cross of St. Patrick, nothing can be allowed to upset his conclusion, this is just what we have *not* taught him in the case of the fire. Indeed we have never set out any list of things about one time and taught him that then something about another time is true no matter what further data he ob-

---

[1] The same sort of explaining gives the meaning of 'Bob has a bee *in his bonnet*' or 'has a new engine *on the brain*', i.e. the explaining of psychological statements, though here the teaching has a double aspect: (1) we explain to the baby that he needn't expect to see an engine on Bob's head, only to hear him keep on saying, 'A new engine for Christmas', but (2) before the baby really understands we shall have to add to our explanation, 'You remember how you could think of nothing but a new wheel-barrow before your birthday'.

tains. We have taught him that everything which tells against
'That was a Union Jack' tells *equally* against 'That was a flag
with a cross of St. George, cross of St. Andrew and cross of St.
Patrick'. Now on the contrary there is *no* statement about how
things now are, i.e. seem, such that we have taught him that
everything which tells against 'There was a fire' tells *equally*
against that statement. This is what we are emphasizing when
we say 'You oughtn't to say that you know there was a fire'.

White. But we are doing this in a very confusing way, we
are not playing fair and we are suddenly altering our way of
speaking. It is true we are not as the Subjectivist suggests
breaking a definition, severing a connection between symbols
which ordinarily is absolute, infinitely strong, but we are
infinitely weakening an infinite set of stronger though never
infinitely strong connections. For we are weighing the confident
tone differently, we are using the confident tone with infinite
strictness; that is, only when no further data can come in; that
is, never with statements for which further data can always
come in. And we are using the prefix 'I know', which is a substitute for the confident tone, with absolute strictness. We are
not thereby refusing to apply an expression where conditions
necessary and sufficient for its application are present; it is true
that the sets of conditions, of data, which we define, are none of
them absolutely connected with the statement we question.
Therefore we never break an infinitely strong connection but we
infinitely weaken stronger and stronger connections and we do
this in a way very confusing to the baby —and to ourselves.
For even if we say 'You don't *know*' as opposed to 'You *don't*
know' the fact remains that the words we use, as opposed to the
emphasis we use, are those we use when we have important adverse information not available to the baby. Even if we thus
carefully emphasize 'know' or say 'You oughtn't to say that you
know' it is still confusing. For these are words which we
ordinarily use when we have noticed that the baby hasn't paid
sufficient attention to a feature of what was before him which
should have made him suspicious. It is true that our new use
grows out of such a scientifically cautionary use. But it is a de-
generate offspring; for it reflects no different suspicion on our part.
We are not being practical at all. We are emphasizing a subtle

feature of our use of 'know' and of the confident tone and of the
future tense and of thing-words, we are bringing out a connection between the essence of things and time and knowledge. We
are doing this in a very surreptitious way, and this the baby and
the bloodstock breeder very properly bring out by asking what
price we are prepared to take about there having been a fire,
about the colt's being a Tetrarch, about the rat's being a rat.

If, as a reason for our dubious tone where no one else speaks
dubiously, we say 'Knowledge, real knowledge, requires the
knower to really know the whole pattern it is claimed he knows',
then although we are not breaking an absolute connection,
denying a correct definition (because the only one we deny is
the Subjectivist's incorrect one), we *are* trying to create one,
we are offering an incorrect definition. For though the Subjectivist is wrong in saying that to really know the better sets of
data suffices, the Sceptic is wrong in insisting that knowledge of
all the data is necessary. As to why the one asks too much and
the other too little and as to what it is that *is* necessary—to
answer these questions is to look for the secret of these very old
temptations, the temptation to say that we can never know
what lies behind what seems and the temptation to say that to
know what seems is to know what is, the first an endless suspicion, the second a lying anodyne. And that investigation we
must postpone. To repeat: If a Sceptic defines 'real knowledge
of a thing' as 'knowing all the endless pattern of it' then he misdescribes our use of 'know' and misdescribes it in a self contradictory way whatever the illuminating things he may thereby
be doing.

He may proceed more subtly. If he never tells what perfect
knowledge is and never demands a view, whether prospective or
retrospective, of all things for ever, but merely for ever demands
a better view, then he not only does not break a definition, he
also does not offer a wrong one, much less a self-contradictory
one. What does he do?

Is it that, as opposed to misdescribing language, he merely
misuses it like one who admits that if x is taller than y and y than
z then that implies that x is taller than z and admits that Henry
is, in fact, taller than Bert and Bert than Alfred and yet raises
his eyebrows over our conclusion, Henry is taller than Alfred?

What he is doing is something like this, and it is misusing as
opposed to misdescribing language; but it is different and less
crude. 'Somewhere beyond the seven seas lie the Islands of the
Blest.' Scepticism is superstition with the signs reversed. The
superstitious man says, 'We can never know that there aren't
fairies'. Whatever we do he says, 'That doesn't prove there
aren't any'. And he is always right. He never admits a statement
and denies what follows from it. What he does is to raise his eyebrows and say, 'May be, may be not', where none of us would.
We remember the man who never said, 'To know that there is
a measle germ we should have to see the invisible', but always
said, 'Still we don't know that there is a measle germ'; and we
remember the man who never said, 'To see an event we should
have to see it in an instant', thus self-contradictorily misdescribing
our use of 'see an event', but always said, 'That took too long'.
Grown up people when asked by children 'When are we going
to the circus?' never reply 'Never' but always 'Some day'.
When we are seven or so we are reassured by this but in time
we come to understand.

Symposium: Other Minds

To return to Françoise, ... if then in my anger at the thought of being pitied by her I tried to pretend that on the the contrary I had scored a distinct success, my lies broke feebly on the wall of her respectful but obvious unbelief. ... For she knew the truth.'—Proust.

' ... it was she who first gave me the idea that a person does not (as I had imagined) stand motionless and clear before our eyes with his merits, his defects, his plans, his intentions with regard to ourself exposed on his surface, like a garden at which, with all its borders spread out before us, we gaze through a railing, but is a shadow, which we can never succeed in penetrating, of which there can be no such thing as direct knowledge, with respect to which we form countless beliefs, based upon his words and sometimes upon his actions, though neither words nor actions can give us anything but inadequate and as it proves contradictory information —a shadow behind which we can alternately imagine, with equal justification, that there burns the flame of hatred and of love.'— Proust.

Sometimes, looking out of the window with someone, we see what he sees, hear what he hears and feel how he is feeling. And some people, it is said, sometimes do this when the other person is far away. Remembering this we may wonder how we ever came to ask 'Do we know, and how do we know, the thoughts and feelings of another?' Then we remember how we came to the doubt by calling seeing what he sees as we look out of the window, not 'seeing what is in his mind' but 'seeing the objects he sees', the laurels in the rain, and thinking of this, speaking of this, not as 'seeing what is before his mind' but as 'seeing in our mind images which tell us of the objects and correspond closely to the images in his mind which tell him of the objects', or, cutting out the objects, we speak of this seeing what he sees as 'seeing in our mind images corresponding to images in his mind', or, cutting out his images, we speak of 'seeing in our mind images from which we guess at later images in our mind' which later images we call 'the confirmation of our guess at what he's seeing'. Once we've done this, we shall describe in the same way seeing telepathically what he sees. This too we shall call 'guessing from shadows now at shadows to come' and be half sick of shadows. And when this web is woven, it's hard to be free of it, though it's we who wove it.

When I began a course of lectures this year with the question' What are mental facts?' at once someone protested 'But how do we know there are any?', which comes to 'How do we know when a man's angry, or when a dog smells a rat?' So I said 'You might as well ask "How do we know when a kettle's boiling?" Surely we know water's boiling when we see it bubbling?'

'But that's different' someone said, meaning of course that the way a creature's growls are a reason for thinking him angry, or his smiles for thinking him pleased is different from the way the bubbling of water is a reason for thinking it boiling.

And no doubt it is different. Bubbles tell us water's boiling because we've so often made tea, or rather, bubbles tell us water's boiling, partly because bubbles are part of boiling, and partly because bubbles have been associated in our experience with the other parts of boiling. Now if anger were, like boiling, just a pattern of physical incidents, then a dog's growls would be a reason for thinking him angry and about to bite in the very way that bubbles in water are a reason for believing that it's boiling and will make tea. But anger is more than the pattern of physical incidents which others observe when a creature's angry. And so the reason for thinking him angry is more complicated than the reason for thinking he's growling and that if you move he'll fly at you. Conversely, the reason is more complicated, and so the conclusion is too. We know a creature's angry not merely by looking at what he's doing and remembering what usually follows, like the doctor anticipating the course of a disease he never felt and which, if you like, the patient too cannot feel. On the contrary, we know a creature's angry by the way we feel as we look at him and the way we have felt when we have acted rather as he is acting. And since the reason for thinking a creature angry involves all this, thinking it involves it too, and therefore 'He is angry' is not a description merely of the creature's physical state like the words 'It's boiling' are of water's physical state.

Many people will say here 'Well of course! We all know "He's angry" unlike "It's boiling" refers not merely, and even not at all, to the physical state of the creature it's about, it refers primarily to his inward state, to the state of the soul or mind which resides in his body'.

And no doubt they are entirely right. Entirely. The trouble is that what they say provides no answer to the questions 'How does one know of another creature that he's angry? Does one know?' It's not that what they say does not suggest an answer. It does and that a bad one. For it suggests the answer 'We know the state of the soul in a body which isn't ours in the way we know the state of the inhabitant of a house we never enter—by analogy'. And this won't do at all.

In the first place, when one argues from the lights behind the blinds and the clatter of the cups that the people opposite are having tea, this is based not merely on having noticed in one's own house a connection between these things, but also upon having observed this connection in the houses of others which one has entered. Without this support the argument would be much feebler, and much feebler still had one never stepped outside one's own front door. And now the whole falsity of this comparison begins to dawn on us. For it's not merely that a condition fulfilled in the case of inference from the outward state of a house or a motor car or a watch to its inward state is not fulfilled in the case of inference from a man's outward state to his inward state, it is that we do not know what it would be like for this condition to be fulfilled, what it would be like to observe the state of the soul which inhabits another body. And it follows that knowing what in me accompanies the drawing of my sword is not related to my knowing what in my neighbour accompanies the drawing of his sword as knowing what in my house accompanies the drawing of the blinds is related to knowing what in my neighbour's house accompanies the drawing of the blinds.

It is the breakdown of this comparison, it is the failure of the answer 'We know the thoughts and feelings of others by analogy' which has tempted some to the desperate paradox 'We know a man's angry like we know a kettle's boiling—from the steam we guess at bubbles and the rest, and from the bubbles and the rest it's a deduction that it's boiling. In the same way, from a face we guess at hidden tears and then distress is a deduction.' For though this comparison too is defective, giving as it does too simple a model for the logic of thoughts and feelings, it has the great merit of bringing out how misleading is the old model so embedded in our language, the model of the house and its inhabitant, the outward sign and the inward state. The old model suggests that even were we in no doubt as to what a man had done and the circumstances in which he had done it and in no doubt as to what he would do next, we might still be in doubt as to how he felt, in the way we might be in doubt as to what was going on inside a machine although we knew all about its outside and what it would do next. And the new comparison, though defective, begins to show us how inappropriate is this suggestion.

Can we find another comparison which shall combine the merits of the old with the merits of the new? Can we say for example that we know the feelings of another like we know the weight of thistledown, of what's too light for us to feel, or like we know the power of another creature or thing? This comparison has in it something of the comparison to the house we can't enter. For we speak of weight we can't feel by analogy with weight we can, we use the words 'weighs this' 'weighs that', and we justify our metaphor, support our conclusion, by analogy. Indeed we might suddenly feel that what analogy suggests is perhaps not so and that we never really know the weight of things we can't feel. But here we instantly realize that the doubt is not a doubt, because our conclusion as to weight is not a conclusion but purely deductive, because given the premisses all is over bar the calculation and there is no finding the conclusion wrong or right.

Of course the words 'finding, feeling the weight of what can't be felt' could be so used that we could easily imagine doing this. We might come to feel the weight of thistledown, only then it would no longer be light as air, and so no longer thistledown. We might come to feel the weight of things the weight of which we can not now feel, but then they'd no longer be things the weight of which we couldn't feel. We shall soon see what lies in the future, but by then it won't lie in the future. We can imagine a man doing what we now can seldom do, something which people have called 'looking into the future'. This man doesn't examine seeds and with his experience predict the crop we may anticipate, he gazes in a glass and sees the flowers of the future. If this is to be called 'looking into the future' then when someone says we can't see into the future what he refers to is the familiar fact that few of us can do this. But if this sort of thing is rejected as being no more than seeing the shadows the future casts upon the present, then indeed we can not know the future.

Likewise we can imagine a man doing what we now can seldom do, something which people have called 'looking into the mind of another'. This man doesn't examine present symptoms and predict how the patient will go on. He sees scenes in a glass or in his mind's eye and knows they are what another sees, he feels distress and knows that another is in distress. If this is to be called seeing what another sees or feeling what he feels, if this would be real knowledge of the thoughts and feelings of another, then when someone says 'We can not know the feelings of others' what he refers to is the familiar fact that few of us can do this. But if this sort of thing is rejected as being no more than seeing the shadows of what is in another's mind upon the walls of our own, or as making two minds one, or as making what is seen partly public and so no longer mental, then indeed we can not know the thoughts and feelings of another. Once more the Agnostic is entirely right—like he was about what lies in the future. Once more what he says is true, necessarily true, because it's a tautology in that natural development of language which its proof encourages us to adopt—a tautology but fortunately a pathological one and so illuminating.

'But' someone will say 'the objects in the mind of Mr. So-and-so are different, since someone observes them. Mr. So-and-so does. And when we talk of really knowing what they are, we are not talking of knowing the unknowable, but simply of knowing them in the way Mr. So-and-so knows them'.

We know things in the future and the weight of things, the weight of which we cannot feel, by 'deductive analogy'— 'deductive' because the conclusion doesn't go beyond what supports it, 'analogy' because from like cases we argue to the case before us. But the hypothesis of feelings in others which we can't feel is not like the hypothesis of weight we can't feel, not even like the hypothesis of unconscious feelings, feelings which no one can feel.

These hypotheses, it is true, are like that of feelings in others in that it is wrong to describe them as mere picturesque re-descriptions of the phenomena in the cases they are used to explain. Nevertheless, for these hypotheses we may well bring out the confusion there is in questioning the existence of the unobservable entities they involve, by calling them '*connecting descriptions*'. A hypothesis of this sort, it is true, is not established merely by ascertaining the phenomena in the case which calls for it, since the connection, the analogy, must be established too. But the more these two jobs are done the less does one who questions the hypothesis ask a question. With the objects before the mind of Mr. So-and-so it's different. For these someone can observe. Mr. So-and-so can. It might seem for a moment that 'Mr. So-and-so has a cold' or 'Has Mr. So-and-so a cold?' mean nothing to us once we know how he's sneezing and are confident he'll cough. But they mean much more to Mr. So-and-so. And therefore, since we speak his language, they must mean much more to us. So the old comparison of the casket none can open but the owner, of the house with the closed doors and mock windows, is after all the best and the soul a ghost we are never quick enough to see.

Undoubtedly there's something in all this. There's something wrong with the comparison of mental things to the utterly 'unobservables'. But what? And must we lose the ground we had gained and go back to gazing at the windows of the house that's haunted?

When counsel claims that what his client sells is a cordial, or like a cordial, we may come at the cash value of his engaging description by recalling the reasons he has offered for it—how sweet, how pleasing in appearance, is what his client sells—like the old cordials. Undoubtedly like the old cordials. At the same time his client's product may differ from the old cordials in features which in certain connections are very important.

Now what are the likenesses between the logic of claims about the contents of caskets and the logic of expressions of thoughts and feelings, statements about thoughts and feelings? And are they incompatible with those differences which the Behaviourist emphasizes in his crude way as important in meeting metaphysical doubt about thoughts and feelings, differences which I have tried to continue to emphasize in a less offensive way? What were the reasons offered us for saying 'After all, what is going on in my neighbour's head is like what is going on in his house or the casket he won't open for me, and not like the weight of what I can't feel, which I cannot really know only because there's nothing which would be called really knowing it'?

The reasons were these. 'He will have a cold' or 'He will be in pain' or 'He will see a dagger' mean more to the man they are about, it was said, than any story however complete of the symptoms of the predicted states; he can tell in a way others can't whether these predictions are fulfilled; he can check them by direct 'observations'. It seems an obvious inference that when these statements are made in the present tense he can tell by direct observation whether they are correct, and indeed there seems no need to *infer* this, for surely if one says to a man, rather oddly perhaps, 'You are in pain', then doesn't he know how right one is in a way one doesn't oneself? It seems an obvious inference too from the fact that 'He will be in pain' means more to him it is about than any prediction of his symptoms, that it means more to the rest of us who speak the same language. And again there seems no need to infer this, for surely when a doctor says 'Mr. So-and-so will be in pain in about an hour's time' he means to say of him what he means to say of himself when he says 'I shall feel pain in about an hour's time'—a thing one might say after an operation before the anaesthetic had worn off. And this sentence means more to the speaker than any prediction of symptoms. And this more that it means is what the speaker can verify by observation. So when the speaker says of someone else 'He will be in pain' he means to predict more than cries and moans and yet he means to predict the existence, not of something unobservable, but of something which will be observed and of the same sort as he himself has observed. So when we say we cannot really know the thoughts and feelings of another, we do not speak of something in principle unobservable like an unconscious feeling, or the weight of something still too light to feel, but of something unobservable like things done behind closed doors.

I believe that here in the fact that there is something that it is not self-contradictory for one man to know directly, while it is self-contradictory for others, we have a characteristic difficulty of the logic of the soul. Here is a feature of the assertions we make about the thoughts and feelings of others which leaves us still troubled about their logical propriety long after like troubles about other things have been removed. We have doubted the propriety of our confidence in the hypothetical entities of science, in the old and universal hypothesis of matter, in all assertions as to what is right and wrong, good and bad. These doubts come from taking the logic of these things to be like the logic of a taste we may lack, of a substance behind the shadows, of a mechanism we cannot see, and they go when we recognize the defects of these false models of the transcendental. But something about thoughts and feelings forces us back to the old model for them and makes them seem the least transcendental of all things. And yet here too the old model is unsatisfactory. There would be no difficulty were it not.

Before this impasse memory of other difficulties may encourage us. In the case of doubts about right and wrong when we found the model of the moral sense defective it was not that we found a new model which was faultless. When we grasped the essence of the variable, when we removed the mystery of the universe of discourse and the worlds of fiction, we didn't do so by saying what these were, thus making the variable still constant and the unreal real still. But neither did we in these cases show how different was the logic of these from what we wished to make it by producing a new comparison that was perfect. On the contrary we were satisfied by recognizing that these things had a logic all their own, that we could not stop at any of the comparisons on the way, although our destination could never have satisfied us without the journey. So in our present difficulty

when someone tries to persuade us to go back we must remember why we started and critically examine his persuasions.

Let us examine a third time the argument which leads us
back to thinking of our ignorance of the feelings of another as
more than the temporary fact that we seldom or never know
what a man's feelings are without seeing his face or hearing him
speak and also as more than a timeless tautology like our
ignorance of the future or the weight of what's too light to feel.
The argument begins with 'It will be admitted that "He will
be in pain" means more to the man it is about than any prediction of his symptoms', and it is not for nothing that it *begins*
with this. It does so because there is something about the way the
sentence works on one person, the person it's about, which is
different from the way it works on others and which makes it
much more impossible to say that it means no more to him than
a prediction of his symptoms than it is to say this of others who
hear the sentence and are not by it led to expect pain but only
sensations as of symptoms of pain. And no doubt it is this
difference which is the source of the curious expression 'means
for him', an expression which becomes futile in view of the
principle upon which the argument next relies, namely that
what a sentence means to one man it must mean to everyone
else who uses the same language.

Another odd thing strikes us. If we ask what more than symptoms it is that 'He will be in pain' means to the man it is about,
the answer is 'A certain sensation'. What sensation? Pain. But
how can this be *part* of what is meant by a statement which is
simply to the effect that he will have that sensation?

If in order to avoid the last paradox we say that 'He will be
in pain' means nothing about symptoms to the man it is about,
then are we to say that it means the same to the rest of us, and
therefore nothing about how he will look? It is true that teaching the meaning of 'He will be in pain' is not merely a matter of
pointing out symptoms to the learner as in teaching the name of
a mechanical disorder; it involves also saying to him when he is
in pain 'Now you are in pain', but nevertheless pointing out the
symptoms is part of the teaching. And these two parts of the
teaching are reflected in the understanding of 'He will be in
pain'. It is true that it cannot be understood by one who has

never felt pain any more than 'smells of cheese' or 'He smells cheese' can be understood by one who can't smell. But it is also true that it is not understood by one who does not understand how it is decided whether it is true or false, that is by one who does not know the relevant symptoms. It is even more ridiculous to say that 'He will be in pain' means nothing about how he will look than it is to say that 'He will burst into tears' says nothing about how he will feel. For the latter sentence can be used even when his having felt quite cheerful is nothing against it. But take away all symptoms from the meaning of 'He will be in pain' and immediately there is nothing we would call B's finding that C was right in saying 'A will be in pain'.

If, in order to avoid these paradoxes, we say that 'He will be in pain' means one thing to the man it is about and another to everyone else, then this is paradoxical in itself and it leads to the following oddity.[1] What does it mean to the man it is about and not to others? A certain sensation surely? In fact pain, his pain. And isn't this what it means to everyone? Doesn't it lead everyone to expect that he will be in pain? Doesn't it lead everyone to expect his pain, to expect pain? Clearly there is an ambiguity here. 'So-and-so is expecting pain' may be used and most usually is used to mean that he is expecting to be in pain. But it may be used to mean merely that he is expecting that someone will be in pain. If we could set out the difference between these two processes we should set out the difference between the way 'He will be in pain' works on the man it is about and the way it works on others. And this would show how it happens that it is absurd to talk of others checking the prediction in the way he checks it. Let us set down as unprovocatively as possible some of the main features of how such sentences as 'I will be hungry', 'You will be hungry', 'He will be hungry' and 'He is hungry', 'You are hungry' and 'I am hungry' work.

Suppose a mother says to a child 'You will be hungry by 11 o'clock'. Then (1a) The child will decide whether the prediction was correct by waiting with his eye on the clock till 11 a.m. and then if he begins to feel hungry saying 'You were right, I am hungry', and if he does not feel hungry saying 'You were wrong'. It is at once apparent that what we have called his

[1] See pp. 50–55.

deciding whether the prediction was correct consists largely in
having that sensation, being in that state, which was predicted
in the statement about him. Is it any wonder that *others* cannot
check *that* statement in *that* way? We may add under this head
that he will not be surprised to find himself complaining that
he is hungry or eating biscuits. (1b) Had his mother made the
same prediction about his brother and not about himself he
would again have waited with his eyes on the clock, only then
he would not have waited for hunger but for symptoms in his
brother. (2a) And this is what his brother will do in order to
verify the prediction about him: I mean of course that the
brother will wait for symptoms in the child not in himself. (2b)
Had his mother made the same prediction about his brother
and not about himself, then his brother would have waited for
hunger, I mean of course hunger in himself, that is I mean
would have anticipated feeling hungry. (3) When the clock
reaches 11, the sentence 'You will be feeling hungry at 11'
ceases to tell the person it is about anything. In other words
'You, Alfred, are hungry' can tell the person to whom it is
addressed nothing, but 'He, Alfred, is hungry' can tell others
much. This again shows up how much knowing, directly
knowing, that a mental prediction is fulfilled is being in the
mental state predicted.

It is no wonder that these facts lead to trouble when we try
to sum them up in our usual logical notation.[1]

For in that notation a sentence must mean the same to any
two people provided it is unambiguous and they are both using
the same language. This implies of course that 'A will be
hungry' either (1) means to A and the rest of us symptoms in A
and only symptoms, or (2) means to A and the rest of us not
only symptoms but also a certain sensation not of symptoms, or
(3) means to A and the rest of us only a certain sensation.

Each of these alternatives illuminates a feature of the logic of
sensations. But they are all paradoxes.

If we say that (1) 'A will be hungry' means only symptoms
both to A and to others so that his waiting for stomach sensa-

---

[1] That is when we try to describe the logic of private, singly observable, things
with the notation suitable to describing the logic of public things. There is also
trouble when we try to describe the logic of utterly unobservable things in the
notation we have for describing the logic of universally observable things.

tions is no part of his learning the correctness of the prediction we do not have to say that others can't learn its correctness in the way he can. But to refuse to call his waiting for a sensation of hunger and saying 'You were right' or 'You were wrong' according to whether he feels hungry or not 'part of his learning whether the prediction was correct' is outrageous: and to say that 'A will see snakes' means to him nothing but symptoms does not do justice to the fact that 'A will see snakes (hallucinatory)' works for him so very like 'A will see snakes (real)': it does not do justice even to the way such a sentence works on others.

If on the other hand we say (2) that 'A will be hungry' or 'A will see snakes' means to A and to others not merely symptoms but also a sensation for A, or say (3) that it means both to A and to others nothing about symptoms but only a sensation, then not only are these statements in themselves paradoxical but both imply that one can never really know the thoughts and feelings of another. The proof, which is almost the same for both, is as follows:

1. According to (2) A learns the correctness of 'A will be hungry at 11' simply by waiting for a feeling of hunger and for symptoms in himself of this. According to (3) he learns the correctness of the predictions simply on the basis of feeling hungry.

2. A person, B, really knows the sensation of another, A, only if he knows them in the way A knows them, that is only if he knows the correctness of a prediction as to A's sensations in the way A knows it, that is only if he learns its correctness in the way A does.

3. Now when B hears a prediction such as 'A will be hungry at 11' either like A he waits for hunger (or for hunger and symptoms in himself) and simply on this basis judges the prediction or he does not. If he does, he misinterprets the prediction as being about himself. If he does not, he learns its correctness not in the way A does.

Therefore a person, B cannot learn the correctness of a prediction about a person, A's, sensations in the way A himself does. Therefore no one really knows the sensations of another.

The third part of this proof may be set out more fully as follows: If when B hears someone say to A 'Snakes at 6' he doesn't wait for snakes but for symptoms in A then he interprets the prediction correctly and checks it like we all would. But then he doesn't check it like A would. If on the other hand, when B hears someone say 'Snakes at 6' to A, he waits for a sensation as of snakes, then either he takes the sensation as of snakes (or the sensation and symptoms in himself) to fulfil the prediction or he does not. If he does, then he misinterprets the prediction and therefore does not come to know its correctness in the way A does. But if he does not, then either he checks the prediction not in the way A does or he misinterprets the prediction. For if B, upon seeing snakes, does not look only for symptoms in A but looks for them in someone else or in everyone else then he has misinterpreted 'Snakes at 6' to mean 'Snakes for C' or 'Snakes for everyone!' that is, roughly, 'Real Snakes'. But if upon seeing snakes he looks only for symptoms in A in order to check the prediction then he doesn't come to know its correctness like A does. Or does he? Some would say he does, since like A he waits for a sensation of snakes, and like A he looks for symptoms in A. Others would say he doesn't, because he doesn't look for symptoms in himself while A does look for symptoms in himself.

Shall we say that a man can't make the movement another makes, can't do what another does, because if A scratches his head then either B scratches his, A's, head too, and therefore he doesn't do what A does since he doesn't scratch his own head, or B scratches his, B's, head, and therefore again doesn't do what A does since A scratches A's head? Or shall we say that B does what A does if A scratches A's head and B scratches B's head? Or shall we say that B does what A does if A scratches A's head and B scratches A's head? These things are so simple that we can keep control of the notations and use or refuse the paradoxes without harm and at our convenience. With the notations for describing the peculiarities of sentences about sensations this is not so easy but it's possible. And in particular it's easy to see that if the case in which B knows A is hungry by feeling hungry himself and then finding symptoms in A is called 'B's knowing A's sensation in the way A knows it', then the proof that we never know the mind of another can no longer be based entirely on self-evident premisses but requires also the premiss that in fact no one ever does know the sensation of another in the extraordinary telepathic way described. And when this premiss is needed, immediately the conclusion diminishes from the paradox that we *can't* know the minds of others to the statement of fact that we *don't*.[1]

For it becomes the statement that no one has telepathic knowledge of the mind of another. For it then *is* this statement put in the paradoxical and misleading form that no one knows, no one really knows, the mind of another.

The pure paradox that we *can* never know the mind of another emphasizes the differences between everythng we do call or might be tempted to call one person's learning the correctness of a prediction about the mind of another and what we call a person's learning the correctness of a prediction about his own mind. It does this by using these differences to persuade us to call *nothing* knowing the correctness of a prediction about the mind of another in the way he knows it himself.

And this is easily done. For a person, A, is said to learn the correctness of a statement to the effect that he, A, will have a sensation largely by having that sensation, while another person's, B's, having that sensation is of course not called his learning the correctness of the statement about A. And if asked who knows best how a man feels, he himself or someone else, we readily answer 'The man himself'. It then remains only to call the way a man knows his own feeling, his own mind, the only real, direct, way of knowing his mind, and it follows at once that no one can have direct and real knowledge of the mind of another. Reached by this route 'We cannot know the mind of another' is a necessary truth in that natural development of ordinary language which its proof persuades us to adopt.

The statement of fact that we never *do* know the mind of another is also something of a paradox. For of course, in the most usual use of words we do all sometimes know how a particular person is feeling although at times we do not, and it is only in a new sense of 'knowing the mind of another' that we seldom or never do this although we can conceive of ourselves doing it quite often. The semi-paradox that we never *do* know

---

[1] I have here added to the first draft of this paper in response to Mr. Ayer's criticism that it was obscure.

the mind of another emphasizes how what is ordinarily called 'knowing the mind of another' differs from a knowledge we may imagine ourselves to have, a knowledge which comes by having a feeling or image or sensation just like that which we attribute to another and basing on this our beliefs about his mental state in the way we base on the images and feelings of memory our beliefs about the past. The semi-paradox emphasizes these differences by using them to persuade us to call only this imagined sort of knowledge 'real knowledge of the mind of another'. This is easily done. For clearly such knowledge would be more like the knowledge a person has of his own mind than is our common knowledge which is based on what we can see of his face and what we can hear him say. And as we have noticed when considering the pure paradox there is in us all an inclination to call a man's knowledge of his own mind the best and most real knowledge of that mind.

Those who say 'We never do really know the mind of another', having persuaded us to deny the title of 'real knowledge' to what we ordinarily call by this name by holding up a new ideal knowledge to which we should confine the title, then remark that we seldom or never attain to this ideal. And they are quite right. We seldom or never do. It's a fact—a familiar fact.

When someone says, 'We never know the mind of another' we need to ask him[1] whether (1) he wishes to say that the sort of thing we would ordinarily call 'knowing the mind of another' doesn't happen—if so he makes in quite ordinary language a statement of fact which is false, or whether (2) he wishes to say that the particular sort of intimate, telepathic knowledge of another's mind which would give us knowledge of his mind comparable to our knowledge in memory of the past seldom or never occurs—if so he makes in a readily acceptable caricature of ordinary language a statement of fact which is true, or whether (3) he wishes to say that we cannot know the mind of another in exactly the way he does himself—if so, in a readily acceptable extreme caricature of ordinary language he makes a statement which is necessarily true, couldn't conceivably be false.

Nearly always the truth of the matter will be that the sceptical

[1] Cf. A. J. Ayer, 'The Terminology of Sense Data', *Mind*, October 1945.

speaker is neither definitely doing one of these things nor definitely doing another. He is like a man who has moved a piece, a chessman perhaps, upon a board before us, but when we move in reply, explains that he is not playing exactly the game ordinarily played with the pieces he uses and that further he has not quite settled what modifications of the ordinary game he plans to play. We shall not come to conclusions with him till this is settled. Is he making a statement of fact or is he making a statement which is necessarily true? He will resent this question for he will feel that with it we are trying either to force him to plod beside the scientist always subject to the vagaries or nature or to banish him to the *a priori* where blows indeed no wind of chance and *ipso facto* no breath of life. He is convinced that somehow he is revealing something about the world and yet making a statement which has all the necessity, all the immunity to chance, of a logical or mathematical statement.

So he may be. For a tautology may reveal something about the world. A tautology made without modifying ordinary language may do this. Still more may one like 'Tigers burn bright in forests at night'. To see the world we must connect things and as we connect them more or in a new way so we see old things anew. Even a logical statement, which by definition cannot involve any modification of linguistic conventions and which therefore in a sense cannot connect things in a new way, but can only underline connections already made, can reveal to us what we had not realized. Thus the equation: 'God exists' means 'Something is divine' disconnects 'God exists' from 'God knows' and 'God loves' and so breaks the power of an analogy suggested by the shape of sentences and very confusing, as we know, in certain connections. Still more can a metaphysical statement, which may modify language, connect or disconnect things in a new way. And when the philosopher says 'We can never know the mind of another' the proof he offers makes us realize that, when from a man's face or what he says we guess he's angry, we are not like one who from the outside of a house guesses that it is inhabited *and could make sure*.

Unfortunately the words 'We cannot know the mind of another' also suggest that when from a man's face or words we guess at his feelings we *are* like one who from the outside of a house guesses that it is inhabited, but can not make sure, because he can't unlock the door or because the windows, though seemingly transparent, are not, or because he lacks the power of gazing in a crystal and so ascertaining what goes on behind closed doors. And thus the very words used to break the power of the analogy of the house and its inhabitant are in conformity with that analogy and encourage it.[1] This is why it is so very necessary to be clear as to whether one wishes to use them to make the scientific statement that we lack telepathic knowledge or to make the metaphysical and tautological statement aimed against the confusing analogy, embedded in our language, of the house and its inhabitant.

To sum up then: The words 'We can not know the mind of another' or better 'We can not really know the mind of another' may be used to reveal something about the world and at the same time to say something which can't be false. But this is not done, cannot be done, by making a statement of fact which has all the necessity of a tautology.

True, one who says 'We cannot know the mind of another' may use these words to make the statement of fact that we lack telepathic knowledge and if he does he is making that statement in a modification of ordinary language in which it is necessarily true that we lack knowledge of the minds of others *unless we have telepathic knowledge*. But if so he is still making a statement which may at any time become false, because we may come to have the power we lack.

And again, one who says 'We cannot know the mind of another' may use these words to make a statement which is necessarily true because made in a modification of ordinary language in which absolutely nothing is to be called 'knowing the mind of another in the way he knows it himself' and absolutely nothing is to be called 'knowing the mind of another' except in in the way he knows it himself. But if the sceptical

---

[1] This is characteristic of the expression of metaphysical advances. Thus to say 'Matter does not exist' is to speak as if matter were something over and above sensations, which is just what those who say it mean to deny. Schlick said that we now know that there are no such entities as numbers and thereby spoke as if they were things, though fabulous, the very way of speaking his statement was directed against. Wittgenstein did the same when he said 'We have the idea that the meaning of a word is an object'. The ghost of this habit lingers when we say 'Material things are logical fictions', 'Numbers and meanings are logical fictions'.

speaker is using words this way then at once he is not making a statement of fact, he is not telling us of something we have missed. For then his statement that we can't know the mind of another has become like the statement that we can't possess the heart of another when we have decided that this description is not to be applied until that other has no desire apart from our own and is then still not to be applied because then that other is no longer other.

Once more then we reach the result that the words 'the impossibility of knowing the mind of another' may stand either for something like the difficulty, or if you like, the impossibility of knowing the future from a crystal or for something like the impossibility of knowing the future just as we do the present, either for a prolonged accident or for a timeless necessity, either for a fact or a tautology, but not for something which is both. This is the result we reached on p. 136. The difference is that now we know the proof and therefore the point of the tautology and that now we can hold to it. We can now hold to it because we have seen how it is that, while there is one person for whom it is not impossible that he knows what is in the mind of a certain person, it is impossible for everyone else. For we have noticed how there is a language, and one we are half inclined to use, in which, while it is not self-contradictory to say that A knows the mind of A, it is self-contradictory to say of anyone other than A that he knows the mind of A.

But now alas, just when all seems well, a new whisper disturbs our complacency: 'How *can* two people attach the same meaning to a statement when the one can check it in a way in which it is impossible for the other to do so? How *can* two people be concerned with the same proposition, the same fact, when the one can ascertain the truth of that proposition in a certain way, while it makes no sense to talk of the other ascertaining its truth in that way? This is the same difficulty, coming from the eccentric logic of sensations, as that we have just investigated. But one who puts the difficulty this way pretends to have another way out and leads us to a different

destination. He says: 'Face the difficulty at once and say that a
sentence such as "A will be hungry" means something different
to A from what it means to the rest of us. You will then not be
forced into admitting that we can never know the feelings of
another. For you will be able to claim that we do know the
statements we make about the feelings of another in the sense
that *we* attach to them'. It's not till later that we find that in
order to preserve our knowledge we have followed a guide who
leaves us in an isolation even more profound—not indeed among
enemies whose words may be all lies but in a place where for
ever there is beside our own voice only the chatter of the
monkeys.

We have caught a glimpse of this person before. It was when
we considered the paradoxes we have now worked till they are
no longer paradoxes and noticed how they depended upon
the principle 'A sentence must mean the same to any two
speakers unless it is ambiguous'. He had then only a rather
freakish air because he just hinted that we might deny this
principle. Now he's becoming bolder. Is he a friend or an
enemy?

When we dealt with the riddle 'Can one man do what another
man does?', we set out what makes paradoxical the answer
'Yes' and in doing so set out what leads to the answer 'No': and
in setting out what makes paradoxical the answer No', we set out
what leads to the answer 'Yes'. Likewise in setting out the paradox involved in 'A sentence must mean the same to any two
speakers' and in "Mr. So-and-so will have a cold" means the
same to any two speakers' we have set out what now seems to
force us towards ' "Mr. So-and-so will have a cold" means more
to him than to us', and therefore towards 'A sentence need not
mean the same to any two speakers'. And if we now welcome this
last paradox and set out what is involved in it, we shall see how
we can still deny it and insist that 'Mr. So-and-so will have a
cold' means the same to him as to everyone else and that every
sentence means the same to any two speakers of the same
language.

Suppose someone says 'We can't know what lies byond the
horizon'. We reply 'Don't be absurd. What you mean no doubt
is that we can't know what's beyond the horizon like we can

what's before us. And that's a tautology. For it's self-contradictory to talk of knowing the remote just as one knows the near'. He may reply 'But it can't be self-contradictory, because there may[1] be someone doing this, e.g. observing a fire in Fleet Street, at the very moment that one cannot oneself. And such a person is learning the truth of a statement with the same meaning as that one is wondering about. Now it cannot be sensible to talk of one person's knowing something in a certain way and absurd to talk of another person's knowing that thing in that way'. Let us now meet this by saying that 'Fire in Fleet Street' doesn't mean the same to people in different places. For this is true in a sense fatal to the Agnostic. And no harm is done if we are careful.

Imagine that people all over the country hear on the wireless 'A fire is now raging in Fleet Street'. Those in Fleet Street have a different and more direct means of checking this statement than those in Brighton or even those in Streatham. Those in Fleet Street have only to open their windows or their eyes, and they will be disappointed if upon doing so they see no flames. But the newspapermen on holiday by the sea will be astonished if they find the front in flames. They may use their eyes of course and observe their editor mount a bus for the station, like people on the Euston road may watch the engines hurry from opposite St. Pancras' Church. But, unlike those on the spot, they can not instantly, by opening their eyes, obtain sensations ultimately and overwhelmingly connected with the words 'Fire in Fleet Street'.

Let us say that the news means something different to listeners far from the scene from what it means to those who are there, and that it means to those at Brighton charred timbers and hurrying firemen in 60 minutes by the Southern Electric, to those in the Strand flames from the window, to watchers in Fleet Street nothing, since it tells them nothing.[2] Only if we say

---

[1] This is one respect in which the puzzle about things in the distance differs from the puzzle about things in the soul. For things in the soul we may say *must* be known. Further the description of an event as Mr. So-and-so's anger tells who may know it but 'Fire in Fleet Street' does not.

[2] The peculiarity of a man's knowledge of his own sensations I have tried to bring out in Other Minds VII.

(*a*) The different meanings of 'Big Ben points to 12' to persons at different distances is given by 'To a person 100 miles away this means Big Ben pointing to

this, that the words have different meanings to listeners in different places, we must remember that they all speak the same language, that the case is not like that of people who being in different places speak a different dialect. On the contrary, were the news to have the same effects on a man in Brighton as it has on one in the Strand so as to give us some inclination to say that it means the same to him as it does to the man in the Strand, then we should say that the man in Brighton didn't understand English, that the words didn't mean the same to him as to the rest of us and therefore not the same as to the man in the Strand. We should say 'The man in the Strand correctly understands them to mean a fire in Fleet Street, the man in Brighton incorrectly understands them to mean a fire in Brighton or a general fire, a fire everywhere. He attaches the wrong significance, or no significance, to the spatial suffix "Fleet Street" or "here" '. In the same way if a man were to hear the words 'Voices in Joan of Arc's ears' and then listen for voices, we should say that the words meant for him something different from what they mean for the rest of us and in that way something different from what they mean for Joan of Arc. We should say 'He incorrectly takes the words "Voices in Joan of Arc's ears" to mean voices in his own ears or public, real voices, voices in everyone's ears: he attaches the wrong significance, or no significance, to the personal suffix "in Joan's ears", "in Joan's mind" '. Again we have asked 'Does "Voices in Joan of Arc's ears" mean more to Joan of Arc than it does to others, and if so what more does it mean?' The answer is 'It doesn't mean more,

---

2 o'clock in two turns of my clock with the speedometer at 50, to a person 50 miles away this means Big Ben pointing to 1 o'clock in one turn of my clock with the speedometer at 50, etc.', or by 'This means to a person 100 miles away Big Ben pointing at 4 o'clock in 4 turns of my clock with the speedometer at 25, etc.'. These accounts of course are simplified and neglect grit in clocks and defective speedometers. The full account involves all the laws of nature, which once they are ascertained are put into the meanings of words. It is no miracle that they can then be pulled out again.

(*b*) The description of the different meanings of sentences about the distant can be given in terms of sentences about the present. The description of the different meanings of sentences about sensations can be given only in sentences about sensations. This leads people to fancy that these are being given a circular definition. But no definition is being given. The description of the use of general sentences cannot be given without the use of any such sentence. But this only means that we can't describe their use by a rule for providing substitutes. When we ask 'What is the variable?' or 'What is consciousness?' it is not that general or psychological sentences are unintelligible to us.

any more than "Fire in Fleet Street" means more to those on the spot than it does to others and consequently there is no answer to "What more does it mean?" except that it doesn't mean more.' It follows at once that it is as misleading and wrong to say ' "Voices in Joan's ears, pain in her heart" means nothing to Joan when she is already hearing the voices and feeling the pain, although it means something to others', as it is to say, ' "Fire in Fleet Street", means nothing to those already watching the fire, although it means something to others and what is more its meaning reaches a maximum just before a person reaches the spot'. But although it is dangerous to say these things because in the usual meaning of 'meaning' they are false, they are well worth saying in a modified meaning of 'meaning', in which the meaning of a word to a particular person at a particular place at a particular time is a matter of what, if he knows the language, it must do to him then and there. For then these paradoxical statements about meaning something different, meaning more, meaning nothing, express what can otherwise be said only with another expression, such as 'works differently for', 'does more work for', 'does nothing for', which expression is again liable to be misunderstood. It is liable to be misunderstood in the way 'means more' is liable to be misunderstood, and although less liable to be misunderstood in this way, that is as attacking the truth that any sentence must mean the same to any two speakers of the same language, it is more liable to be misunderstood as referring merely to the fact that 'Fire in Fleet Street' may mean more to a man whose business is there than it does to one whose business is elsewhere, that is to unconventional, unsymmetrical differences. There is indeed at this juncture no substitute for luck and goodwill except industry—industrious description of the detailed differences between hearers and equally industrious description of the likenesses, and this will involve not merely a description of the use of the particular expression giving trouble such as 'He hears voices', but also a description of other expressions in the same linguistic constellations, such as 'I hear voices', 'You are hearing voices', 'You will hear voices', 'Everyone will hear voices', 'There will be voices', and at last the whole language.

And what point have these descriptions which are so apt to

mislead or so laborious? None—unless we wish to answer the question with which we started 'How do we know that a man is angry? Surely we do know this and yet how can we, since all we really know is how he frowns and growls?' But if we wish to free ourselves of that puzzling question and positively to gain that sort of new view of the world which a new language and a new grasp of language gives, then these dangerous or tedious descriptions are not merely useful but essential. For without referring to the facts we have dangerously described as sentences having different meanings for different people, we could not understand how true it is nor how it's true that no one can know what lies beyond the horizon or behind the windows of the soul. For without referring to these facts we could not understand how it is also true that, while one person may know these things, others cannot.

And it's not until we have understood these things that we ask 'Why is it that familiar facts and truths have been so confusingly expressed?' Have we perhaps missed the deepest meaning of these metaphysical doctrines so absurd and so profound?

'Let us consider letters', Virginia Woolf writes. 'Life would split asunder without them. "Come to tea, come to dinner, what's the truth of the story?, have you heard the news?, life in the capital is gay, the Russian dancers..." These are our stays and props. These lace our days together and make of life a perfect globe. And yet, and yet... when we go to dinner, when pressing finger-tips we hope to meet somewhere soon, a doubt insinuates itself; is this the way to spend our days? the rare, the limited, so soon dealt out to us—drinking tea? dining out? And the notes accumulate. And the telephones ring. And everywhere we go wires and tubes surround us to carry the voices that try to penetrate before the last card is dealt and the days are over. "Try to penetrate", for as we lift the cup, shake the hand, express the hope, something whispers, Is this all? Can I ever know, share, be certain? Am I doomed all my days to write letters, send voices, which fall upon the tea-table, fade upon the passage, making appointments, while life dwindles, to come and dine? Yet letters are venerable: and the telephone valiant, for the journey is a lonely one, and if bound together by notes and telephones we went in company, perhaps—who knows?—we might talk by the way.'[1]

This isolation which we may defeat but cannot vanquish, does it find voice in the old puzzle as to whether we really know what is in the mind of others? Does the contradiction in the philosopher's request for perfect knowledge of others reflect a conflict in the human heart which dreads and yet demands the otherness of others?

[1] *Jacob's Room*, p. 91.

Synopsis of Paper: Other Minds

How do we know a man's angry? Not like we know a kettle's boiling—by deduction from the physical symptoms. For in knowing another man's angry we use the analogy of our own feelings. But this is not to use analogy like we do when we know they're having a party opposite; for then we may ourselves be wrong; that is, to such knowledge is opposed a non-analogical, direct, knowledge.

Do we know a man's angry like we know the weight of thistledown? Here the weight isn't known merely from the symptoms on the scales, but from this in conjunction with having felt the weight of other things we have weighed. We can, of course, imagine ourselves feeling the weight of thistledown, or, if you like, we can't, because it would then no more be light as air and so no longer thistledown. If one speaks the first way, then 'We can't really feel the weight of thistledown' means that we don't—a thing everybody knows. If one speaks the second way, then 'We can't know the weight of thistledown' is an eternal truth—because it's a tautology in that natural development of ordinary language to which we are encouraged in its proof.

'We can't know the anger, the feelings of another' is also either a familiar fact or a pathological and illuminating tautology.

Someone will protest that a man's anger, the contents of another's mind are not like quite unobservable things, which cannot be known differently from the way we know them only because there's no sense in such different and more direct knowledge. For they are not things nobody can observe, they are not things nobody can know differently from the way we know them. For somebody does know them differently. The man in whose mind they are does. And if it is not absurd for one man to do this, then surely it is not absurd for another?

But it is. For it is from feeling angry that a man knows that someone who said he'd be angry is right. And *we* can't in *that* way know that *that* prediction is right—we *can't*. For our feeling angry would have nothing to do with the case. Or, rather, it might be a clue (we might have telepathic powers), but it wouldn't show us the rightness of that prediction like the feeling of the man the prediction is about shows him its rightness, or like it would show us the rightness of a like prediction about ourselves.

The Concept of Mind

This paper is not a review of Professor Ryle's book *The Concept of Mind* but it is an attempt to criticize and at the same time to continue it. Before coming to the criticism, may I say how much I admire the power, the simplicity and the grace of Ryle's work. It is an achievement and a part of the progress of philosophy.

Wittgenstein said that we have the idea that the soul is a little man within, and also that we have the idea that within us is a mental mechanism. Ryle says (p. 22) that he will be concerned with the dogma of the ghost in the machine. He has assembled a thousand instances to illustrate the influence and demonstrate the menace of the myth, the myths, of the hidden stream, the concealed mirrors, the private pictures, the invisible incidents, the flames of passion fanned by the winds of fancy.

I am not suggesting that Wittgenstein's treatment of the metaphysics of mind is not very different from Ryle's. He did not neglect what Ryle never adequately recognizes, the difference between the method of verification of statements about thoughts and feelings and the method of verification of statements about the movements of wheels, levers, limbs, electricity and the wind that bloweth where it listeth, visible to none though we hear the sound of it.

To come to the ghost: Stuart Hampshire, in his excellent review in *Mind* of Ryle's book, says that Ryle has given the impression that philosophers have foisted this myth, these myths, on the masses, and that this impression is a false one. He is right, surely? Philosophers have made us aware of the myth and in such a way as to increase its power, not free us from it. But it wasn't they who impregnated our talk and thought with this myth. And this is important to the explanation of its merits and demerits.

Hampshire points out that Ryle often draws attention to the

evils of the myth in a misleading way. He says: 'On what grounds does Professor Ryle decide that there are no acts "answering to such verbs as 'see', 'hear', 'deduce' and 'recall'"'. Ryle here has put his point in the old form: 'There are no such things as so-and-so's'—compare 'There is no such thing as matter', 'Belief in the causal connection is superstition', 'There are no such things as infinite numbers', 'There are no such things as numbers', 'Universals do not exist', 'We have the idea that the meaning of a word is an object' (Wittgenstein). Russell began to put part of Ryle's point when he wrote 'Empirically I cannot discover anything corresponding to the supposed act' (*Analysis of Mind*, p. 17). No sea serpents in the depths of the ocean, no acts behind the 'presentational continuum' (an old phrase from Ward's *Principles of Psychology*).

The old form for putting a metaphysical point, namely, 'There are no such things as so-and-so's", tempts people to object in the old inappropriate but powerful way in which Moore objected to 'There are no material things'. Moore said: 'I have two thumbs. Thumbs are material things'. It also tempts people to reply in the newer inappropriate way: 'The question "Are there any so-and-so's?" asked metaphysically is meaningless'.[1]

Moore forces those who say 'There are no so-and-so's' to hasten to explain that they mean 'There are no so-and-so's over and above such-and-such's, that so-and-so's are nothing but such-and-such's, that so-and-so's are logical fictions though not fictions, that they are logical myths not myths. (This is still not what they mean but it is a great improvement.) And Ryle has explained that this is what he means to say. He writes (p. 22): 'I am not, for example, denying that there are mental processes. Doing long division is a mental process and so is making a joke. But I am saying that the phrase "there occur mental processes" does not mean the same sort of thing as "there occur physical processes", and therefore that it makes no sense to conjoin or disjoin the two.'

To conjoin or disjoin the two is to make what Ryle would call a 'category mistake' comparable to that made by a child who,

[1] For example Carnap, 'Revue Internationale de Philosophie,' January 15th, 1950, p. 25.

having observed the passing of men and guns, asks 'And has the division passed, too?'

He says (p. 22): 'The "reduction" of the material world to mental states and processes, as well as the reduction of mental states and processes to physical states and processes presupposes the legitimacy of the disjunction "Either there exist minds or there exist bodies (but not both)".' This shows that he does not mean by the reduction of X's to Y's the claim that there are not X's over and above Y's but the claim that there are no X's, only Y's. Thus the average man is not reducible, in Ryle's sense, to individual men. He does, however, often use words which suggest that he does wish to say that in the sense in which the average man is reducible to individual men the mind is reducible to the body, that in the sense in which the passing of a division is reducible to the passing of men and guns, mental processes are reducible to bodily processes, that consciousness is to its manifestations as electricity to its manifestations.

And now two things emerge—one is, I submit, a confusion and the second an inadequacy in Ryle's work—a serious inadequacy.

The confusion is one which has lasted since James's exposition of his theory of emotions and of thought. He didn't make clear whether what he was concerned with was the connection between (1) statements about emotions and (2) statements purely about the bodily changes associated with emotions, or with the connection between (1) statements about emotions and (3) statements about the feelings and sensations of the bodily manifestations associated with emotions. It is true that statements only about the bodily changes associated with an emotion are not sharply separated from those which are also about the sensations of those changes. 'He is shivering', even 'His breathing is harsh', usually tell not only of bodily changes but also of how he feels—though not when he is plainly under an anaesthetic. 'He is walking very fast' many philosophers would call a description of bodily performance and 'He is thinking about the trade cycle' a description of a mental performance. And yet both are both—like the novelist's 'He turned away, his eyes filled with tears'. Ryle sets this fact in the light. But though many statements which philosophers would call descriptions of bodily performance are not merely that, and there are no statements about sensations to which nothing about bodily symptoms is relevant, it remains true that a philosopher who is concerned with 'How do I know I am wishing for this, fearing that, thinking of so and so, since all I know is that my heart is fluttering or feels as if it is, that I have a sinking feeling, that I hear as it were a voice? How can I from these presentations that float on the stream of mental activity know the condition of the currents in it?' is concerned with a very different problem from that which concerns the philosopher who asks 'How do I know from the fluttering of Bill's heart that he has a feeling as of his heart fluttering?'

There are two myths: the myth of the stream of pure spiritual activity on which or in which float patches of oil, sensations and images, and the myth of the inner, mental, spiritual, sensual, stream which drives the bodily machine and is in its turn affected by that machine. The reduction of the spiritual to the sensual is Sensationism about mental events. It corresponds to Sensationism about material events. The two combined give Neutral Monism. The reduction of the sensual and, with it, the spiritual to the material is Materialism. In both cases only when categorical statements about that which is to be reduced are presented as involving hypothetical statements about that to which it is reduced are the doctrines not obviously utterly absurd.

This brings us to the second point—Ryle's insufficient explanation of the purpose of his demonstration of the omnipresence in our minds of the model of the hidden stream, his insufficient explanation of the purpose and merits of that model, and the consequent insufficiency of his explanation of the defects of that model.

All this begins to emerge if we ask 'What is the dispute between Ryle and Hampshire? One of them says "Our language is riddled with the myth of the ghost in the machine", the other says "Certainly, certainly our language is riddled with the myth of the ghost in the machine".' Only the tone of voice is different.

Plain men and philosophers have continually presented the peculiarities in the way classes of statements are known as a

peculiarity in their subject matters, as a peculiarity in the sorts
of things to which they refer, that is, they have presented the
peculiarities of the ultimate logical characters of statements in
the form of myths of other worlds—the world of legend, the
universe of fiction, the womb of Time, the realms of logical
space. But what's the harm? What's the harm of a myth im-
pregnating our language? And what is the harm of developing
and rendering explicit that myth?

To plain men, by and large, no harm. It is true, perhaps, that
for every class of statements there are outlying areas on the
manifold of discussions in which they appear where the myth
in them bedevils discussion. And with some classes of statements
these areas are more important to us and larger than with other
classes. This is true, I think, of ethical statements and also more
than we realize of statements about minds. But exactly how it
is that misleading models of statements about minds mislead
discussion carried on *in* these statements it is not easy to bring
out, any more than it is easy for a psychoanalyst to assemble in
a moment the evidence to prove that a person is dominated and
harmed by a model from the past, by the idea, for example, that
They are all against me.

It is easier to bring out how a myth harms discussion *about*
a class of statements, that is, it is easier to bring out how the
myth suggested by a language in which a class of discussions is
conducted befuddles those who step back and consider the discussions themselves—in short, metaphysicians. For the be-
fuddlement shows in curious scepticism, in talking of a class of
statements as myths without realizing that speaking in this way
one is misleadingly employing a myth—that of proving a myth
a mytn, that of proving harpies fictions.

Ryle, of course, realizes that minds aren't myths like harpies
or sea serpents—that it is to use a myth to call them myths. And
he says so. And his proof of the prevalence of the myth or myths
he speaks of is not invalidated by his sometimes expressing himself in terms of that myth. The proofs a philosopher offers of
'There are no integers' are not invalidated by the fact that he
puts his point in terms of the very myth he purposes to extin-
guish. Ryle's point is that statements about minds are not
related to what in the end gives a man a right to make them,

as statements about a temporarily hidden mechanism to that which makes us guess it is present.

Nevertheless, it seems to me that Hampshire is not being merely doctrinaire when he claims that Ryle's exposition is in places obscured by being put in terms of the logical model the fascination of which it is designed to destroy and does destroy. Had Ryle put his point more often in terms of a misleading pattern for the ultimate logic of a class of statements he would have said more of the purpose of exposing the inadequacy of that pattern.

He may reply 'The purpose of saying that our language is riddled with this myth is to say that our language is riddled with this myth; the purpose of saying that we continually talk as if the logic of statements about thoughts and feelings were what it is not is to say just that'. He may say that he doesn't wish to put his point in the form 'Philosophers, metaphysicians, have got into difficulties about how we know what we claim to know about minds. These difficulties are removed by noticing how we are dominated by the idea that a mind is a hidden stream'.

Again Ryle may reply that my accusation is false and that he has made it clear that he aims to give such an apprehension of the logic of the soul that one will not be troubled by such questions as 'How does a man know from the images and feelings which float on the surface of the stream of spiritual activity the currents in that stream or whether it exists at all? How does a man know from the behaviour and surroundings of another the feelings of the other?' 'How does a mental state explain a bodily act?'

But I submit that he has not. The peculiarity of the soul is not that it is visible to none but that it is visible only to one. Unless we understand this we cannot understand why people have so persistently clung to the model for the logic of the soul which gives rise to scepticism not only about the mental acts of others but also about their aches and pains, feelings of quickened heart beats, sensations as of voices, daggers, snakes.

Ryle rightly stresses the fact that pictures in the mind are not like pictures in a gallery, that statements about what is in or on the mirror of the mind have a different logic from those about what is in the mirror on the mantelpiece and that sensation, or

the 'observation of the presentational continuum', has a different logic from the observation of a film, and that knowledge
that one is observing the presentational continuum or this or
that in it, for example knowledge that one is seeing as it were
snakes, has a different logic from knowledge that one is observing
a film or this or that in it. He rightly insists that if we talk of
sensations as observations and then of these observations as
reasons, everything falls into confusion if we expect the same of
these reasons as we expect of the reasons garnered from the
observation of the scenes of a show.

I don't think he explains clearly *how* things fall into confusion
and how solipsism and subjectivism are born, but that is not my
point. My point is that, though the sources of solipsism are also
sources of doubt about the minds of others, there is also a source
of this doubt other than those sources of it which also lead to
solipsism. And this source lies in the facts covered by the words
'The soul is visible only to one'.

What are these facts? They are the facts which lead people
to say that a person has a way of knowing how he feels which
no one else has, has a right to say what he does about how he
feels which no one else has ever had or ever will have.

But what are the facts which have led them to say this? And
do these facts justify the Sceptic in saying 'No one but Bill
really knows how Bill feels. No one but Bill has any real reason
for saying anything about how Bill feels'.

First, what are the facts which have led people to say that a
man can know himself in a way others can't? They are the same
as those which have led people to say that other people have
a peculiar difficulty in knowing how a man feels.

One might think that the special facility and the special
difficulty lie in the fact that while Bill, if he is in pain, has every
right to say that Bill is in pain, Arabella has not because she is
in pain the right to say Bill is in pain. Bill, when he feels a
choking in his throat has a reason for saying he is angry,
while Arabella has not because she has a choking in her throat
a reason for saying that Bill is angry.

But isn't this an accident? Suppose Arabella, having a pain
or a choking feeling, says with confidence 'Bill is in pain' or
'Bill is angry' and suppose that she is again and again right. We

should say 'Extraordinary thing, she knows from her own feelings that Bill is in pain or angry—as if she were Bill himself'. Were she never to learn of the success of her telepathy we should not say that her confidence was reasoned and hardly that it was reasonable, any more than we say this of the young antelope who instinctively knows that lions are dangerous. But we should say that she had every reason for her confidence once she had learned of the unvaried correctness of her claims, like the antelope that has been repeatedly clawed. Again, from a sensation of snakes in blue or in a monogram B, I, L, Arabella might know that Bill was having a sensation as of snakes or was in for the horrors.

Under such circumstances we would say that Arabella has an extraordinary knowledge of Bill's mind, that she can see into his mind, that while the rest of us have to guess from external signs at what is in his mind, she can know what is in his mind as well as he can himself and in the way he does himself. Like Bill, because she has a sensation as of snakes, she has a right to say 'Bill sees as it were snakes'; a choking feeling in her throat, angry words coming to her mind, give her the right to say 'Bill is angry' as they do Bill himself; other pictures, other feelings, give her the right to say 'Bill's in love'.

But the philosophical sceptic says 'Do they *as* they do Bill himself?'. No doubt some people do, much more than others, know how another person is feeling by 'feeling themselves into' the other person, and the connection between this and telepathy deserves attention. But the question at the moment is 'Does the philosophical sceptic when he says that a person, A, never really knows how another, B, feels refer to the fact that it seldom or never happens that one person knows the mind of another as we have imagined Arabella to know Bill's mind, that is altogether from feeling as she feels Bill feels?

And the answer is No. For in so far as a person is referring to this fact, whether or no he is right is to be settled by investigation and experiment, not by philosophical reflection. If someone says philosophically 'One can never really know the mind of another, only the way he lays back his ears and frowns' and we say to him 'That is upon the whole true but it is said that sometimes a person knows the mind of another without at all relying upon external signs and for good or ill this sort of thing may become more common', then the philosopher will reply 'I don't think you quite understand. I am not denying that there occur the most striking instances of telepathy, of a person knowing from his or her own feelings the mind of another. But such a person wouldn't be really and directly knowing the mind of another. Even one with such insight as Arabella's would not because she saw as it were snakes have that right to say that Bill sees as it were snakes which Bill has because he sees as it were snakes'.

It might now be thought that what the philosopher refers to is the fact that while what gives Bill the right to say that he sees as it were snakes or is in for the horrors is *his* sensation of as it were snakes, what gives a telepathic person the right to say that Bill sees as it were snakes or is in for the horrors is *her* sensation of as it were snakes. I am sure that some sceptics about the minds of others would seek to prove their point this way. But this proof proves that no one really knows there's a snake in the grass just as much as it proves that no one really knows that there's a snake in Bill's mind. And therefore let us now ignore this proof; for we are concerned with a Sceptic who finds in some feature of our knowledge of the mind of others a reason for saying that we never know the minds of others, which reason does not plunge him into Solipsism and make him say we can never know whether or no there's a snake in the grass.

We must now again try to say what that feature is. It is this: While one can from one's own sensation as of a snake have a right to say that there is a snake in the grass *in the way any*one can, one cannot from one's own sensation as of a snake have a right to say that there is a snake in someone else's mind *in the way he* can because of his sensation as of a snake. And the familiar but complicated facts to which this refers are the following: Suppose that a certain person, Arabella, upon seeing as it were snakes, says 'Bill sees as it were snakes'. Upon being asked, Bill says he sees no such thing. Arabella is impressed by this but doesn't regard it as proving her wrong; instead she asks the rest of us whether we can see snakes, and when we say 'Yes, we can', she says 'There you are, Bill sees them'. 'But', we say, 'look, he has blundered into them'. 'Ah,' she says, 'he saw them all right. I can see them, you can see them, the camera can see them. That settles it'. In this story we have indeed arranged that Arabella shall know as well as Bill what Bill sees and that the rest of us can do so too. And with this we have arranged too much. For if Arabella uses the words 'Bill sees as it were snakes' in the way described, then with them she makes a statement of a well-known sort, a statement whose familiar features now begin to show through its disguise, the statement 'Snakes, real, live, snakes'.

We must tell a different story if we are to tell one of how Arabella knows as well as Bill the snakes in his mind. We must tell a story in which it doesn't turn out that what she is talking about are real snakes. And we can easily do this. Suppose that Arabella, elated by many proofs of her telepathic powers, now on a new occasion says 'Bill sees snakes'. We ask Bill and he says he does not see snakes. We may, because of Arabella's past successes as a telepathist, suspect that Bill is lying and that later he will say he did see snakes. But if he does not and this happens again and again and Arabella pays no more attention to the evidence we offer against her statements than she would have done had she made them of herself then we say 'When Arabella says "Bill sees snakes", although she uses Bill's name, what she says amounts to "I see snakes" or "I see snakes and have a feeling about Bill". She has lost her power of insight into Bill's mind and conceals this from us and from herself by using still the words "Bill sees snakes" while using them in such a way that all that counts in a dispute as to whether he does is just the same as what counts in a dispute as to whether she does'.

If we talk about Bill as Arabella does and ignore or treat lightly Bill's protests, then, of course, we may say, as she, perhaps, does, that she knows better than Bill how he feels or what he fancies.

'Exactly so,' says the Sceptic, 'when Arabella's statement becomes really one about herself she knows better than anyone else whether it is right, but while it is still about Bill she doesn't know it to be right like she would were it about herself, that is, like Bill does.'

It is true that the circumstances which make us say of a statement, S, made by A, that A has a right to make it just like B has a right to make a statement about how things seem to him, are also the circumstances which make us say that S is not about how things seem to B but about how things seem to A. It thus appears that it is perfectly true that A cannot make a statement about how things seem to B and have a right to say it just like B has.

Now it is not unnatural to express this by saying that A never has that reason for a statement about how things seem to B which B has. And it is not unnatural to express this by saying that when one person makes a statement about the mind of another then he never has all the reason one could have for such a statement.

And this leads to 'No one ever knows anything about the mind of another'. For though we often speak of a person knowing something even when he hasn't all the reason he could have for what he says—for example, we say that a man knows that a stream is flowing because he sees the mill wheel turning—in these cases we speak of knowledge only because, though on the particular occasion in question the person of whom we speak hasn't all those reasons one could have for what he says, on other occasions he has been better placed and has had, not only the reasons he has on this occasion, but also those which one better placed would have—he has seen beneath the wheel the water. Further, it is only because one who sees a mill wheel turning has on other occasions had other reason to say that the water is high today that we allow that now seeing the mill wheel turning, he has a right to say 'The water's high today'.

Now we have said that no one who makes a statement about the mind of another *ever* has the right to make it which that other has, that therefore he never has had all the reason one could have for the statement he makes.

It is tempting to infer that no one ever knows anything about the mind of another and even that no one ever has any right to assert anything about the mind of another, since it is not true of him that on some other occasion he has been better placed and had then the reason, the ground, the data, the premiss, he now lacks.

But we must notice that if we express the facts referred to by 'The soul is visible only to one' by saying that a person, A, never has all the right, all the reason, one could have for a statement about the mind of B, then we are using these words here very differently from the way we use them when we say of one who sees only a mill wheel that he hasn't on this occasion all the reason one could have for what he says about the mill stream. One who sees only the mill wheel could have all the reason one could have for what he says about the stream and could have all the reason he could have for what he says about the stream. One, A, who has all the reason one ever has for a statement about the mind of another, B, couldn't have all the reason one could have for what he says—not in the sense of 'has all the reason one could have' which requires that he should have the reason B has, in the sense which requires that, like B, he need not look to the face of another for confirmation of what he says. For such a requirement guarantees that what he says is not about another but about himself. When we say of one who sees only the mill wheel that he hasn't all the reason one could have for what he says about the stream one contrasts him with someone better placed. But if because of the facts about statements about the minds of others of which the Sceptic reminds us we say that no one ever has all the right one could have, all the reason one could have, for a statement about the mind of another, then we contrast ourselves with no one, in earth or heaven. If we use 'has all the right he could have' in the way the Sceptic does, then 'A has all the right he could have for a statement about the mind of B' becomes self-contradictory. And if we wed in the usual way 'has all the reason he could have' to 'has all the right he could have' then 'A has all the reason he could have for a statement about the mind of B' becomes self-contradictory. And if we then wed in the usual way 'knowledge' to 'sometimes has all the reason he could have', then 'A has knowledge of the mind of B' becomes self-contradictory and the paradox that no one ever knows the mind of another a necessary truth.

It is not unnatural to describe the facts about the usage of statements about people, particularly about what is in their minds as opposed to what is in their stomachs, by saying that the person the statement is about can have a right to make it which no one else has. It is tempting then to say that the person the statement is about can have reason to make it which no one else can have. It is tempting then to say that he can know the statement to be true in a way no one else can and then to say that no one else can really know it to be true. But we do not in fact in connection with statements about the thoughts and feelings use the expression 'has all the right *a* person could have' like we use 'has just the sort of right some person could have, including the person it is about'; still less do we use 'has all the right *one* could have' in this way; still less do we use 'has all the right *he* could have' in this sense in which no one could have all the right he could have. Nor do we use 'has all the reason one could have' in this way. Still less do we use 'one knows how he feels' in this way, that is, in such a way that one could not, because one could not without having reason for saying it in that sense in which it is senseless to say that one could. That is, we do not use these expressions in such a way that 'No one has real right, real reason to make, real knowledge of, statements about the minds of others' is a necessary truth. In other words, when in the course of life we say 'Arabella knows how Bill feels, Clarissa does not' we do not mean to deny that, were Arabella to make a statement about how Bill feels according to how *she* feels just as Bill does according to how *he* feels then she would be making a statement not about Bill but about herself. So if we express the fact that it is ridiculous to speak of her doing this by saying that Arabella must always lack reason Bill could have and therefore reason one could have, for statements about the mind of Bill, we must remember that this form of words means the facts it refers to and no more, and that these are not facts from which it follows that she never knows the thoughts and feelings in Bill's mind. When we claim that someone knows the thoughts and feelings of another we do not deny any of those facts about what ultimately gives a right to make statements about thoughts and feelings to which the Sceptic draws our attention. And therefore what the Sceptic says does not show that what we claim could not be true nor that what we claim is false.

This does not show that what we claim is true; it does not settle the question whether sometimes we do know what is in the mind of another. This is a question of fact and not of philosophy. But the fact is we do.

Metaphysics

1. Sometimes we say that a thing is so, sometimes only that it seems so. We say 'There's a snake in the grass', 'It looks as if there's a snake in the grass', 'It looks to me as if there's a snake in the grass'. We say 'It's hot in here today' and 'Today it feels to me hot in here', 'It's admirable, at least it seems to me admirable'.

Of course the form of words a person uses doesn't guarantee that he is really talking about what is really so nor that he is really talking about what appears to be so. For a man may say 'There are snakes in the grass' or 'under your chair' and then when one says 'I see no snakes. You're wrong I think' he may reply 'I don't mean real snakes. I mean it looks to me just as if there are snakes under your chair'. Again a man may say 'It's wonderful' and then when one says 'Will you feel it so wonderful in the morning?' he may reply 'I mean that at the moment it seems to me wonderful'. And on the other hand a man may say 'It seemed to me futile' and then carry on the conversation just as if he had said 'It was futile'. So we can't tell for sure from the words a man uses whether he is talking about appearance or reality. That is a matter of how he carries on the conversation. If, when someone says 'There's blood on my hands' he pays attention to how things seem to others in the way a woman does if she says 'There are mice in the kitchen' but gives this up when no one but she can see or smell them, then he, like her, is speaking about real things, not things in his mind. But if he pays no attention to how things seem to others then he is speaking not about how things are but about how they seem.

Of course, if someone says 'To most people it seems that this is so' he is in a way talking about how things seem and not about how they are. But in a way he is still talking about how things are and not merely about how they seem. For he is not saying 'To me it seems that to most people it seems that this is so' but

245

that to most people it seems that this is so. And for this he must pay attention to how things seem to others. And he must do this in two ways. He must pay attention to whether things seem to others as he says they do and thus to whether it seems to others that it seems to others as he says it seems. If someone says 'This seems to everyone just the thing' he is not saying 'It seems just the thing' in the way he is when he takes no notice of how it seems to anyone but him.

Even if someone says 'To me this seems so' he may not be talking merely about how things seem as he would be if he said 'To me from here this seems so'. For he may say 'To me this looks the larger' and then, because when viewed from another place what from the first place looked the larger no longer looks the larger, say 'I was wrong. It's the other which to me looks the larger'.

Even if someone says 'From here this seems to me so' he may still not be talking about how things seem. For he may say 'From here this looks to me rose-coloured' and then, because later it looks grey, say 'I was wrong. From here it looks to me grey'.

Only one who says 'It seems so' without regard to how things seem to others or will or would seem to him at some other time or in some other place is really talking only about what seems.

2. Now no one, ever, anywhere, has then reason to say that this or that is so beyond the reason he has for saying that then and there to him it seems so.

Some have concluded that no one ever really knows how things are, only how at the moment they seem to him.

Others have concluded that to know how things are is only to know how they seem.

3. The first, the Sceptical Solipsist, reasons as follows:

No one anywhere at any time has reason to say that a thing is so beyond the reason he has for saying that then and there to him it seems so.

Therefore no one anywhere at any time has for what he says as to what is so the reason another could have, nor the reason one could have at another place, nor the reason one could have at another time.

Therefore no one anywhere at any time has for what he says as to what is so all the reason one could have.

Therefore no one anywhere at any time really knows that a thing is so. For to really know that a thing is so one must have all the reason one could have for saying that it is so.

'Admittedly,' says the Sceptic, 'admittedly, we don't always use the word "know" so that only if a man's reasons are all they might be do we say that he knows, but sometimes we do.' 'And anyway', says the Sceptic, 'that is what I mean. We would sometimes say of a man that he knows that a vehicle is approaching from behind when we are well aware that all he has to go upon is what he sees in a mirror. But sometimes we would say that though such a man has excellent reason to think that a vehicle is approaching he doesn't really *know* this—not like he does when he sees the vehicle itself. And we would sometimes say that a man knows there is a fox in a covert although we are well aware that he can see only the head of a fox. But sometimes, especially if we have been telling stories of practical jokes, we would say of such a man that he doesn't absolutely *know* that a *fox* is there as he would if he saw the whole of a fox and saw the creature slip away. Here we say that he doesn't really know, not because his grounds are wholly indirect, like images in a mirror or shadows on a wall, but because they are incomplete. The head of a fox is part of a fox but not the whole, and it is only indirect ground for thinking that the other parts of a fox are there too. In the same way we would say of a man who sees a partly unfurled map and on it in bold type the word "London" and above that the river and the Strand that he knows it's a map of London, but we would say that he doesn't *absolutely know* it's a map of London—not like one who sees the whole map unfurled and so, knowing the parts are there in proper arrangement, has absolutely conclusive, direct and complete reason to say that here is a map of London. We would say of one who has the measurements of many London children from Mayfair and from Bethnal Green that he knows the height of the average London child. But of course one who has still more measurements knows it better and only one who has the measurement of every child absolutely knows that the height of the average London child is 4 ft. 2 in., only such a man has all the reason one could have for what he says. He could have had reason other than that he has for what he says but that's a different matter. Innumerable sets of data would have given the same conclusion but the data he has couldn't be better than it is.'

The Sceptic is right when he says that we have some tendency to so use the words 'knows' or 'absolutely knows' or 'really knows' only of one who has all the reason one could have for what he says' and that anyway we can easily understand such a way of speaking of knowledge or of real knowledge.

He next submits that when we consider how in the end no man ever has all the reason one could have for what he may assert as to what is so we must admit that no one really knows reality.

4. One who reduces reality to appearance argues as follows:

To know that in every way a thing seems so is to know that it is so. For no one *could* have reason to say that a thing is so beyond those he could have for saying 'It seems so'.

Therefore to say 'It is so' is to say no more than 'It seems so'.

For unless one *could* have reason for saying one thing beyond what one could have for saying another to say the one is no more than to say the other and to say the other is to say the one.

To say 'Here is a fox' is to say more than 'Here is the head of a fox'. But then one could have grounds for 'Here is a fox' beyond those one could have for 'Here is the head of a fox'. One couldn't have grounds for 'Here is the head of a fox' beyond those one could have for 'Here is a fox'. But then the latter implies the former. One could have every reason for 'Here is the Marble Arch' without having every reason for 'Here is London'. One couldn't have every reason for 'Here is Marble Arch, here Piccadilly Circus, here the Strand, there the Elephant and the rest' without having every reason for 'Here is London'. But then while the Marble Arch isn't London, London is the Marble Arch, the Circus, the Elephant and the rest.

To say that every child is 4 ft. 2 in. is to say more than 'The average child is 4 ft. 2 in.' But then one could have reason for the former beyond what one could have for the latter. One could not have reason for 'The average child is 4 ft. 2 in.' beyond the reason one could have for 'Every child is 4 ft. 2 in.'

One could on another occasion have quite different reasons for 'The average child is 4 ft. 2 in.'—that is why one needs more reason for the more specific statement than one does for the less. But one could not have reason for the less specific statement beyond all the reason one could have for the more specific. But then to say 'The average child is 4 ft. 2 in.' is to say no more than one who says 'Every child is 4 ft. 2 in.'

Put the thing another way: If one statement, S, does not imply another, S', then one could have reason for S' beyond what one could have for S. Therefore if one couldn't have reason for S' beyond what one could have for S then S doesn't not imply S', that is to say S does imply S', that is to say to say that S is to say that S'.

Therefore where S' = 'There's a snake in the grass' and S = 'In every way it seems to me here and now there's a snake in the grass' the latter implies the former so that one who says 'There's a snake in the grass' means no more than one who says 'In every way it seems to me here and now that there's a snake in the grass'. He appears to mean more, he appears to speak of something beyond what seems and passes, as one who speaks of spring and of how she has come late this year appears to speak of one who, when the blossom she has brought has faded, still will come again. She has been here before and when we were young we hoped some time to see her. Later we reckoned we never would. Now we know we never could. Now we know that what seemed an impossible hope was not a hope, not a delusion like that of one who dreams that someone is come back, but a logical illusion. For we know now that spring is not more though not less than the flowers of spring, and that one who seeing the flowers asks 'But how do we know that spring is here?' is like one who, seeing children, asks 'But where is the Mean and where the Modal Child round whom I am told these children cluster?' Such questions do nothing but show the power of a logical model, that of the man behind the scenes, the substance and the shadow. This model prevents those who ask these questions from realizing that the answers to the questions they ask follow from the data they allow they have, that these answers are nothing but deductive transformations of the premises they possess.

In the same way one who says 'It looks like a daffodil, it smells like a daffodil, it feels like a daffodil but is it a daffodil?' does nothing but show that he is under the influence of a logical model inappropriate to his logical situation. It's still the model of the man behind the scenes, the substance and the shadow.

5. So argues the Reductionistic Solipsist and so he seems to deliver us from the doubts of Scepticism. And yet is everything all right? Isn't something lost? For if 'It seems so' means as much as 'It is so' then 'It is so' means no more than 'It seems so'. And the result doesn't look so good this way round. Something is wrong.

It is not for nothing that the Sceptic proceeded as if the logical connection between abstractions, like spring and the average child, and that from which they are abstracted is different from the logical connection between realities and the appearances through which from time to time, to one observer and another, the realities are manifested. For the connection is different. It is more like than we realized. But it's different. And it's different in a way that's relevant to the question 'Does anyone ever really know reality?' From the fact that an investigator has such and premisses just suited to a conclusion about an abstraction it follows that that conclusion is correct. But from the fact that to an investigator it seems just as it should for a conclusion about what is so it does not follow that that conclusion is correct. There is something wrong with the reasoning by which the Sceptic steps from this to the conclusion that no one has all the reason he could have for what he says about reality and thence to the conclusion that no one really knows reality. But an account of what is wrong with Scepticism which pretends that the logical relation between appearance and reality is the same as that between an abstraction and the individual things from which it is abstracted is itself wrong. An account which pretends that the connection is deductive, that to say 'It seems so' is to say 'It is so', such an account is itself wrong.

For it isn't true that one who says 'There's a daffodil in the grass' means no more than 'To me it looks, sounds, feels, smells, and tastes as if there is a daffodil in the grass and it looks, sounds, feels, smells and tastes as if to others it looks, sounds, feels, smells and tastes as if there is a daffodil in the grass and as if to others it looks, sounds, feels, smells and tastes as if ... and so on'. And it is possible to say why. It isn't true even that one who says that spring is come means only that there *is* blossom on the trees. For if tomorrow there is snow and silence he may say 'It seemed that spring had come but she had not'. And this is true in general of one who says 'It is so' not 'It seems so'. One could not have reason to say 'In every way it seems so but it isn't so' but one could have reason to say 'In every way it seemed so but it wasn't so'. But more. One who says 'It is so' not only makes a statement more vulnerable to time than 'In every way it seems so', he also makes a statement more vulnerable to the challenge of others. One could not have reason to say 'To me in every way it seems so but it isn't so' but another could. He could have reason to say 'To him', meaning me, 'in every way it seems so but it isn't so'. Descartes couldn't have reason to say 'It is so' which wasn't reason to say 'To Descartes it seems so'. But another than Descartes could. In short, although one who at a certain time and place says that this or that is so and has every reason he could have to say 'Here and now to me it seems so' has all the reason he at that time and place could have for what he says is so and therefore in a sense all the reason one could have for what he says is so, he yet in a sense has not and could not have all the reason one could have for what he says is so. Indeed it is now plain that for a statement as to what is so no one *could* have all the reason one could have. And this is not a contradiction but merely a bewildering way of saying that for a statement about what is so no particular person at a particular time at a particular place could have at that time and place every reason anyone could have at any time or place.

And this is the logical truth referred to both by one who says 'We never know reality, only appearance' and one who says 'Reality is no more than appearance'. Both have before them a man trying to know what is and is not so. Slyly the Sceptic argues 'He hasn't all the reason one could have so he hasn't all the reason he could have' and with these words he not only states the truth on which they are based, namely that one couldn't have the reasons one couldn't have but also *suggests* that each of us is like one who sees only the head of a fox, or rather like one who never sees, never has seen, and never will see fields or trees or men or beasts but only their shadows in a mirror, and so never has, never has had, and never will have, the reason he could have had for what he thinks is so.

Slyly the Reductionist replies 'But one to whom in every way a thing seems so has all the reason one could have to say it is so' and with these words he not only states the truth on which they are based, namely that one couldn't have the reason one couldn't have, but also *suggests* that 'It is so' means no more than 'It seems so,' like 'Spring is come' means no more than 'The snowdrops are out, the primroses soon will be' or like 'It's dark' sometimes *does* mean 'To me it's dark'.

6. All this might lead one to say 'So all the paradoxes that no one can know the future, the past, the distant or anything beyond the meaningless moment of his own sensation, and the contrary paradoxes that the future is the past, the past the future, the distant the near, the real the apparent, are all the products of a logical slip, of a play on the use of "he" and "one", of a mismanagement of variables'.

But the strength of the forces behind the perplexities of the place, time, and personality predicaments are not to be gauged this way. A play upon the use of 'one' and 'he' contributes to the confusion. But the secret of the illumination and the distortion that there is in this metaphysic doesn't lie here. For the metaphysicians are as well aware as anyone else that it is not in general true that if one thing is in a certain relation to another for a certain person at a certain time and place then it must be for any other person at any other time and place. They don't assume that if to A at t at p B is more desirable than C then so will it be to A' and so will it be at t'. They know that love is sensitive to place, time and personality. It is logic they suppose is not and could not be. In other words what they assume is that if for A at t at p R is a reason for C then so it is for A' and at t' and at p'. It follows at once that if for A at p at t nothing is reason for C which isn't reason for C' then the same is true at p' and at t' and for A'.

To put the matter more fully: What metaphysicians do assume is (i) that if for one person something, R, could be reason for a conclusion, C, then so it could be for another person, (ii) that if at one time R could be a reason for C then so it could be at another, (iii) that if at one place R could be a reason for C then so it could be at another.

It is easy to see how reasoning in accordance with these axioms we reach the conclusion of Scepticism that no one at any time has all the reason he could have for a statement such as 'There's a snake in the grass' or the conclusion of Reductionism that any statement such as 'There's a snake in the grass' has a different meaning for every different person and at every different time and at every different place, or the conclusion that either Scepticism or Reductionism is the truth. For suppose A feels cold. Then this feeling gives him reason to say 'To me it feels cold' and also reason to assert what he understands by 'It's cold'. And if someone else, B, feels cold his feeling gives him reason to say 'To me it feels cold' and also reason to say 'It's cold'. But A's feeling isn't B's feeling nor B's A's. So each lacks a reason for 'It's cold' which the other has. Therefore each lacks a reason which another could have for what that other understands by 'It's cold' and therefore (axiom 1) lacks a reason he could have for what another understands by 'It's cold', and therefore lacks a reason he could have for what he understands by 'It's cold', unless what he understands by 'It's cold' is different from what the other understands by this.

Alternatively, we may argue 'No one has reason for a statement S is P beyond those he has for "It seems to me that S is P" and everyone has reason for "It seems to me that S is P" which no one else has. Therefore either everyone *could* have reason for S is P beyond what he has for "It seems to me that S is P" and therefore beyond what he ever *does* have for S is P or "S is P" means something different to every different person, namely "It seems to *me* that S is P".'

Like arguments will show in accordance with axioms 2 and 3 that either (1) no one ever anywhere has all the reason he could have at that time and place for a statement S is P, because he lacks those he could have at another time or place, or (2) because he has all the reason he could have at that time and place for S is P the meaning of 'S is P' is different for every different time and place.

7. Can we deny or must we accept these axioms so obviously true no logic book takes the trouble to state them, so preposterously

false as to generate those caricatures of logic which are the monsters of metaphysics? Must we accept them or can we deny them? We have seen what is involved in accepting them. But to deny them is not merely to deny what is true of every reason contemplated in any logic book from the first page on deduction to the last on induction. It is to deny what is of the very essence of reason.

8. Can we say that the axioms are not applicable to what in the end makes a man say what he does as to what is so—not applicable because what makes him say 'It seems so' and then 'It is so' is a feeling, an experience, a sensation, and not a reason?

But hasn't one who smells cheese reason to say 'Cheese again'? Hasn't one to whom it looks black reason to say 'It's dark' which one to whom it looks like day has not? If these reasons aren't reasons then in the end we have none and are plunged into a scepticism more profound than before.

But they are reasons. And, this admitted, all the machinery of the calculus drives us into the isolation of Solipsism and on to Absolute Scepticism where nothing that could be known can be known and, in dear despair, doubt and denigration meet.

9. But this dilemma is no longer a dilemma. It was but now it isn't. The centuries of work on it have not gone for nothing. We can now grasp what all along we have known but not grasped, namely, what is referred to by one who says 'How things seem provides no reason for claims as to how things are' and what is referred to by one who says 'How things seem provides every reason for claims as to how things are'. We can more and more grasp what lies behind the questions 'Wouldn't one to whom a thing in every way seemed so thereby have every reason he could have to say it is so? If he would not doesn't this imply that he wouldn't know that what he says is so? If he would doesn't this imply that he would have every reason one could have for what he says is so? And doesn't this imply that what he means by what he says is so is that to him and at the moment it seems so?' We can grasp and connect what lies behind the answers to these questions and realize how each answer illuminates what the others obscure and obscures what the others illuminate.

And in this process that which we wish illuminated is illuminated.

10. If the character of our procedure[1] puzzles us we have only to compare it with the dissolution of other more limited and manageable dilemmas. For example: Are infinite numbers numbers or not? At first it appears that they are. For can't we speak of the number of even numbers, of the number of odd numbers and of the number of numbers, and say that the number of numbers is greater than the number of even numbers as the number of people in the world exceeds the number of women? But then is the number of numbers greater than the number of even numbers although for every number there is just one even number which is the double of it and for every even number there is just one number of which it is the double, as when every man has just one wife and every woman just one husband? Or is the number of numbers not greater than the number of even numbers, although beside the even numbers there are odd numbers?

Does this prove that infinite numbers are not numbers? But then as we set out the general truths which apply both to infinite numbers and to numbers which are not infinite don't we demonstrate features of infinite numbers which prove that they are numbers, in spite of the fact that axioms true of all other numbers are not true of them? Of all other numbers it is true (i) that if to every member of one class, C, there corresponds just one member of another, C', and to every member of C' there corresponds just one member of C then the number of members of C is the same as the number of members of C', and (ii) that if there are members of C which are not members of C' but no members of C' which are not members of C then the number of members of C is not the same as the number of members of C'. But these axioms are not true of infinite numbers and therefore if infinite numbers are numbers, the axioms are not true of all numbers.

But to say this suggests that one who says that these axioms are true of all numbers makes a mistake like one who thinks that all isosceles triangles must be equiangular because he has

---

[1] Wittgenstein would no doubt not wish to be associated with this paper. But I feel I must mention how much in it comes out of things he said years ago.

always drawn isosceles triangles as equilateral. It suggests that one who says that infinite numbers are not numbers because they do not obey the axioms which hold for all other numbers makes a mistake like one who says that triangles which are not equiangular are not isosceles, because he assumes they must conform to the truth which holds for all equilateral triangles. And he is not making a mistake like this. For to be equilateral is definitely not of the essence of triangles but to obey the axioms which infinite numbers do not obey is not definitely not of the essence of numbers.

Suppose we come upon people playing a game like chess except that the knights are not in their game allowed to leap over other pieces when they are moved. Shall we say that they play chess and use knights but that they never take advantage of a certain power which knights have and won't allow others to take advantage of this power? Or shall we say that they don't play with knights and even that they are not playing chess? Or shall we say that they are playing chess and are playing with knights and that these knights can't jump, but that it was just an assumption on our part that all knights can jump over other pieces? To say this is to recognize at once the kinship and the difference between the role of the pieces we use as knights and the role of certain pieces used in the game we have come upon. But it is to present this difference in a misleading way. For it suggests that one who says that the game we have come upon isn't chess and that the knights aren't knights is wrong like one who says that a triangle isn't isosceles because it isn't equi-angular, because he has been in the habit of drawing every isosceles triangle as also equiangular, or even like one who says that a wild horse isn't a horse because it doesn't go in harness nor under saddle. But one who says it is of the essence of a knight that he should leap over other pieces and that therefore these knights are not knights isn't wrong like this. For he's quite right—a knight which can't jump isn't a horse without the usual trappings, but a horse on wheels in the plough, *Hamlet* without the Prince of Denmark, wealth which none can buy, a predicate which like existence nothing can lose nor gain, reason which like a feeling one can't give nor yet retain.

I well remember how Moore twenty years ago after lecturing for a year on what is meant by one who says 'This is a black-board' said in conclusion that though it is commonly thought that our reasons for such statements must be either deductive or inductive it seemed to him that our reasons (he meant our ultimate reasons) are of neither of these sorts and yet such that we often know such statements to be true.

This was, I submit, the first move towards recognizing how those reasons which must be different for different people on different occasions are unlike those reasons which must be the same for everyone on every occasion.

Moore would have been the first to admit that this first move needed much examination and explanation.

Asked whether knights which can't jump are knights it is easy to explain the idiosyncrasies and affinities of such knights until the question 'Are they knights or aren't they?' vanishes although it has no answer.

Asked whether the infinite numbers are or are not numbers it is not easy to explain. But it has been done.

Asked whether appearances are reasons or not it is difficult to explain. It is easy to answer 'Yes' and it is easy to answer 'No' and it is easy to answer 'Yes and no'. But it is not easy to explain. And yet whichever answer we give we must explain, if perplexity is to be changed into a new grasp of the logic of appearance and reality. If we answer 'No, appearances are not reasons, how things seem is no reason to think one thing rather than another as to how they are' then we shall have to explain the affinity between (1) the contrast between (*a*) one who, hearing and seeing as it were rain, says 'It's raining' and (*b*) one who says 'It's raining' though he neither sees nor hears anything of the sort and (2) the contrast between (*a*) one who, knowing that a thing has both the shape and the voice of a fox, says 'It's a fox' and (*b*) one who says 'It's a fox' though he knows nothing of the sort the other knows. We shall need to recognize how like is the difference between one who says 'It's a musical box' merely because it has the shape of a musical box and one who says 'It's a musical box' because it has the shape and also the sound of a musical box to the difference between one who says 'It's a dagger' merely because it looks to him as if there is a dagger before him and one who says this because it not only looks but feels to him as if there is a dagger before him.

And if we answer the question 'Are appearances reasons or not?' by 'Yes, one to whom a thing seems so has reason to say "It is so" and the more reason the more it seems so' we shall have to explain the idiosyncrasy of such reason. For we shall have to answer the question 'Has one to whom in every way at the moment it seems that something is so every reason one could have to say "It is so"?'

And if to this question we answer 'No' we shall have to explain that it doesn't follow that one to whom it seems in every way that something is so doesn't know that it is so, because the way the feelings and sensations which make it true that to a particular person it seems so are not, because they could not be, all the reason one could have for a statement as to what is so, is different from the way reasons of the sort 'This is so' may not be all the reason one could have for a conclusion of the sort 'That is so'. If you feel it warm and I feel it warm then since your feeling isn't mine what gives you reason to say 'It's warm' is not a thing which gives me reason to say 'It's warm'—although my hearing you say 'It's warm' gives me more reason to say 'It's warm'. Therefore since in a sense I haven't the reason you have to say 'It's warm' it is also true in *a* sense that I haven't all the reason anyone could have to say 'It's warm'. But it is not true in the sense in which one who sees a fox only in a mirror, or sees only its head, hasn't all the reason one could have to say 'There's a fox,' nor in the sense in which one who is blind or deaf hasn't every reason one could have to say 'Here is musical box'. If, because I am deaf, I haven't the sensation which gives you reason to say 'Here is a musical box' then I haven't all the reason one could have for the statement 'Here is a musical box', and we may say either that I don't really know, can't really know, that what I say is so when I say 'Here is a musical box' or that because I am deaf 'Here is a musical box' doesn't mean to to me what it means to others. But if I am not deaf then though I couldn't have your sensation as of the sound of a musical box I could have just such a sensation. And in these circumstances, although your sensation gives you reason to say 'Here is a musical box' and my sensation gives me reason to say the same and your sensation isn't mine, it is misleading to say that I have not a reason which you have. For to say this suggests that my position is what it would be were I deaf, and sets in motion the machinery that carries us to the conclusion that either I lack reason I could have for what I mean by 'Here is a musical box' or I don't mean by these words what you mean.

On the other hand if we answer 'Yes, one to whom in every way it seems that something is so has every reason one could have to say it is so' we shall have to explain that 'It is so' cannot be deduced from 'In every way to me it seems so' and that 'It is so' does not mean no more than 'In every way to me it seems so'.

If to you it looks, smells, and tastes as if there is cheese on the table and to me it looks, smells and tastes as if there is cheese on the table then in a sense I have every reason you have to say that there is cheese on the table; for as I am not blind and haven't a cold I have the same sort of sensations to tell me there is cheese on the table as you have. But though in such a case we may say that I have the same sensations as you have we may also say that my sensations are not yours nor yours mine and that therefore in a sense I have not the reasons you have. I have not the same reasons as you have in the sense in which I have when you and I have the same figures about the average this or that, or when you have the premisses that there is a thing on the table of the shape and colour of cheese and with the taste and nourishing properties of cheese and I have these premisses too. I have not in the sensations I get the reasons you have in the sensations you get as I have the reasons you have in the premisses, the facts, that you and I both have to go upon. Any premiss that you have is a premiss I have or could have, any fact you have to go upon is a fact I have or could have to go upon; there is not the fact that you go upon and the fact that I go upon. Even the premiss, the fact, that to you it seems that there is cheese on the table may be among my reasons for saying 'There is cheese on the table'. It is when what we are speaking of as your reason for thinking that there is cheese on the table is not the fact that it seems to you that there is cheese on the table but those sensations which make you say that it seems to you that there is cheese on the table, it is then that the reasons you have could not, in a sense, be mine. In this sense no one could have the reason another could have for any statement and in this sense no one could have every reason one could have for a statement as to what is so. It is true that we say such things as 'From the sensation in my old wound I deduced that the weather had changed'. But here that from which one person deduces a conclusion is not something from which any other person could. It is true that Mr. Jackson may say ' "Australia in five days"—means to me that in five days I shall be warm' and that Mrs. Jackson may say the same. But this doesn't mean that 'Australia in five days' means one thing to Mr. Jackson and another to Mrs. Jackson, although each can judge the correctness of the prediction only in accordance with how he (or she) feels, only in accordance with how things look, sound, smell to him, to her.

Or if we say that 'It will be so,' 'It is so' mean something different to every speaker, every hearer, we shall have to explain that this doesn't mean that each statement of the sort 'It will be so', 'It is so' means something different to every speaker in the way that 'He sent two truss of hay' means something different to an Englishman from what it means to a Scotsman and 'There was a contract' means to a lawyer something different from what it means to a layman. Indeed, if we say that each statement of the sort 'It is so' has a different meaning to every different person and at every different time and at every different place at which it is uttered then we shall have to explain that this is true only in a sense in which a statement can not in the *ordinary* sense mean the same for different speakers at different times and places, unless in our new, *solipsistic*, sense it means something different for every different speaker at every different time and place. For if one who at Brighton hears a voice say 'Fire in Fleet Street' looks for flames like one in Fleet Street should, this proves he doesn't understand, this proves that the words have for him a different meaning from that they have to one in Fleet Street who pulls back his curtains or to one in Brighton who, because he understands, pulls out his car, keeps his speedometer at 50 while his clock revolves once, and then anticipates not flames but ashes.

But all this explaining can be done. And then what was a

dilemma is no longer a dilemma, a difficult situation has vanished. Or, if you like, what was a question is become no longer a question.

This doesn't mean that it wasn't a question. It means only that questions of the sort 'Is this so?' which call for reflection no longer call for that reflection to those who have done that reflection *and that this is no less so* when the question hasn't an answer than when it has. The question 'Do these accounts balance?' calls for reflection but it does so no longer when the calculation has been done. Then the question is settled. And this is no less so when a question hasn't an answer. The question 'Was there negligence?' on occasion has no answer or, if you like, has no answer 'Yes' or 'No'. But the reflection it calls for can be as successfully carried through on these occasions as on those occasions on which it has an answer, it can be successfully completed whether or no what happened can be fairly described as 'negligence' or as 'not negligence'.

Put the thing another way. Questions of the form 'Is it so or isn't it?' call for a study of reality. How much that study reveals reality does not depend on how much that study can or cannot be summed up in an answer 'Yes' or 'No' without danger of distortion. This is demonstrated again and again in the courts. We have seen how it is true of the question 'Are infinite numbers numbers?' It is true of the question 'Are questions which have no answers questions?' Whether we say that they are not questions or that they have answers or that though most questions have answers these are questions which have no answers, we must explain. But we can explain. And then the questions 'Are these questions questions?' 'Have they answers?' which questions have no answers, have been answered.

The question 'Does "He is her second cousin" mean "He is a child of a child of the parents of one of her parents"?' has an answer and the study of the question reveals what is involved in being a second cousin, and thus indirectly gives us a better grasp of those situations in which we call one person the second cousin of another .

The questions 'Does the word "here" have different meanings when used at different places?' 'Does the word "now" have different meanings at different times?' 'Does the word "I"

have different meanings in the mouths of different speakers?'
haven't answers. But when we have explained what in each case
there is to be said for the answer 'Yes' and what for the answer
'No' we have a new grasp of the familiar use of the familiar
expressions 'here', 'now' and 'I', just as we may gain a new
grasp of a familiar relationship as we struggle with the question.
'Is he afraid of her or isn't he?' As we answer such questions
we at once gain in awareness of the particular pattern of events
with which we are concerned and also recognize how fear, hate
and love have a hundred heads and as many disguises. We
don't learn this, for we know it, but we gain a new awareness
of it.

The question 'Does "It's raining" mean to everyone "It here
and now looks to *me*, feels to *me*, sounds to *me*, as if it's raining" '
has an answer. For in the usual usage of language the answer
is 'No'. But if we say that this question has an answer and that
the answer is 'No' we must explain that when a metaphysician
paradoxically answers this question with 'Yes', he is not prepared to deny that which makes us in the usual way answer
'No'. On the other hand, if we say that when this question is
asked metaphysically it hasn't an answer we must explain that
the question is not meaningless even when asked metaphysically,
we must explain that in studying what there is to be said for the
answer 'Yes' and what there is to be said for the answer 'No'
we can come to grasp afresh those facts which support each
answer. Paradoxical questions, whether metaphysical or not,
are in a peculiar position. For a question 'Is this so?' is not on a
particular occasion paradoxical unless on that occasion that
question would as ordinarily asked have an answer 'Yes' or
'No'. On the other hand 'Is this so?' is not on a particular
occasion asked paradoxically if it is to be answered in the
ordinary way.

And this tends to lead to confusion in the discussion of these
questions unless both speaker and hearer are aware of the
peculiar character of their own procedure—a thing it is not
easy to be aware of. For in the first place, just as the line between
questions which have not answers and those which have isn't
sharp so the line between paradoxical questions and those
which are not isn't sharp. And in the second place, the reflection

and discussion which a paradoxical question calls for is best carried on *as if* both he who defends the ordinary answer and he who defends the extraordinary answer were speaking literally.

On the other hand, while the paradoxical character of a paradoxical question is not recognized the discussion of it will tend to be chronic and to give the impression that the reflection the question calls for cannot be carried through, just as a misapprehension of the character of questions which have no answers tends to have this effect. The peculiarity of the logical situation both in the case of reasoning about questions which have no answers and in the case of reasoning about paradoxical questions may lead people to say that we cannot reach, cannot know, the answers to these questions, just as the peculiarity of the reasoning appropriate to ethical questions and the peculiarity of reasons in appearance for conclusions about reality has been expressed in this misleadingly lugubrious form.

In the case of paradoxical questions unless their peculiar character is understood it will tend to have a further effect— that of making the paradoxical answers to them peculiarly misleading and dangerous and that of making the platitudinous answers to them seem peculiarly pointless. For unless the paradoxical character of a paradoxical question and discussion is understood the point of the platitudinous answer will be taken to be no more than it would be when not opposed to a paradoxical answer. And unless the paradoxical character of the paradoxical question and of the paradoxical answer to it is understood the paradoxical answer will be confused with the non-paradoxical answer expressed in the same words and definitely false.

Another circumstance makes difficult the management of paradoxical thought. Just as when used non-paradoxically a statement of the form S is P (or S is not P) may (1) express something which could have been otherwise, or (2) express something which could not have been otherwise, so also may such statements when used paradoxically express something which could have been otherwise or express something which could not have been otherwise. And when they express something that couldn't have been otherwise this may be (*a*) because nothing could be S and not P (or S and P) or (*b*) because nothing could be not P (or nothing could be P). To put the matter another way. There are contingent paradoxes and tauto-logical ones. Amongst the tautological paradoxes there are those which are limited and those which are not. One who speaks paradoxically may be using words in such a way that though what he says is not false on the usual grounds it still could be false. For example, one who says 'No man is good—not even St. Francis' may still be using words so that it is not impossible that a man should be good. But he may not be. For he may be so using the words 'good' and 'human' that a creature with evil desires is not good even if he overcomes them while one without such desires isn't human. Then his paradox couldn't be false.

In such a case, however, he may still be using the word 'good' so that though no human being could be good, some-thing could be—an angel or a god. But he may not be. For he may be using the word 'good' so that nothing which has an evil desire is good and nothing which doesn't overcome an evil desire is good. And then plainly nothing could be good. One who for such reasons says 'No man *is* good' speaks mis-leadingly. For his reasons show that no man *could* be good. And one who for these reasons says 'No man could be good' still speaks misleadingly. For he is not contrasting men with any-thing that could be in earth or heaven.

But this doesn't make what he says meaningless. For in his caricature of our idea of goodness he has brought out the con-flicting elements in that idea by accentuating them until the hidden conflict becomes a contradiction and sweet perfection wears a foolish smile.

11. It's this way in metaphysics. Its doctrines are para-doxes when they aren't platitudes. And they are tautologies, truths which couldn't but be true. And they are tautologies which tend towards the unlimited tautology of Absolute Scepticism. Take 'No one really knows the past'. This couldn't but be true in its paradoxical role. For in that role either it refers to the peculiarities of knowledge of the past which make it knowledge of the past or it's a deduction from the wider paradox that no one really knows anything as to what is gone or what's to come, only what is so. And this paradox couldn't but be true; for

either it refers to the peculiarities of knowledge of what was and what will be so or it's a deduction from the wider paradox that no one really knows anything as to what was so, will be so or is so, only what seems. And this paradox couldn't but be true; for either it refers to the peculiarities of knowledge of what was, is, or will be so as opposed to knowledge of what seems or it's a deduction from the wider paradox that knowledge is impossible, since a claim that goes beyond what seems goes too far and one that doesn't go beyond what seems doesn't go far enough. This in its paradoxical role couldn't but be true and has no limit.

But all this no more makes metaphysical questions senseless than it makes other tautological and unlimited paradoxical questions senseless. Such questions have their own sort of sense. But this is only because there is a sort of procedure appropriate to them. Reasons for answers to paradoxical questions are eccentric but they are reasons still.

12. Metaphysical questions are paradoxical questions with the peculiarity that they are concerned with the character of questions, of discussions, of reasons, of knowledge. But this peculiarity does not make it impossible to carry through the reflection they call for so as to reveal the character of that with which they are concerned and thus, indirectly, the character of that with which that with which they are concerned is concerned—time and space, good and evil, things and persons.